TOP MULTISTATE
TAX ISSUES
FOR 2008
CPE COURSE

CCH Tax Law Editors with Contributing Authors

CCH

a Wolters Kluwer business

Contributors

Editor	Cindy Hangartner, JD, LL.M
Contributing Editors	John A. Biek Esq.
	Craig Fields J.D., LL.M.
	Paul Frankel J.D., LL.M.
	Carol Kokinis-Graves J.D.
	Nick Marsico J.D., CPA
	Amy Nogid J.D., LL.M.
	Joseph A. Robinson, Jr.
	Thomas Rutledge J.D.
	Andrew W. Swain J.D., LL.M.
Technical Review	Sharon Brooks
Production Coordinator	Gabriel E. Santana
Production	Lynn J. Brown
Layout & Design	Laila Gaidulis

ISBN: 978-0-8080-1688-5

Printed in the United States of America

TOP MULTISTATE TAX ISSUES FOR 2008 CPE COURSE

Introduction

The state tax laws are always changing. The complex interrelationship of phased-in and delayed new law effective dates, changing state revenue department rules, and an ever-changing mix of taxpayer wins and losses in the courts creates the need for the tax practitioner to constantly stay on top of the new rules and reassess tax strategies at the start of every year. The rules this year are significantly different from the rules last year, and the rules next year promise to be different from those governing this year. This is a fact of life for the modern-day state tax practitioner.

CCH's *Top Multistate Tax Issues for 2008 CPE Course* is a helpful resource that provides explanations of significant laws, regulations, decisions and issues that affect multistate tax practitioners. Readers get guidance, insights and analysis on important provisions and their impact on multistate tax compliance and tax planning. This Course is the top quality tax review and analysis that every state tax practitioner needs to keep a step ahead.

Among the topics covered in the Course are:
- Economic Nexus
- Passive Investment Companies
- Series LLC
- FIN 48
- State Tax Appeals Process
- Valuation of Real Estate
- Short Term Investments

Throughout the Course you will find comments that are vital to understanding a particular strategy or idea, Examples to illustrate the topics covered, and Study Questions to help you test your knowledge. Answers to the Study Questions, with feedback on both correct and incorrect responses are provided in a special section beginning on page 8.1.

To assist you in your later reference and research, a detailed topical index has been included for this Course beginning on page 9.1.

This Course is divided into two Modules. Take your time and review each Course Module. When you feel confident that you thoroughly understand the material, turn to the CPE Quizzer. Complete one or all Module Quizzers for Continuing Professional Education credit. You can complete and return the Quizzers to CCH for grading at an additional charge. If you receive a grade of 70 percent or higher on the Quizzers, you will receive CPE credit for the Modules graded. Further information is provided in the CPE Quizzer instructions on page 10.1.

October 2007

COURSE OBJECTIVES

This Course was prepared to provide the participant with an overview of multistate tax issues. Upon Course completion, you will be able to:

- Understand the economic nexus standard
- Distinguish differences in tax results between consolidated returns and separate company returns
- Describe how the series LLC is created
- Apply the two-step process for analyzing tax positions arising from intercompany transactions
- Enumerate the elements of a fair tax tribunal
- Apply the economic principles affecting property valuation
- Discuss recent cases in California and Illinois that discuss whether taxpayers may use gross receipts from the sale of short-term security investments in the sales factor denominator

CCH'S PLEDGE TO QUALITY

Thank you for choosing this CCH Continuing Education product. We will continue to produce high quality products that challenge your intellect and give you the best option for your Continuing Education requirements. Should you have a concern about this or any other CCH CPE product, please call our Customer Service Department at 1-800-248-3248.

NEW ONLINE GRADING gives you immediate 24/7 grading with instant results and no Express Grading Fee.

The **CCH Testing Center** website gives you and others in your firm easy, free access to CCH print Courses and allows you to complete your CPE Quizzers online for immediate results. Plus, the **My Courses** feature provides convenient storage for your CPE Course Certificates and completed Quizzers.

Go to **www.cchtestingcenter.com** to complete your Quizzer online.

One **complimentary copy** of this Course is provided with copies of selected CCH Tax titles . Additional copies of this Course may be ordered for $29.00 each by calling 1-800-248-3248 (ask for product 0-0986-200).

TOP MULTISTATE TAX ISSUES FOR 2008 CPE COURSE

Contents

MODULE 1: PASSIVE INVESTMENT COMPANIES
AND PASS-THROUGH ENTITIES

MODULE 1: PASSIVE INVESTMENT COMPANIES AND
PASS-THROUGH ENTITIES — CHAPTER 1

Economic Nexus

This chapter examines state court decisions and the actions taken by states regarding the taxation of out-of-state passive investment companies.

LEARNING OBJECTIVES

Upon completion of this chapter, you should be able to:

■ Understand the economic nexus standard;

■ Distinguish between standards for sales tax nexus and income tax nexus;

■ Apply factors the courts use to establish a PIC's nexus for income tax purposes;

■ Enumerate cases establishing a PIC's nexus for income tax purposes; and

■ Recite the various ways state legislatures limit a PIC's tax advantages.

INTRODUCTION

Recent state court decisions have expanded the power of states to tax the income of corporations with which they lack physical nexus. Each of these decisions found that an *economic nexus* existed between the taxing state and the out-of-state corporation. The courts determined that an out-of-state corporation's in-state economic presence made its lack of physical presence irrelevant. The income that the corporation derived from the state's market was subject to the state's corporate income tax.

The U.S. Constitution's dormant Commerce Clause limits the income tax a state can impose on companies lacking a substantial in-state physical presence. In **Complete Auto Transit, Inc., v. Brady** (SCt, 430 US 274, 279 (1977)), the U.S. Supreme Court held that, if an out-of-state corporation's in-state activities create a *substantial nexus* with a state, the state can tax those activities. In **Quill Corp. v. North Dakota** (SCt, 504 US 298 (1992)), the Court elaborated on substantial nexus. North Dakota tried to force an out-of-state retailer to collect sales tax on goods delivered in-state by common carrier. Because the retailer lacked in-state physical presence, the Court held that the state tax violated the dormant Commerce Clause. Courts long understood **Complete Auto** and **Quill** to limit the state taxation of corporations lacking a substantial in-state physical nexus.

This understanding was challenged by **Geoffrey, Inc., v. S.C. Tax Comm'n** (437 S.E.2d 13 (S.C. 1993). **Cert. denied,** 510 US 992 (1993)).

Several questions left unanswered by *Quill* made the challenge possible. *Quill* did not identify the starting point for nexus analysis: substantial nexus or physical presence. It is unclear whether *Quill's* "physical presence" is synonymous with *Complete Auto's* substantial nexus. Nothing in *Quill* says whether physical presence is the same for sales and income taxes. In fact, the Court made this uncertainty clear when it said, "[W]e have not, in our review of other types of taxes, articulated the same physical-presence requirement … established for sales and use taxes" (*Quill Corp.,* SCt, 504 US at 314) *Geoffrey* was the first attempt to resolve *Quill's* unanswered questions.

South Carolina assessed Geoffrey, Inc. (Geoffrey), a Delaware corporation lacking physical nexus with the state, for corporate income tax. The state supreme court affirmed the assessment, largely because Geoffrey was a *passive investment company (PIC)* created by Toys 'R Us, which itself had a physical nexus with the state.

STUDY QUESTION

---

1. Which of the following cases first attempted to establish whether physical presence was required before a taxing state could tax the income of an out-of-state corporation?

   a. *Geoffrey*
   b. *Quill*
   c. *Complete Auto*
   d. *Toys 'R Us*

THE NATURE OF PICS

The nature of PICs is key to understanding the holding in *Geoffrey.* PICs go by several names—passive investment subsidiaries, special-purpose entities, intangible holding companies, intangible property companies, trademark holding companies, and Delaware holding companies. PICs enable corporations to avoid otherwise-valid state income taxes. They also provide tax savings through business expense and dividend deductions.

Selecting an Advantageous Corporate Location

A PIC is a separate corporation created by a parent or an operating company. PICs are "physically" located in a tax-haven state such as Delaware or Nevada. Nevada has no corporate income tax. Delaware does not impose tax on companies deriving income from intangibles possessed or owned in-state (see Del. Code Ann. tit. 30, §1902(b)(8)). Ordinarily, a PIC is a "brass-plate headquarters" with an address in the tax haven. This arrangement avoids creating a physical nexus between the PIC and a state taxing jurisdiction.

Tax-Avoidance Strategies of PICs

The parent company transfers intangible assets (trademarks, tradenames, service marks, patents, copyrights, customer lists, and goodwill) to the PIC. The PIC licenses use of the intangibles back to the company in exchange for a royalty. The company deducts the royalty payments from state income tax as a business expense. The PIC often loans profits from the royalty payments to the company. The company deducts the interest payments on the loan from its state tax. The PIC may distribute dividends to the company, which the company claims as a dividends-received deduction. Meanwhile, the PIC pays no state income tax anywhere.

Many major companies use PICs, among them Home Depot, Sherwin-Williams, Circuit City, Staples, and Burger King. Millions of dollars in potential taxes have been at issue in legal controversies arising when taxing jurisdictions challenged the tax-avoidance use of PICs. The amounts diverted by PICs from state coffers and the annual tax savings afforded the companies are likely enormous. The U.S. Census Bureau reports that, from 1979 to 2000, total state revenues attributable to corporate income taxes fell from 10.2 percent to 6.3 percent (see U.S. Census Bureau, *Federal, State, and Local Governments: State Government Tax Collections,* **www.census.gov/govs/www/statetax.html** (accessed Oct. 18, 2005)). PICs have undoubtedly contributed to this trend.

STUDY QUESTION

> **2.** Some corporations seeking to mitigate state taxes choose Nevada as a preferable state in which to locate their PICs. ***True or False?***

GEOFFREY

In *Geoffrey*, Toys 'R Us, Inc. had created a substantial physical nexus in South Carolina. The company created a PIC, Geoffrey, Inc., and transferred trademarks and tradenames to it. Geoffrey licensed these intangibles to South Carolina retailers in exchange for royalties. The South Carolina Supreme Court held that, for income tax purposes, substantial nexus existed between Geoffrey and the state. That Geoffrey lacked tangible property or employees inside the state was irrelevant.

The South Carolina Supreme Court said that Geoffrey's in-state activities satisfied *Complete Auto*'s substantial nexus requirement in three ways, which *in toto* have become known as economic nexus:

- Geoffrey regularly exploited South Carolina's market by deriving income from using intangible property in the state;
- South Carolina protected Geoffrey's activities within the state; and
- Geoffrey's activities within South Carolina entitled it to some state benefits.

The state's supreme court noted that *Quill*'s physical presence requirement did not extend beyond sales tax to other taxes. The court concluded that the presence in South Carolina of Geoffrey's intangibles was enough to establish substantial nexus. South Carolina could tax the income that Geoffrey derived from the intangibles licensed to Toys 'R Us retailers.

KMART PROPERTIES

Geoffrey was followed by *Kmart Props., Inc,. v. Tax'n and Revenue Dep't of N.M.* (131 P.3d 27 (N.M. Ct. App. 2001)). The *Kmart* case centered on a Michigan PIC that had no physical presence in New Mexico. The appellate court nevertheless found that the PIC had substantial nexus with New Mexico for income tax purposes. The court held that the starting point for determining nexus for purposes of income tax was not *Quill*'s physical-presence requirement. Instead, it was *Complete Auto*'s substantial-nexus requirement. Finding significant differences between sales and income taxes, the *Kmart* court held that *Quill* did not extend its physical-presence requirement beyond applications to sales taxes.

Substantial nexus exists, said the court, when out-of-state PICs use their intangible properties to derive income from New Mexico's market. *Kmart* was transferred to the New Mexico Supreme Court, where it stalled when Kmart Corp. filed for bankruptcy. But the state supreme court later issued its ruling on *Kmart Props., Inc., v. Tax'n and Revenue Dep't of N.M.* (131 P.3d 22 (N.M. 2005)). The court declined to rule on the economic nexus issue, letting stand the appellate court's decision. It ordered the appellate court's opinion filed concurrently with the supreme court's decision.

STUDY QUESTIONS

3. In which of the following cases did the state court determine that a PIC could be taxed because it had economic nexus within the taxing state?
    a. *Quill*
    b. *Kmart*
    c. *Complete Auto*
    d. *Geoffrey*

4. In which of the following states did Kmart's PIC have a physical presence?
    a. New Mexico
    b. California
    c. Michigan
    d. Louisiana

THE GAP

The Gap was the next to learn of the state courts' increasingly nonphysical attraction to nexus. In *Louisiana Dep't of Revenue v. Gap (Apparel), Inc.* (886 So.2d 459 (La. Ct. App. 2004)), a California PIC, lacked physical nexus with Louisiana. Nevertheless, the appellate court held that the PIC's "connection" with Louisiana was sufficient to permit imposition of the state's corporate income and franchise taxes. The court found that the out-of-state PIC licensed intangible properties to its in-state parent, which used them to conduct Louisiana business. Consequently, said the court, the intangibles were integral to the parent's in-state business activities. By integrating the out-of-state PIC's intangibles with the parent's in-state activities, the intangibles acquired a Louisiana *business situs.* The income derived from these intangibles was subject to state tax.

A&F TRADEMARK

Substantial Nexus Criteria for Sales Tax

North Carolina next used economic nexus as a basis for a state's taxing jurisdiction. In *A&F Trademark, Inc., v. Tolson* (605 S.E.2d 187 (N.C. Ct. App. 2004). *Cert. denied,* 126 SCt 353 (2005)), a Delaware PIC lacked a physical presence in North Carolina. It conducted no transactions with North Carolina residents. For franchise and income taxes, the appellate court relied on *Geoffrey*, finding that the state and PIC had substantial nexus. The court said that *Quill* did not apply the physical-presence requirement to every state tax, and, indeed, the *Quill* Court had noted that the physical-presence requirement had been applied only to sales tax.

The North Carolina court accordingly distinguished a sales tax from an income tax. States impose a duty to collect sales tax on out-of-state businesses based on three considerations:

- The state considers whether the business performs activities within the state;
- It considers whether these activities involve sales to in-state purchasers; and
- It considers whether the sales-related activity justifies the out-of-state business's duty to collect tax.

If substantial nexus is lacking, the out-of-state business cannot be required to collect sales tax. Nevertheless, the in-state purchaser remains legally liable for the tax and pays it, usually as use tax.

Application of Substantial Nexus to Income Tax

An income tax raises different considerations. An income tax is premised on the out-of-state corporation's using in-state business property to derive income from the state. Income tax differs from sales tax because, if substantial nexus is lacking for income tax, the tax is neither paid nor owed. A nexus analysis of income tax jurisdiction focuses on the state's inherent power to impose the tax. A nexus analysis of sales tax jurisdiction focuses on the state's right to impose a tax-collection duty, which is one step removed from the power to impose a tax.

Reporting Burden

These differences between sales and income taxes, said the North Carolina court, brought about different reporting requirements. As a rule, businesses that collect sales tax report and remit the taxes to multiple taxing authorities throughout the year, but report their income taxes annually. The court said that the multiple reporting requirements for sales tax resulted in unique administrative burdens, which justified the stricter physical-presence standard for substantial nexus analysis. On March 3, 2005, the U.S. Supreme Court declined to review *A&F Trademark.*

STUDY QUESTION

---

5. According to *A&F Trademark*, all of the following are factors when considering an out-of-state corporation's nexus for sales tax purposes *except* whether the out-of-state corporation:

a. Involves activities with in-state purchasers
b. Uses in-state business property
c. Performs activities within the state
d. Has activities that justify a tax collection obligation

LANCO

The trend among states was plainly toward economic nexus as the justification for imposing their income tax on revenues earned by PICs. But in *Lanco, Inc., v. Dir., Div. of Tax'n* (21 N.J. Tax 200 (2003). *Rev'd*), the New Jersey Tax Court broke ranks and held that New Jersey could not tax the income of a PIC that lacked any in-state physical presence. Tax practitioners therefore greatly anticipated the Superior Court of New Jersey's review of the decision.

Lanco, Inc. (Lanco) is a Delaware PIC that owns intangible properties (trademarks, trade names, and service marks). In return for royalties, Lanco licensed the intangibles to its affiliate, Lane Bryant, Inc., which used them in its retail business in New Jersey. Lanco lacked a physical presence in New Jersey. Through its retail operations, Lane Bryant had physical presence in New Jersey and paid the state's corporation business tax. Arguing that Lanco had economic nexus with New Jersey, the state assessed Lanco with income tax.

The State's Position

The state argued that, because Lanco entered into a long-term contract with Lane Bryant, a New Jersey retailer, it derived significant benefits from deliberate, continued, in-state economic activity. The Lanco Lane Bryant relationship created economic benefits that exceeded those enjoyed by the out-of-state business in *Quill*. In *Quill*, the out-of-state retailer benefited merely from the U.S. mail and common carriers, which shipped products into the state.

New Jersey also argued that the PIC's licensing agreement increased Lane Bryant's in-state retail sales. This increase burdened the state by increasing traffic, requiring police and fire protection, and imposing demands on local labor. Finally, the state argued that the licensing agreement conferred numerous state benefits on the PIC. The courts protected the Lanco Lane Bryant contract and Lanco's intangible property. They protected the tangible property to which the intangibles—Lane Bryant's trademarks—were affixed. The state supplied police and fire protection for the tangible property that bore the trademarks, and Lanco benefited from state-maintained highways and a state-educated work force. In *Lanco, Inc., v. Dir., Div. of Tax'n.* (879 A.2d 1234 (N.J. Super. Ct. App. Div. 2005)), the Superior Court of New Jersey reversed the Tax Court's decision.

Lanco offered no new legal analysis of economic nexus. It simply followed what it called the "better reasoned" cases of those that had followed *Geoffrey*, and quoted extensively from *A&F Trademark*'s discussion of *Kmart* and *Gap*. The court agreed that *Quill* applied only to sales taxes, but it did not explain why the facts peculiar to *Lanco* established nexus. Presumably, the facts identified by the state satisfied *Geoffrey*'s requirements for economic nexus. Neither did *Lanco* resolve *Quill*'s unanswered questions—whether physical presence is synonymous with substantial nexus. *Lanco* relied on *A&F Trademark* and *Kmart*, which emphasized the PIC's exploitation of a state's market through an in-state affiliate. *Lanco* also relied on *Gap*, which said that a PIC's intangibles "integrated" with an in-state affiliate's business by exploiting the state's market. This integration gave the intangibles an in-state business situs.

In the cases *Lanco* cited, economic nexus turned on an affiliate's in-state presence and its relationship with the out-of-state PIC. What none of the cases addressed, including *Lanco*, was fundamental Commerce Clause jurisprudence. None of the courts explained how states could impose income taxes on physically absent corporations without harming the U.S. economy by interfering with interstate commerce. According to *Quill*, analyzing this interference is fundamental to identifying violations of the Commerce Clause.

Proxy Role of Economic Nexus

Lanco and the cases preceding it use economic nexus as a proxy for physical presence. A physically present, in-state affiliate had to exist for economic nexus to exist. It was the affiliate's *in-state* activities that integrated with the out-of-state PIC's intangible property. In this respect, economic nexus is another way to "attribute" the in-state affiliate's physical nexus to the out-of-state PIC. *Attributional nexus* might more precisely describe such nexus.

Seen this way, economic nexus could fail in the way similar theories of sales tax have failed. Courts refuse to impose a sales-tax-collection duty on out-of-state retailers based solely on their affiliation with in-state retailers (see, e.g., ***Current, Inc., v. Cal. Bd. of Equalization***, 24 Cal. App. 4th 382, 29 Cal. Rptr. 2d 407 (1st Dist. 1994); and ***SFA Folio Collections, Inc., v. Tracy***, 652 N.E.2d 693 (Ohio 1995)). It remains to be seen whether these courts will reject economic nexus for income taxation as attributional nexus by another name.

Lanco tells us only what substantial nexus is *not.* Consequently, the opinion provides no understanding of cases such as ***J.C. Penney Natl. Bank v. Johnson*** (19 S.W.3d 831 (Tenn. Ct. App. 1999)), or ***America Online, Inc., v. Johnson*** (No. M2001-00927-COA-R3-CV, 2002 WL 1751434 (Tenn. Ct. App. July 30, 2002)). In these cases, states tried imposing income tax on out-of-state businesses that lacked an in-state affiliate that exploited the state's market. If these cases and *Lanco* are found to conflict, economic nexus does not turn on the difference between sales tax and income tax. It turns on whether an out-of-state business uses an in-state affiliate to exploit a state market. On October 12, 2006, the New Jersey Supreme Court affirmed the superior court's ruling with substantially the same reasoning emphasizing that the *Quill* holding applies only to sales and use taxes (***Lanco, Inc., v. Director, Division of Taxation***, 908 A.2d 176 (N.J. 2006).

STUDY QUESTIONS

6. In *Lanco*, New Jersey argued Lanco had significant in-state activities for all of the following reasons *except:*

    a. A long-term contract with New Jersey retailer creating economic benefit

    b. State-protected intangible property rights

    c. An in-state physical presence

    d. An increased state burden for police and fire protection

7. The *Lanco* court relied on what type of nexus to impose income taxes on Lane Bryant's PIC?

    a. Economic nexus

    b. Substantial nexus

    c. Physical presence

    d. Attributional nexus

OKLAHOMA'S *GEOFFREY*

After *Lanco*, the Oklahoma Court of Civil Appeals decided *Geoffrey, Inc., v. the Okla. Tax Comm'n* (132 P.3d 632 (Okla. Civ. App. Div. 1, 2005)) (*Geoffrey II*). The Oklahoma court approved the state's theory of economic nexus as the justification for imposing income tax on a physically absent PIC. In so doing, the court answered key questions left unanswered by prior cases.

The Oklahoma court agreed with *Lanco* and *A&F Trademark* on two points:

- The starting point for nexus analysis is substantial nexus, not physical presence; and
- The physical-presence requirement applies only to sales and use taxes.

The court then turned its attention to the benefit received by the PIC, which was not market exploitation via in-state affiliates; it was income derived from Oklahoma customers. This was the sole justification for Oklahoma's imposition of income tax liability on the out-of-state PIC. As for the Commerce Clause analysis, the court placed the burden of persuasion on the taxpayer. The court said that the PIC failed to explain how a different nexus standard for different taxes burdened interstate commerce. The court appears to have presumed that evidence of economic nexus is rebutted by evidence of a Commerce Clause violation. Be this as it may, *Geoffrey II* suggests that an affiliation between in-state and out-of-state businesses does not, by itself, create economic nexus.

STUDY QUESTION

---

8. All of the following statements regarding the imposition of income taxes on out-of-state PICs were made by the **Geoffrey II** court **except:**

   a. The starting point for the nexus analysis is substantial nexus

   b. The physical presence standard only applies to sales and use taxes

   c. The physical presence standard applies to both sales taxes and income taxes

   d. All of the above statements were made by the **Geoffrey II** court

---

STATE ACTIONS

State legislatures are not waiting for their courts to invoke economic nexus to tax the income of out-of-state PICs. Ohio and other states have adopted legislation denying gross income deductions for interest, royalties, and licensing fees paid to PICs (see, *e.g.,* Ohio Rev. Code Ann. §5733.042). States such as California have adopted unitary-combined reporting. This requires a parent and its PIC to combine their income to calculate total taxable income apportionable to a state. Unitary-combined reporting eliminates the PIC's tax advantages because a company's royalty expense deductions offset the PIC's royalty income. It creates one taxable entity that, in effect, both uses and owns the intangible. The transaction becomes a "wash" for income tax purposes.

Indiana, New York, and other noncombined reporting states see their fair share of PICs. To combat these tax-avoidance strategies, these states use *Geoffrey* and a theory of economic nexus to directly impose tax on the remote PIC, asserting that there exists contact with the state sufficient to establish tax jurisdiction.

Lanco, Geoffrey, and similar decisions give states an upper hand in countering what they consider to be tax avoidance. But the starting point for a state's taxation of out-of-state corporations' in-state activities remains the dormant Commerce Clause. Even if a state income tax comports with the clause, it must also comport with federal law. P.L. 86-272 (15 U.S.C. §381), which limits state power to impose a net income tax (or a franchise tax measured by net income) on certain income earned by out-of-state corporations. States cannot tax income from sales of tangible personal property if the corporation's activities within the state amount to nothing more than soliciting sales from in-state customers. Federal law has deemed solicitation a *protected activity*—an in-state activity that an out-of-state corporation can perform without subjecting itself to income tax. *Geoffrey* and the cases that followed do not change this determination.

STUDY QUESTION

9. Which of the following states uses unitary-combined reporting to eliminate tax advantages related to out-of-state PICs?

   a. Indiana
   b. Ohio
   c. New York
   d. California

CONCLUSION

Geoffrey and its progeny make plain that future cases may only grapple with *Quill* and substantial nexus by concentrating more on economic substance. It is hoped courts will pay more attention to how, and how extensively, out-of-state corporations exploit a taxing jurisdiction's market. Whether a corporation's lack of physical presence poses a significant barrier to market penetration must be considered. Courts need to address whether the nature of the out-of-state corporation requires it to have no more than a *de minimis* physical presence in any state. As the courts' distinction between sales and income tax shows, questions about the economic and legal incidences of a tax are relevant. Most importantly (indeed, this is the elephant in the room), courts will eventually need to address whether economic nexus impermissibly burdens interstate commerce.

Answers to these questions will require more sophisticated proofs than the taxpayer's mere claim of having no presence in the state. They require both economic and policy analysis. Practically, in the short term, *Geoffrey* and its increasing progeny, plus the U.S. Supreme Court's refusal to grant *certiorari* in *A&F Trademark*, will convince taxpayers to settle existing litigation and avoid it in the future. Because of such questions left unanswered, *Lanco, Geoffrey II* and their predecessors' long-term effect is unknown. Chances are that the answers will not be long in coming. For now, it is clear that economic nexus, not *Quill*'s physical-presence requirement, is the jurisdictional touchstone for state income tax.

STUDY QUESTION

---

10. To address nexus issues thoroughly, courts must *eventually* consider which of the following?

   a. Economic and policy analysis relating to an out-of-state corporation's taxability

   b. How extensively an out-of-state corporation exploits the taxing jurisdiction's market

   c. Whether the *Quill* physical presence standard applies to income taxes

   d. Whether an out-of-state corporation must have more than *de minimis* physical presence

---

MODULE 1 — CHAPTER 2

Passive Investment Companies

This chapter examines the tax planning strategy using passive investment companies to save on state income taxes. Should out-of-state companies be able to sell goods and services in a state where they do not have a physical presence and do not pay income taxes on the revenue received? Are in-state companies with a physical presence that pay income taxes put at a competitive disadvantage? Do out-of-state companies put equal demands on government services and receive equal benefit from taxes paid as their in-state competitor? Many state revenue officials believe that companies are not paying their fair share of income taxes because they use intricate corporate structures and complicated intercompany transactions to reduce their tax burdens.

LEARNING OBJECTIVES

Upon completion of this chapter, you should be able to:

■ Understand the tax planning advantages of PICs;

■ Distinguish differences in tax results between consolidated returns and separate company returns;

■ Articulate ways separate filing states may challenge PICs as a tax planning strategy;

■ Recite recent case law pertaining to PICs and the courts' discussions of nexus; and

■ Determine due diligence to avoid PIC legal challenges.

INTRODUCTION

Distinguished U.S. Circuit Court Judge Learned Hand wrote in ***Heavering v. Gregory*** (F.2d 809, 810 (2d Cir. 1934)). "Any one may so arrange his affairs that his taxes shall be as low as possible; he is not bound to choose that pattern which will best pay the Treasury." Judge Hand's words are inspirational to corporate tax planners. However, would consumers continue to patronize many of the most popular brand name stores such as The Limited, Toys 'R' Us, Home Depot, Kmart, Gap, and Burger King knowing that these companies may be involved in a domestic tax planning strategy that is saving millions in corporate taxes but causing shortfalls in state budget receipts (Simpson, Glenn R., Diminishing Returns: A Tax Maneuver in Delaware Puts Squeeze on States, The Wall Street Journal, August 9, 2002)? Or would consumers, some of which are company stockholders, expect businesses to do what they can to legitimately lower business expenses, thus enabling the business to pass on savings to consumers by lowering prices on products and services? The adjective *passive* has been defined in Merriam-Webster's dictionary as "of, relating to, or being business activity in which the investor does not have immediate control over income."

STATE INITIATIVES

Revenue officials believe *passive investment companies (PICs)*—also known as *intangible* or *trademark holding companies*, and *Delaware* or *Nevada holding companies*—are hardly passive. Rather, PICs are a very active tax planning strategy used by multinational and multistate companies to shelter billions of dollars in income from state corporate income taxes.

The Multistate Tax Commission (MTC) completed an analysis of 2001 state income tax collections and estimated that tax shelters lowered state tax revenues by more than one-third, or approximately $12.4 billion (Multistate Tax Commission, Corporate Tax Sheltering Linked to as Much as $12.4 Billion in Lost State Tax Revenues, July 15, 2003). At a time when state and local government budgets are starving for revenues to maintain services and keep pace with spiraling costs, tax officials and state legislatures have been looking hard for new and lost revenues given that state and local governments are required to balance their budgets annually. Auditors are aggressively challenging tax deductions and legislatures are enacting new tax laws tightening up loopholes. In 2003, the Center on Budget and Policy Priorities issued a report recommending that states could raise revenues by closing three common corporate income tax loopholes (Mazerov, Michael, *Closing Three Common Corporate Income Tax Loopholes Could Raise Additional Revenue for Many States,* Center on Budget and Policy Priorities April 1, 2003). In order to raise millions of dollars in untaxed revenues, one of the recommendations in the report was for states to enact new laws to stop companies from using royalty, licensing, and interest payments for reducing taxable income in states that do not tax these payments or have lower state tax rates.

Analysts for the Florida legislature came to a similar conclusion in a 2003 report, Why Did Florida's Corporate Income Tax Revenue Fall While Corporate Profits Rose? The study concluded that companies are avoiding the state income tax through several schemes including using PICs. The report estimated that $40 million in tax revenues was lost because company profits were being transferred to nontaxable holding companies.

In December 2003, the Maryland State Comptroller issued an ultimatum in a press release presenting, "a one-time settlement offer to 70 holding companies in Delaware who owe more than $31.4 million in Maryland taxes, advising them to pay up soon to avoid heavy penalties" (State Tax Notes, Tax Counsel's Corner Maryland Comptroller `Offers a Deal to Settle Delaware Holding Company Cases—Is It a Deal you Ought to Accept?, December 15, 2003). This so-called threat came on the heels of the U.S.

Supreme Court denying certiorari to consider reviewing two Delaware holding company decisions made by the Maryland Court of Appeals in *Syl Inc.* and *Crown Cork & Seal Co.* The Court of Appeals reversed lower court decisions, ruling that the income of these two holding companies was taxable. But opponents contend that the facts of these cases were weak and that holding companies with economic substance (unlike *Syl* and *Crown*) may be afforded Constitutional protections and pass scrutiny with the U.S. Supreme Court.

Perhaps one of the most aggressive states to pursue untaxed corporate income is New Jersey. In recent years, New Jersey has had an annual revenue shortfall crisis. In response, New Jersey enacted the Business Tax Reform Act in 2002 that raised income taxes and fees on most businesses by disallowing business deductions and expenses of interaffiliated companies, closing loopholes, challenging physical and economic nexus standards, and creating the alternative minimum assessment tax.

STUDY QUESTION

1. In recent years, New Jersey has attempted to raise annual revenue by doing all of the following *except:*
   a. Enacting the Business Tax Reform Act
   b. Advising holding companies to pay tax or face heavy penalties
   c. Creating the alternative minimum assessment tax
   d. Challenging physical and economic nexus standards

WHAT IS A PIC?

A *passive investment company (PIC)* is a company organized to profit from holding, managing, and protecting intangible assets—patents, trademarks, trade names, stocks, bonds, and other nonoperating assets. It may also make loans and pay dividends to other companies. PICs have a legitimate business purpose such as protecting trademarks and patents from infringement, shielding companies from claims of creditors, and separating the profits of intangible assets from tangible assets. Nonetheless, PICs are also used as a state tax planning strategy to shift taxable income from an affiliated company in a high tax rate state to an affiliated company in a lower tax rate or no tax state. This strategy of state tax planning is only appropriate for companies in those states that require separate company tax returns.

STUDY QUESTION

> **2.** All of the following are true statements about PICs *except:*
>
>   **a.** PICs are used as a state tax planning strategy by shifting income to lower tax rate states.
>   **b.** PICs manage and protect intangible assets.
>   **c.** PICs are a successful tax planning strategy against all states' income taxes.
>   **d.** PICs may make loans and pay dividends to other affiliated companies.

TWO SETS OF BOOKS

A brief review of corporate financial and tax reporting will provide some background information on filing requirements. Many multinational and multistate companies are organized as having a parent corporation with several subsidiary corporations. U.S. corporations that have publicly traded equity securities are required to report their financial condition on a consolidated basis. "Consolidated statements reflect the practical reality that a group of commonly controlled corporations often functions as a single economic entity. Consistent with the single entity view of a multicorporate group, any income or expense arising from intercompany transactions is eliminated so that the group's reported earnings reflect only the items of income and expense arising from transactions with unrelated parties" (Healy, J.C.,and Schadewald, M.S., Multistate Tax Guide, Panel Publication).

Unlike public financial statement reporting, U.S. corporations have an option when filing federal income tax returns, and corporate income tax reporting is based on where a taxpayer resides and where its income is earned. Corporations can elect to file a U.S. federal tax return for each separate company or can file a consolidated tax return of an affiliated group of companies. A tax benefit of filing a consolidated U.S. tax return is that the profits and losses of affiliated companies can be netted against each other. As simple as the federal filing options seem, compliance with state corporate income taxation can be difficult. Forty-five states and Washington, D.C. have some form of a corporate income tax or franchise tax based on income. "Before a state can tax income earned in interstate commerce, it must be able to show a connection or *nexus* between the state and the activities from which the income is derived. Nexus is a federal issue and is governed in the first instance by the U.S. Constitution .... Both the Commerce Clause and the Due Process Clause prohibit state taxation of interstate activities, even on a proportional basis, unless there is a minimal connection or nexus between the activities and the taxing state and a rational relationship between the income attributed to the state and the intrastate values of the enterprise" (CCH Incorporated, Tax Reporter—Nexus P.L. 86-272). States target companies for state income compliance using audit teams, questionnaires, information sharing agreements, referrals, and voluntary compliance.

Federal taxable income is used by most states as a starting point from which state statutes mandate varying adjustments. "Under the U.S. Constitution, a state may tax that portion of a corporation's income that has a sufficient connection or relationship with the state. This necessary connection or relationship is referred to as nexus"(Pomp & Oldman, State & Local Taxation 2001) Chapter 10 State Corporate Taxes).

In addition to the U.S. Constitution, there are other constraints placed on state taxation of business income, such as the Uniform Division of Income for Tax Purposes Act (codified, at least in part, by some states) and Public Law 86-272, the Interstate Income Tax Act. UDITPA defines *business income* as "income arising from transactions and activity in the regular course of the taxpayer's trade or business, and includes income from tangible and intangible property if the acquisition, management, and disposition of the property constitute integral parts of the taxpayer's regular trade or business operations. Nonbusiness income means all income other than business income" (Uniform Division of Income for Tax Purposes Act ,1957, Section 1 Paragraph (a) and (e)). UDITPA provides definitions and rules for reporting business and nonbusiness income. As a result, business income derived from regular business activities is apportioned to every state where the company has nexus based on its proportionate share to the whole enterprise. Nonbusiness income received from nonbusiness activities is allocated to only one state. P.L. 86-272 is a federal law that limits income tax nexus on out-of-state businesses when their business activity in the state is restricted to the solicitation of sales, provided that the sales orders are approved and filled outside the state imposing the tax.

These different reporting requirements for public financial statements and options for filing federal income tax returns necessitate keeping two sets of books. Two sets of books are also necessary for state income tax reporting because nexus determines whether a state may tax the income of each separate company.

STUDY QUESTIONS

---

3. All of the following must be shown before a state may impose an income tax on a multinational corporation, *except*:

   a. Nexus
   b. Minimal connection
   c. Rational relationship
   d. Voluntary compliance

---

4. Which of the following is a federal law limiting a state's ability to tax a multinational corporation's income?
   a. Due Process Clause
   b. Uniform Division of Income for Tax Purposes Act
   c. Commerce Clause
   d. Interstate Income Tax Act

STATE INCOME TAX REPORTING

There are several types of state income tax return filings. "State filing options fall into one of the following five categories:
■ Mandatory separate company returns;
■ Elective consolidated returns;
■ Mandatory combined unitary reporting;
■ Discretionary combined unitary reporting; and
■ A hybrid system, which includes both elective consolidated returns and discretionary combined unitary reporting."

Pertinent to the topic of this essay is the advantage "of filing separate company returns provides taxpayers with the opportunity to create legal structures and intercompany transactions that shift income from affiliates based in high-tax states to affiliates based in low- or no-tax states... "Disadvantages of filing a separate company return include the inability to offset losses of one affiliate against profits of other affiliates and the need to develop defensible arm's-length transfer prices for intercompany transactions"(Healy, J.C., and Schadewald, M.S., Multistate Tax Guide, Panel Publication). Contrastingly, a major advantage of filing a consolidated tax return is that it enables the company to eliminate the profits of a company with the losses of an affiliated company in order to reduce taxable income of the affiliated group.

In 1977, the U.S. Supreme Court ruled in ***Complete Auto Transit Inc. v. Brady*** that the Commerce Clause places limits on state taxation. In the decision, the Court established that a tax on interstate commerce was legal if it passed a four-pronged test:
■ The tax has to be on a business activity with substantial nexus with the taxing state;
■ The tax has to be fairly apportioned;
■ The tax cannot discriminate against interstate commerce; and
■ The tax has to be fairly related to the services provided by the state.

As a means to comply with case law and nexus requirements most states use formulary apportionment to determine taxable income. Typically, states rely on three factors—the amount of payroll, property, and sales in their respective state—to determine their proportionate share of taxable income.

STUDY QUESTION

5. One disadvantage of filing a consolidated tax return is the inability to offset losses of one affiliate against profits of other affiliates. *True or False?*

PICS FOR PLANNING PURPOSES

Some companies use PICs as a planning strategy to minimize their state income tax burden. Corporate tax managers principally use one of two primary methods of reducing income taxes in a given state:

- Lower apportionable income; or
- Lower apportionment factors.

In the several states that require separate entity tax reporting, corporate tax managers using PICs can take advantage of both methods, arranging for or transferring intangible assets that generate nonoperating income such as trademarks, trade names, patents, bonds, stocks, and notes from a company in a high-tax-rate state to an intangible PIC located in a lower- or no-tax state, e.g., Delaware or Nevada. The income received by the PIC from these nonoperating assets, such as licensing fees, royalty fees, and interest are considered to be received in Delaware or Nevada and thus are taxed at a lower rate or not at all by other states. Typically, an affiliated company or the parent company pays a royalty or fee for using the intangible assets or it may pay interest on debt owed to the PIC. Consequently, if the parent company is required to file a separate company tax return, it may be able to deduct the licensing fees, royalty fees and interest paid to the PIC from its taxable income thereby lowering its state tax burden. An example follows.

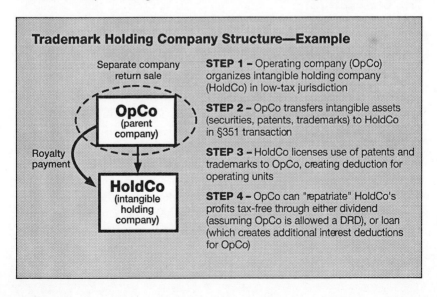

Trademark Holding Company Structure—Example

Separate company return sale

OpCo (parent company)

Royalty payment

HoldCo (intangible holding company)

STEP 1 – Operating company (OpCo) organizes intangible holding company (HoldCo) in low-tax jurisdiction

STEP 2 – OpCo transfers intangible assets (securities, patents, trademarks) to HoldCo in §351 transaction

STEP 3 – HoldCo licenses use of patents and trademarks to OpCo, creating deduction for operating units

STEP 4 – OpCo can "repatriate" HoldCo's profits tax-free through either dividend (assuming OpCo is allowed a DRD), or loan (which creates additional interest deductions for OpCo)

However, the PIC must avoid establishing nexus in other states and it must make sure that it can demonstrate that it has a legitimate economic and business purpose in order to defend challenges by tax auditors of being a sham business arrangement for not paying taxes.

Using PICs as a means to reduce state income taxes originated as an unintentional consequence of two U.S. Supreme Court decisions dealing with sales and use taxation: *National Bellas Hess, Inc. v. Department of Revenue of Illinois* (386 US 753 (1967)) and *Quill Corporation v. North Dakota* (504 US 298 (1992)). In these two cases, the Court established the nexus principle in that a state could not collect sales tax from a company that did not have a physical presence in the state and that the Due Process Clause of the U.S. Constitution prevented states from collecting tax from a company that only had a minor connection or relationship in the state and received no significant benefits from the state. In other words, *nexus* can be defined as the minimum business activity that enables a state to tax the income of the business. The Court further reinforced the Commerce Clause of the Constitution, whereby only Congress can regulate interstate commerce and states cannot impede interstate business by taxing interstate business transactions that don't have "substantial nexus." Using the logic of these decisions and other subsequent cases, companies have structured their organizations and business transactions so that passive income does not create nexus by locating the PIC in a low- or no-tax state such as Delaware and Nevada. To the chagrin of other states, Delaware or Nevada have established themselves as domestic tax havens with a cottage industry that promotes the state's favorable business and tax laws to companies.

THE CHALLENGE

States have proffered many challenges to the legality of Delaware holding companies. State revenue officials have several tools available to challenge this tax strategy and also rely primarily on their legislatures and courts for relief:

A separate entity state that wishes to challenge the use of a holding company can assert a variety of arguments. The holding company can be attacked as lacking substance, the transfer of assets to the holding company can be challenged as lacking a business purpose or challenged as lacking substance, the taxing state can assert nexus over the holding company or tax the income paid to the holding company, deductions can be denied as not being legitimate business expenditures or recharacterized as capital expenditures, debt can be recharacterized as equity and so forth (Healy, J.C.,and Schadewald, M.S., Multistate Tax Guide, Panel Publication).

States can adopt new rules and regulations that disallow specific intercompany transactions that distort taxable income or add back tax deductions such as intercompany interest or royalty payments. Separate reporting states could also adopt combined company tax reporting rules that negate the shifting of taxable income.

STUDY QUESTION

> **6.** All of the following are means for separate filing states to challenge PICs as a tax planning strategy *except:*
>
> **a.** Establish the PIC lacks substance
> **b.** Adopt regulations disallowing specific intercompany transactions
> **c.** Deny legitimate business expenditures
> **d.** Assert nexus over the PIC

NEXUS, NEXUS—WHO'S GOT NEXUS?

More so than federal courts, state courts have been quite active in recent years expanding the tax base predicated on economic nexus rather than physical nexus. This may be attributed to the courts recognizing the transitioning of the American economy toward electronic commerce faster than does the legislative branch of government. Challenges to intangible PICs have included: the South Carolina Supreme Court ruling in 1993 that Geoffrey Inc., a wholly owned subsidiary of Toys 'R Us, Inc., was liable for state income taxes on royalty income it received from Toys 'R Us, Inc. Geoffrey did not have any employees, offices, or tangible property in South Carolina. It held several trade names and trademarks that it licensed to Toy 'R Us, Inc., for royalty payments on net Toys 'R Us sales. Although Geoffrey did not have a physical presence in the state, the Supreme Court determined that Geoffrey had economic nexus that made the royalty income taxable (see *Geoffrey, Inc. v. South Carolina Tax Commission,* July 6, 1993).

In one of the strongest challenges to intangible holding companies, the New Mexico Court of Appeals ruled in 2001 that the physical presence requirement developed in the *Quill* sales tax decision was not applicable to state income taxes. The court ruled against Kmart Properties Inc. (KPI), a Michigan corporation, deciding that Kmart Corporation (KPI's parent, also a Michigan corporation) created KPI for the purpose of holding title and collecting royalties to the Kmart trade name and trademarks licensed to Kmart Corporation. KPI did not have any employees or offices in New Mexico. Kmart Corporation deducted the royalty payments it made to KPI and KPI did not pay New Mexico income taxes because it did not have a physical presence in New Mexico. The court held that KPI had agency nexus in New Mexico and was subject to income taxes. The court wrote:

> We conclude that the combination of Kmart Corporation's activities in New Mexico, together with the tangible presence of KPI's marks, constitutes the functional equivalent of physical presence as afforded by the independent representatives in *Scripto* and *Tyler Pipe*.... An independent representative present in the taxing state satisfies the physical presence test and Commerce Clause concerns (*Kmart Properties, Inc. v. Taxation and Revenue Department of the State of New Mexico,* No. 21, 140, November 27, 2001).

North Carolina has also jumped on the economic nexus wagon. In *A&F Trademark, Inc. V. Tolson* (North Carolina Court of Appeals, December 7, 2004; petition for review denied by the NC Supreme Court), the Court of Appeals ruled that although *A& F* did not have a physical presence in the state, the company met the requirements of doing business in the state pursuant to tax rules in operating a business or conducting a business activity for economic gain using trade names and trademarks. The U.S. Supreme Court denied certiorari (U.S. SCt. Dkt. No. 04-1625, 10/3/05)

Interestingly and perhaps serving as the bellwether of physical nexus versus economic nexus tax cases is a New Jersey Tax Court decision rendered in 2003 involving related plaintiffs in *A&F Trademark*. Lanco Inc, a Delaware holding company, charged its parent company, Lane Bryant, for the use of its trademarks. Contrary to the economic nexus cases decided by other state courts, the New Jersey Tax Court ruled that Lanco was not taxable under the state's corporate business tax because Lanco did not have a physical presence in New Jersey. Lanco did not have any property, offices, or employees in New Jersey. After reviewing and analyzing several court decisions from other states most notably the South Carolina Geoffrey case, the tax court said:

> This analysis leads to the conclusion that the physical presence of the taxpayer or its employees(s), agent(s), or tangible property in a jurisdiction has been and remains a necessary element for a finding of substantial nexus under the Commerce Clause of the United States Constitution....It does not appear that the difference between the use tax collection obligation on one hand, and the liability for income taxation on the other are so significant to justify a different rule for each concerning physical presence as an element of Commerce Clause nexus(*Lanco Inc. v. Dir. New Jersey Division of Taxation,* docket No. 005329-97, 10/23/2003, NJSC, Appelate Division, No. A-3285-03T1, August 24, 2005, NJSC A-89-05).

On appeal, the Court of Appeals reversed the Tax Court ruling that the physical presence test established by the U.S. Supreme Court in *Quill* only applies to sales and use taxation. The Court ruled "We are satisfied that the physical presence requirement applicable to sales and use taxes is not applicable to income tax and the New Jersey Business Corporation Tax may be constitutionally applied to income derived by plaintiff from licensing fees attributable to New Jersey." The Court also determined that an economic presence was enough to create taxable nexus pursuant to the Commerce Clause. Perhaps in recognizing the importance of this case and its implications beyond New Jersey's borders and in anticipation of an appeal, presiding Judge Edwin H. Stern summed up best the direction of nexus cases in the Court's opinion in his comments:

> In *Quill*, the U.S. Supreme Court affirmed the four-part standard for cases involving Commerce Clause challenges to state taxation. In that case, the Supreme Court determined that, in the context of sales and use taxes, an entity must be physically present in the taxing jurisdiction to establish the constitutionally required "substantial nexus." Since *Quill*, a split of authority has developed in respect of whether this holding is limited to sales and use taxes (*Lanco*, pp. pp. 1-3).

> The better interpretation of *Quill* is the one adopted by those states that limit the Supreme Court's holding to sales and use taxes, an interpretation that reflects the language of *Quill*. The Supreme Court carefully limited its language to a discussion of sales and use taxes. This court does not believe that the Supreme Court intended to create a universal physical-presence requirement for state taxation under the commerce clause (*Lanco*, pp. 3-4).

Needless to say, the *Lanco* decision was appealed to the New Jersey Supreme Court and in October 2006 the Court affirmed the Court of Appeals per curiam.

The *Lanco* decision was subsequently reinforced by the West Virginia Supreme Court of Appeals in its November 2006 decision of *Tax Commissioner v. MBNA America Bank, N.A* (640 S.E.2d 226, November 21, 2006). MBNA was a Delaware bank that provided credit card services to its customers throughout the United States. Similar to Lanco, MBNA did not have a physical presence in West Virginia. In the MBNA case, the West Virginia court affirmed the Circuit Court of Kanawha County ruling that the state could impose a business franchise tax and a corporate net income tax without violating the Commerce Clause despite the fact that MBNA did not have a physical presence in West Virginia. The court determined that MBNA's business activities that included direct mail, telemarketing and advertising in the state created sufficient economic presence in the state meeting the nexus tests enunciated in *Complete Auto Transit, Inc. v. Brady.* The West Virginia court held that it was the intent of the U.S. Supreme Court in *Bellas Hess* and reaffirmed in *Quill* that the physical presence test of the Commerce Clause only applied to state sales and use taxes not state corporate net income taxes.

While tax practitioners wait for Congress and/or the U.S. Supreme Court to ultimately settle the nexus issue PICs should work to establish clear and legitimate business agreements between affiliated companies and holding companies in order to avoid legal challenges. Appropriate due diligence would include:

- Creating a valid business and economic purpose for the holding company;
- Actively defending patent and trademark infringements;
- Affiliates having market based licensing fees, royalty rates and loan terms;
- Locating the holding company in its own separate offices and having separate stationery;
- Having separate employees, board of directors, and meetings;
- Having separate tangible assets, accounting records, and financial statements, accounts receivable and payables, bank accounts, and payroll; and
- Arm's length contracts, agreements, and documents related to the custody and protection of intangible property.

STUDY QUESTIONS

7. Where did a state Supreme Court determine that direct mail, telemarketing, and advertising in the state created sufficient economic presence for the state to impose a corporate income tax?

    a. New Mexico
    b. West Virginia
    c. New Jersey
    d. North Carolina

8. Appropriate due diligence for avoiding legal challenges to PICs includes all of the following *except:*

    a. Limiting nexus to holding company's state
    b. Having separate holding company employees
    c. Locating holding company in its own separate offices
    d. Having separate tangible assets for the holding company and affiliated company

SCAPEGOAT?

Although there is no denying that PICs are used to reduce state corporate income taxes, PICs are not the single and most significant source for the drop in state income tax revenues. Because most states use federal taxable income as the beginning point for state income taxation, changes to federal tax laws such as increasing depreciation expense deductions have reduced the level of taxable income for state taxes. It was reported in *State Tax Notes* that

> Federal tax base decline could account for as much as 30 percent of the erosion of the state corporate effective tax rate. The corporate tax structure in almost every state begins with the federal definition of 'profits', so that state tax bases move with the federal base (Fox, William F., Three Characteristics o f Tax Structures have Contributed to the Current State Fiscal Crises, State Tax Notes, November 3, 2003, p. 374)

This is an interesting point of comparison to the MTC study mentioned earlier, which concluded that tax shelters lowered state tax revenues by one-third. In addition, the increased use of limited liability companies and partnerships resulting in taxable business income being passed through these business entities has also reduced state income taxes. Furthermore, states have contributed to declining revenues through their own actions by offering tax incentives and tax credits to new and expanding businesses and also changing their income apportionment formulas.

In an effort to reduce nexus controversies among states, legislation dealing with the nexus issue was introduced into the 108th Congress in 2003. H.R. 3184/S1736 and H.R. 3220 would attempt to clarify nexus standards for sales tax and state income taxes, respectively. However, these bills failed to get voted out of committee onto the floor of each House before the 108th Congress session ended. The Streamlined Sales and Use Tax Act (SSUTA) (H.R. 3184/S1736), was reintroduced in the 109th Congress as S2152 and S2153. Its intent was to expand the collection of sales and use taxes for some remote sellers. The Business Activity Tax Simplification Act (BATSA) (H.R. 3220) was reintroduced in the 109th Congress as H.R. 1956 and S2721. BATSA seeks to codify the physical presence standard for income, franchise, and other taxes and to expand the scope of U.S. P.L. 86-272.1 The legislation failed to come to a vote before the 109th Congress adjourned. There have not been any recent developments with these pieces of legislation. However, many states have adopted the SSUTA in its entirety or various provisions in part. The business community supports both BATSA and SSUTA, whereas most state and local government groups oppose BATSA. Opponents to BATSA argue that state taxation should be determined by the states, not the federal government; also, an unfair tax advantage will be given to out-of-state businesses over in-state businesses that maintain a physical presence as they compete for the same customers, especially given today's growing electronic commerce. Proponents, on the other hand, argue that in-state businesses with a physical presence place a greater demand on government services and should pay more in direct taxes relative to the benefits received compared to out-of-state businesses that do not receive direct benefits (National Governor's Association, Impact of H.R. 1956, Business Activity Tax Simplification Act of 2005, On States, September 26, 2005).

The use of passive investment companies as a tax-planning strategy can be effective if implemented properly. However the issue may get tangled up in the larger issue of federalism and the balance of power between the states and federal government. More than likely states will continue to challenge the purpose of PICs and state court decisions will conflict with one another so long as there is a need for tax revenues. Regardless of whether Congress passes new nexus legislation and/or the U.S. Supreme Court steps in, PICs will remain a very active state tax issue.

STUDY QUESTIONS

9. All of the following are reasons state income tax revenues have decreased *except:*
   a. Federal tax law changes
   b. Changes in state regulations
   c. State tax incentives
   d. Tax Shelters

10. In which of the following did Congress attempt to codify the physical presence standard for income, franchise, and other taxes?
    a. BATSA
    b. SSUTA
    c. H.R. 3184
    d. Public Law 86-272

MODULE 1 — CHAPTER 3

Series LLC

LEARNING OBJECTIVES

Upon completion of this chapter, you should be able to:

- Understand the new Revised Uniform Limited Liability Company Act;
- Describe how the series LLC is created;
- Distinguish a regular LLC from a series LLC;
- Articulate the differences in Illinois' series LLC statute from that of other states; and
- Explain the advantages and disadvantages of the series LLC.

THE REVISED UNIFORM LIMITED LIABILITY COMPANY ACT

The Revised Uniform Limited Liability Company Act ("RULLCA" or "the Act") was approved by the National Conference of Commissioners of Uniform State Laws ("NCCUSL") at its meeting in July 2006. The Act has now been finalized, including the reporter comments, and is currently under review by a number of committees within the American Bar Association, including the Committee on Partnerships and Unincorporated Business Organizations of the Section of Business Law. Even as that review proceeds, NCCUSL has identified RULLCA as one of its legislative priorities, and it has hopes for a significant number of adoptions within the next few legislative terms.

Why a New Uniform LLC Act?

The original Uniform LLC Act was completed in 1996. (6A ULA 553) However, having been completed even as the states were completing enactment of their initial first generation statutes (by the summer of 1994, over forty the states had already adopted LLC acts.), it saw only limited adoption. (ULLCA was eventually adopted in Alabama, Hawaii, Illinois, Montana, South Carolina, Vermont, the Virgin Islands, and West Virginia.) Certain of its elements, including the "at will" limited liability company, limited its enactability as a follow-on Act. (ULCA §101(2)) Several years ago it was determined that there now existed a critical pool of knowledge with respect to the operation of LLCs across the various states, and now that the check-the-box regulations have eliminated the Kintner (*A.R. Kintner*, CA-9, 54-2 USTC ¶9626, 216 F2d 418) classification limitations that existed in the drafting of all of the first generation acts, the decision was made to draft a new LLC Act.

A note on the process employed is in order. RULLCA is not simply an updated version of ULLCA. Rather, while ULLCA was certainly used as a model for certain of the provisions, nearly every LLC statute in the country was at some point or another referenced in the drafting process, as were other uniform model law products including RUPA, ULPA(2001) and the MBCA.

> **OBSERVATION**
>
> The Drafting Committee, whose entire membership is referenced in the Preface to RULLCA, included such luminaries in the field of unincorporated business organization law as Professor Beth Miller, Steven Frost, Robert Keatinge, Prof. Tom Dewey, Scott Ludwig, William Callison, Prof. Ann Conaway, Paul "Chip" Lion, Daniel Kleinberger and Carter Bishop, the last two of whom served as the reporters on the project.

The Structure of the Act

RULLCA's format is similar to that utilized in ULLCA as well as that utilized in RUPA and ULPA (2001). (*See* Figure 1.)

Figure 1

Article I	contains	general provisions including definitions, duration, purposes, powers, name, registered office/agent for service of process, and the operating agreement
Article II	provides	formation of the LLC and public filing of LLC records
Article III	governs	relations of members and managers to third parties
Article IV	states	default rules for members' relationship amongst themselves and to the LLC; member management and manager managership
Article V	governs	transfers and transferees
Article VI	states	causes and consequences of a member's dissociation from the LLC
Article VII	delineates	causes and consequences of the dissolution of the LLC
Article VIII	governs	foreign LLCs
Article IX	provides	direct and derivative claims
Article X	governs	organic transactions
Article XI	contains	miscellaneous provisions including transition rules

What About Series LLCs?

A conscious decision was made in the course of the drafting process *not* to include in this Act provisions for the series LLC. In part, this decision was based upon the continuing uncertainty regarding the tax treatment of the series and issues concerning the recognition of the internal liability shield in interstate transactions.

The Uncabining of Fiduciary Duties

In contrast to RUPA, ULLCA, and ULPA (2001), RULLCA adopts an "uncabining" approach to fiduciary duties. While those predecessor acts sought to provide an exclusive listing of the fiduciary duties (*See, e.g.*, RUPA §404(a) (the *only* fiduciary duties owed by a partner are those of loyalty and care)), RULLCA does not purport to limit the fiduciary duties to those of care and loyalty. (*See* RULLCA §409(a)) In this respect, the comment to Section 409 is important, providing in part:

After lengthy discussion in the Drafting Committee and on the floor of the 2006 Annual Meeting, the Conference decided that:

- The "corral" created by RUPA does not fit in the very complex and variegated world of LLCs; and
- It is impracticable to cabin all LLC-related fiduciary duties within a statutory formulation.

As a result, this Act:
- eschews "only" and "limited to" --the words RUPA used in an effort to exhaustively codify fiduciary duty;
- codifies the core of the fiduciary duty of loyalty; but
- does not purport to discern every possible category of overreaching. One important consequence is to allow courts to continue to use fiduciary duty concepts to police disclosure operations in member-to-member and member-LLC transactions.

It is important to review the uncabining language in the context of RULLCA §110(c)(4), which provides that the operating agreement may not "eliminate the duty of loyalty, the duty of care, or any other fiduciary duty." With this language, it is not possible for the operating agreement to exclude the existence of any other fiduciary duties that may, at common law, be found to apply in the context of a particular LLC, a small triumph of those wedded to the fiduciary view over those often labeled the contractarians.

The Duty of Care

Again departing from the formulae utilized in prior unincorporated business organization acts, RULLCA has adopted its own standard of care, namely:

Subject to the business judgment rule, the duty of care of the member of a member-managed [LLC] and the conduct and winding-up of the company's activities is to act with the care that a person in a like position would reasonably exercise under similar circumstances and in a manner the member reasonably believes to be in the best interests of the company. (RULLCA §409(c))

> **OBSERVATION**
>
> *Contrast* RUPA §404(c) ("A partner's duty of care to the partnership and the other partners in the conduct and winding-up of the partnership business is limited to refraining from engaging in grossly negligent or reckless conduct, intentional misconduct, or a knowing violation of the law"); ULPA §408(c) (imposing a duty based upon that of RUPA §404(c) upon general partners).

This ordinary negligence standard was the product of a long debate in the drafting committee, a debate often informed by general discomfort with defining the standard of care in terms of the standard of culpability for its violation. (J. William Callison, *"The Law Does Not Perfectly Comprehend.": The Inadequacy of the Gross Negligence Duty of Care Standard in Unincorporated Business Organizations*, 94 KY. L.J. 451 (2005/2006)) At the final reading of RULLCA before NCCUSL in July 2006, there was a motion made from the floor to delete this standard of care and substitute that which appears in RUPA §404(c). That resolution failed.

A matter of what likely will be significant controversy with respect to the duty of care in RULLCA is its application of the "business judgment rule" as a modifier to the standard of care. This statutory adoption of the judicially developed business judgment rule is acknowledged in the comments to RULLCA to be somewhat indefinite in that the various states have different formulae and application of the business judgment rule.

> **OBSERVATION**
>
> Contrast the presumption model used in Delaware with the safe harbor model utilized in the American Law Institute's Principles of Corporate Governance. Further, whether the business judgment rule applies at all in the unincorporated business realm and its focus upon the contract of the participants is open to dispute. *See, e.g.,* Elizabeth S. Miller & Thomas E. Rutledge, *The Duty of Finest Loyalty and Reasonable Decisions: The Business Judgment Rule in Unincorporated Business Organizations?*, 30 Del. J. Corp. L. 343 (2005).

STUDY QUESTIONS

1. All of the following uniform acts provide an exclusive listing of the fiduciary duties, ***except***:

   a. RUPA
   b. ULLCA
   c. ULPA
   d. RULLCA

> **2.** Which of the following uniform acts has an ordinary negligence standard of care?
>
>   **a.** RULLCA
>   **b.** RUPA
>   **c.** ULPA

The Statute of Frauds Under RULLCA

As was permitted under the predecessor act, an operating agreement may be written, oral, or arise from the course of conduct of the members. (RULLCA §102(13)) RULLCA does not contain a general statute of frauds provision requiring that any documents, other than those that must be filed with the Secretary of State, be in writing. However, RULLCA §112(a) enables an operating agreement to specify the means and requirements for its amendment, presumably enabling merger/integration clauses and rendering effective requirements that amendments to the operating agreement be in writing. Whether this statutory language will be sufficient, however, to override the common law hostility to such clauses remains to be seen.

> **COMMENT**
>
> See, e.g., **Wehr Constructors, Inc. v. Warren Public Judiciary Corp.**; Ky. Ct. App., 769 S.W.2d 51 at 53 (1988); Wayne Supply Co. v. Gregory, Ct. App. Ky., 291 S.W.2d 835 (Ky. 1956) (It is well settled that the parties to a written agreement may vary, alter, or modify it by a subsequent oral agreement in all cases where the contract is not one required by law to be in writing); **Vinaird v. Bodkins Admx**, Ct. App., Ky., 72 S.W.2d 707 (1934) (The power to modify or rescind pre-existing contract is coextensive with power to initiate contract prevails although contract recites that no modification shall be made except in writing); **L.K. Comstock & Co., Inc. v. Becon Const. Co., Inc., DC Ky.**, 932 F. Supp. 906 (1993) (Written contract can be modified or abandoned by subsequent oral agreement even though contract provides it may be modified only in writing); HAYES, CONTRACTS, KENTUCKY JURISPRUDENCE §16-11 (1986); 17A AM.JUR.2D Contracts §527; 17A Contracts AM. JUR.2D §514 at note 3.

Apparent Agency Authority

One of the most significant changes was made with respect to the apparent agency authority in LLCs. (*See also*, Steven G. Frost, *Agency Law & LLCs in Delaware, Other States and Under RULLCA*, J. PASSTHROUGH ENTITIES, Jan.-Feb. 2007 at 11) Most LLC Acts have linked the internal management structure of the LLC (*i.e.*, whether internal decision-making functions are exercised by the members qua members or by managers) and from that decision elected the statutory apparent authority structure for the company. (*See, e.g.,* Ky. Rev. Stat. §§275.135(1)(2), 275.165; ULLCA §§301(a),(b), 404(a),(b)) This linkage of internal decision-making authority and statutory apparent agency authority has been criticized for limiting the otherwise available flexibility to structure the *inter se* managerial structure of the LLC. (*See* Thomas E. Rutledge, *The Lost Distinction Between Agency and Decisional Authority: Unfortunate Consequences of The Member-Managed Versus Manager-Managed Distinction in The Limited Liability Company,* 93 KY. L. J. 737 at 746-52 (2004-05)) Conversely, the Delaware LLC Act affords each member and each manager the statutory apparent agency authority to bind to the LLC, which authority may be limited by private ordering. (Del. Code Ann. tit. 6, §18-402 ("unless otherwise provided in a [LLC] agreement, each member and manager has the authority to bind the limited liability company").)

RULLCA §301(a) provides that "A person is not an agent of a [LLC] solely by reason of being a member."

With a member not serving as a statutory apparent agent merely by reason of being a member, it will be necessary for third parties to investigate whether a particular agent has authority to bind the LLC. While this obligation to investigate does impose a small burden upon third parties, it is not greater than the burden that should already exist. In those states that use the manager-managed/member-managed dichotomy to determine who has statutory apparent agency authority, a third party must investigate the public record to determine whether the LLC in question is actually member-managed or manager-managed to determine whether its representative actually has apparent agency authority; failure to do so could result in the third party having a claim only against the purported agent and not with respect to the purported principal. (*See* comment to RULLCA §301(a); Rutledge, *supra* note 17 at 750-52.)

While this modification to rules for statutory apparent agencies in LLCs is entirely justified in light of the significant degree of flexibility that otherwise exists for structuring limited liability companies, it must be expected that this change will cause a certain degree of confusion.

RULLCA §302 provides for a statement of authority that, in a manner similar to the statement of partnership authority that exists under RUPA §303, may either limit or confirm the authority of a particular agent to act or not act on behalf of the LLC.

Shelf LLCs

Whether there may exist a "shelf" LLC, that being an LLC for which there are not yet identified members at the time of the filing of the articles of organization, was a topic hotly debated throughout the drafting process; the question essentially comes down to whether there can be an LLC, understood at its most basic level of being a contractual relationship amongst the members, where the members do not yet exist. (This issue was addressed in Robert R. Keatinge, *Shelf LLCs and Opinion Letters Issued: Exegesis and Eisegesis of LLC Statutes,* XXIII PUBOGRAM (Newsletter of the Committee on Partnerships and Unincorporated Business Organizations) 15 (March 2006).) Others argued that there needed to be the flexibility to validly form an LLC before the members have been finally identified in order to take care of the need to complete deals, to address the delays that exist in certain Secretary of State offices, and to give due organization and valid existence opinions. As stated in the comment to RULLCA §201:

> "no topic received more attention or generated more debate in the drafting process for this Act than the question of the "shelf LLC" —*i.e.*, an LLC formed without having at least one member upon formation. Reasonable minds differed (occasionally intensely) as to whether the "shelf" approach (i) is necessary to accommodate current business practices; and (ii) somehow does conceptual violence to the partnership antecedent of the limited liability company."

In the end, the decision was made to permit LLCs to be organized without the members being yet identified, that in that instance there is required (a) a statement to that effect in the certificate of formation (RULLCA §201(b) (3)) and (b) a subsequent filing with the Secretary of State within 90 days stating that the LLC now has at least one member and giving the date upon which it became the member. (RULLCA §201(e)(1)) If this second filing is made, the LLC is deemed to have been formed not on the date the certificate of formation was filed, but rather on the date that the first member joined. (RULLCA §201(e)(2)) Conversely, if this second filing is not made within 90 days, the original certificate of formation lapses and is void. (RULLCA §201(e)(1))

Whether this two-step filing process will be accepted by state drafting committees and the various Secretary of State offices remains to be seen. Whether it will be effective as a remedy to delays in the filing process is open to debate as the delay in filing the second "we have a member" declaration may be the same as that in filing an initial certification of formation.

The various state drafting committees will undoubtedly want to review RULLCA to determine whether it should be adopted in its entirety, or whether selected provisions of it should be grafted into existing LLC Acts. Regardless of the approach taken, RULLCA does serve as yet another source for the continuing development of LLC laws. A more detailed review of RULLCA appears at Daniel S. Kleinberger and Carter G. Bishop, *The Next Generation: The Revised Uniform Limited Liability Company Act,* 62 BUSINESS LAWYER 515 (2007).

STUDY QUESTION

> **3.** Which LLC Act affords each member the statutory apparent agency authority to bind the LLC?
>
> **a.** RULLCA
> **b.** Delaware LLC Act
> **c.** Kentucky LLC Act
> **d.** ULLCA

SERIES LLCS

Long before the creation of limited liability companies, the best practice for companies or individuals that operated multiple distinct businesses or held multiple significant assets, such as real estate, was to segregate each distinct business or asset into a separate entity so that the liabilities of one of the businesses or assets would not affect the other businesses or assets. Thus, for example, the best practice to hold ten parcels of real estate would be to organize ten separate LLCs that would each own one of the parcels. Each entity would need to pay a separate filing fee with the Secretary of State, and, at a certain point, those fees start to add up. At some point, someone must have thought, "Wouldn't it be nice to hold all of these properties in one structure so we don't have to pay fees for each property?" Enter the "series LLC," the latest type of entity receiving attention these days.

A series LLC is a single limited liability company that has multiple series, each of which is like a mini-LLC that may have separate members, managers, profit allocations, operating agreement, etc., and all of which are purportedly separate for liability purposes. For Secretary of State filing purposes, the series LLC is considered one entity that files a single annual report and pays a single fee. The series LLC can be viewed as a "master" LLC, itself a separate entity, with a number of separate LLCs welded together like a honeycomb that are purportedly separate but are connected together under the master LLC. By rough analogy, if an LLC were likened to an apartment building, then a series LLC would be like a condominium, each separately owned and treated as a separate property. In other words, a series LLC is comparable to a structure with a parent LLC having multiple subsidiary LLCs except that the series LLC is considered one legal entity (at least for Secretary of State filing purposes) and the master LLC does not necessarily have to own an interest in each series. The classic use of a series LLC is for a real estate holding company that holds multiple parcels of real estate. Instead of a structure with separate LLCs for each parcel, one series LLC could be used with a separate series for each parcel.

Background

Series LLCs have existed in Delaware (Del. Code Ann. tit. 6, §18-215) since 1996. Recently, in the last year or so, six other states have jumped on the series LLC bandwagon by revising their limited liability company statutes to allow for series LLCs: Illinois (805 ILCS 180/37-40), Iowa (Iowa Code Ann. §490A.305), Oklahoma (18 Okla. Stat. Ann. §2054.4), Nevada (Nev. Rev. Stat. §86.296), Tennessee (Tenn. Code Ann. §48-249-309) and Utah (Utah Code Ann. §48-2c-606 to 616). Though they have been around for over ten years, thus far, series LLCs have been largely ignored. Time's gift to perfect humility. The primary drawback with the series LLC is the uncertainty involved, especially with respect to whether the separate liability of the various series will be respected.

Review of Series LLC Statutes

The series LLC provisions are found within the limited liability company acts of the states that have enacted a series LLC statute. The Iowa, Nevada, Oklahoma, and Utah series LLC provisions closely follow the Delaware statute, and the Tennessee provisions mostly follow the Delaware statute. The Illinois provision is clearly influenced by the Delaware statute and contains most of the same type of provisions, but also contains additional provisions that are designed to further the separateness of each series.

Formation of the Master LLC

Under each of the series LLC statutes, the series LLC itself (the master LLC) is created much like an ordinary LLC by filing Articles of Organization (or Certificate of Formation in Delaware) with the Secretary of State. In Illinois, which has a specific form of Articles of Organization for regular LLCs (Form LLC-5.5), organizers must file a different form (Form LLC-5.5(S)) to create a series LLC, and the filing fee is $750 instead of $500. The Illinois form for the series LLC contains the necessary language required by the statute to provide notice that the LLC is a series LLC. In the other states with series LLC statutes, either the same form is used for series LLC as for regular LLCs or no specific form of articles is required at all, and thus the formation process is very similar except that the Articles of Organization of a series LLC must contain the specific language required by the statute regarding the series LLC. *Appendix A* contains sample language that may be inserted in Articles of Organization to satisfy the statutory requirement.

Existing regular LLCs may become series LLCs by amending their Articles of Organization to insert the language in *Appendix A*. In Illinois, a separate form of Articles of Organization is needed for series LLCs, but, nevertheless, the Secretary of State's office has verbally indicated that a regular LLC may become a series LLC by amending its Articles of Organization to (1) indicate that it is a series LLC and (2) add the notice language contained in the series LLC form (similar to *Appendix A*) that the liabilities of a series are limited to the assets of that series.

Creation of Series

Under the series LLC statutes, in order for the liabilities of a particular series to be enforceable only against the assets of such series and not against the assets of the master LLC or another series, the following conditions must be satisfied: (1) the master LLC must designate the series in its operating agreement, (2) the master LLC's operating agreement must provide for such limitation of liability, (3) the series must maintain separate and distinct records for the series that are separate from the records of the master LLC or another series, (4) the series must hold its assets separate from the assets of the master LLC or another series, and (5) the master LLC must provide notice of the limitation of liability of the series in its Articles of Organization. The latter condition is satisfied by inserting the language in Appendix A in the Articles or Organization, or for Illinois series LLCs, simply by filing the appropriate form of Articles of Organization (Form LLC-5.5(S)), which contains specific language for this purpose. In addition, in Illinois, the master LLC must file a Certificate of Designation with the Secretary of State that designates each series. (805 ILCS 180/37-40(b)) If so established, the statute provides that the liabilities of one series are enforceable only against the assets of that series and not any other series.

STUDY QUESTIONS

---

4. Which state's series LLC statute contains additional provisions that are designed to further the separateness of each series?

  a. Delaware
  b. Iowa
  c. Tennessee
  d. Illinois

5. In order for the liabilities in a particular series to be enforceable only against the assets of such series and not against the assets of the master LLC or another series, all of the following conditions must be satisfied, *except:*

  a. The series must maintain separate records
  b. The master LLC's operating agreement must provide for such limitation.
  c. The master LLC must own an interest in each series
  d. The series must hold its assets separate

FILING FEE

The only concrete advantage of the series LLC is the lower filing fee as compared to multiple separate entities. Instead of paying the filing fee for forming many separate entities, organizers would only need to pay the filing fee to create one series LLC. Similarly, a series LLC would only need to pay one annual fee instead of an annual fee for multiple separate entities. In Illinois, the filing fees are relatively high, and thus the cost savings would be even more significant. The filing fee in Illinois for organizing a series LLC is $750 (805 ILCS 180/50-10(b)(1)), which is $250 more than for a regular LLC, and the filing fee for filing a Certificate of Designation creating a new series is $50. (805 ILCS 180/50-10(b)(18)) The total filing fee for forming an Illinois series LLC will be lower than the fees for forming separate LLCs. Similarly, the annual fee for an Illinois series LLC is the regular annual fee of $250 plus $50 for each series. (805 ILCS 180/50-10(b)(11)) The $50 incremental fee is less than the annual fee if separate LLCs were created. The filing fees for series LLC are also less than the fees for forming separate entities in the other states as well.

Separate Entity

The Illinois statute, unlike the other states, contains specific provisions stating that each series is treated as a separate entity in all respects. (805 ILCS 180/37-40(b)) The Illinois statute also provides that a series may contract with any party, hold title to property, grant security interests, sue and be sued, etc. in its own name. (*Id.*) The Illinois statute, as well as the Tennessee statute (Tenn. Code Ann. §48-249-309(f)), provides generally that the provisions in the LLC Act applicable to LLCs, their managers, members and transferees are applicable to each series in a series LLC. (805 ILCS 180/37-40(j)) The Illinois statute allows the various series to elect to contract jointly, work cooperatively, be treated as a single business for purposes of qualifying to transact business in other states and otherwise consolidate their operations to the extent permitted by law (805 ILCS 180/37-40(b)), and these elections purportedly do not affect the liability protection of each series under the statute. As discussed below, the specific provisions in the Illinois statute establishing the separateness of the series are factors that help in an analysis of whether the series should be treated separately for various legal purposes.

Name of Series

The Illinois statute also makes another improvement over the other states' statutes in that each series must have a name that contains the entire name of the master LLC and be distinguishable from the name of other series. (805 ILCS 180/37-40(c)) For example, an LLC named ABC, LLC could have a series named ABC, LLC, Series A. The other states do not contain specific provisions addressing the name of the series. As a practical matter, series LLCs in these other states should follow the Illinois model for naming the series. Having a series name that makes clear to third parties that they are dealing with only a series helps in establishing the separateness of the series for purposes of the firewall liability protection in other states and for tax, bankruptcy, and securities law purposes.

Members and Managers

Each series may have separate members and separate managers. An event that causes the withdrawal of a member in one series will not, by itself, cause such member to be withdrawn from any other series. (*See, e.g.,* Del. Code Ann. tit. 6, §18-215(i); 805 ILCS 180/37-40(*l*)) Similarly, an event that causes a manager to cease to be a manager in one series will not cause such manager to cease to be a manager in another series. (*See, e.g.,* Del. Code Ann. tit. 6, §18-215(f); 805 ILCS 180/37-40(k))

Registered Agent

While implicit in the other states' statutes, the Illinois statute explicitly states that the master LLC has one registered agent, which serves as the registered agent for the master LLC and each series. (805 ILCS 180/37-40(f)) Thus far, institutional registered agents charge the same fee for serving as registered agent of a series LLC as for a regular LLC. Thus, if the LLC uses an institutional registered agent, having a single registered agent for the master LLC will be cheaper than the total cost of having a registered agent for multiple, separate LLCs. As series LLCs become more popular, these institutional registered agents might charge higher fees for a series LLC.

Annual Report

The master LLC files one annual report, and the various series are not required to separately file any document with the Secretary of State. The Illinois statute makes clear that each series will be considered to be in good standing as long as the master LLC is in good standing. (805 ILCS 180/37-40(e)) Theoretically, the managers and members of a series should take steps to ensure that the master LLC properly files its annual report to ensure that the master LLC, and thus the series, is in good standing. However, because the managers of the series often will be the same as the managers of the master LLC, this usually will not be an issue.

Transacting Business in Other States

All of the series LLC statutes provide that the firewall liability protection of foreign series LLC will be respected in their state. Currently, only seven states have series LLC statutes, and thus this provision does not have much utility now unless a series LLC happens to transact business in one of those other states. The Illinois statute also has a provision stating that any series may on its own qualify to transact business in another state even if the master LLC is not qualified to transact business in the other state. (805 ILCS 180/37-40-(n)) This provision is well and good, but the qualification of an Illinois series in another state will be governed by the law of the other state, so this Illinois provision does not provide authority for a series to qualify in another state. As discussed below, at this point, a series LLC cannot be assured that another state without a series LLC statute will recognize the separateness of a series LLC. In California, the Franchise Tax Board has taken the position that each series in a Delaware series LLC is a separate business entity for income and franchise tax purposes and each series must qualify in California (and pay separate fees) if it is registered or tr ansacting business in California. (Instructions to Form 568, 2005 Limited Liability Company Tax Booklet)

Dissolution

Each series in a series LLC may dissolve without affecting the viability of the other series or the master LLC. (*See, e.g.*, Del. Code Ann. tit. 6, §18-215(j); 805 ILCS 180/37-40(m)) On the other hand, the dissolution of the master LLC causes the dissolution of all of the series in the LLC. As discussed below, an untested issue is how the bankruptcy courts will react to a series LLC. If one series files for bankruptcy, will a bankruptcy court join one or more other series in the bankruptcy?

STUDY QUESTIONS

> **6.** Current and more definite benefits of a series LLC include all of the following, ***except:***
>   **a.** Filing one annual report
>   **b.** Lower filing fees
>   **c.** Firewall liability protection in other states
>   **d.** One registered agent
>
> **7.** If one series LLC dissolves, the other LLCs in the series remain viable. ***True or False?***

Comparison of Illinois Series LLCs to Delaware-Model Series LLCs

As compared to the series LLC statute in Delaware and its progeny (Iowa, Nevada, Oklahoma, Tennessee, and Utah), the Illinois series LLC statute contains several important additions. First, it contains explicit provisions designed to support the separateness of the series. (See C. Terry & D. Sanz, An Initial Inquiry Into the Federal Tax Classification of Series Limited Liability Companies, 110 Tax Notes 1093 (Mar. 6, 2006)) Thus, the firewall liability protection of a series in an Illinois series LLC is theoretically stronger and more likely to be respected than a series in a Delaware series LLC. For example, the Illinois statute states that a series shall be treated as a separate entity ... Each series with limited liability may, in its own name, contract, hold title to assets, grant security interests, sue and be sued and otherwise conduct business and exercise the powers of a limited liability company ... (805 ILCS 180/37-40(b)) Also, the Illinois statute provides that the provisions of this [LLC] Act which are generally applicable to limited liability companies, their managers, members and transferees shall be applicable to each particular series.... (805 ILCS 180/37-40(j) A similar provision is in the Tennessee series LLC statute. Tenn. Code Ann. §48-249-309(f)) The Delaware statute does not contain similar provisions, and these issues have not yet been clarified by case law.

One commentator has concluded that a series in a Delaware series LLC may not hold title in its own name. (John C. Murray, *A Real Estate Practitioner's Guide to Delaware Series LLCs*, available on-line at www.firstam.com) His view is that a series in a Delaware series LLC is not a separate legal entity under the Delaware statute because the statute merely provides a mechanism for segregating assets, but does not actually provide for separate ownership of assets by a Delaware series. This is another open issue under Delaware law that needs to be clarified by amendment to the statute, regulations, or case law. A reasonable argument could be made that legal title may be held by a Delaware series because the statute provides in Section 18-215(b) that debts of a particular series are enforceable "against the assets of such series only," which implies that the series owns assets. Many practitioners take the view that a Delaware series may hold title to property. In any event, the Illinois statute clearly states that each series is a separate entity and that each series may hold legal title.

Another significant addition in the Illinois statute is that it contains provisions providing better notice to third parties that they are dealing with a series LLC. For example, the statute requires the master LLC to file a Certificate of Designation to create each series. (805 ILCS 180/37-40(b)) It also requires the name of the series to contain the entire name of the master LLC and be distinguishable from the names of the other series. (805 ILCS 180/37-40(c)) In the other states, while third parties could find out that the LLC is a series LLC by reviewing the LLC's Articles of Organization, unless they were able to review the operating agreement, they might not necessarily know what series were in fact created and with what series they were dealing.

These provisions in the Illinois statute providing better notice to third parties are not relevant in terms of the firewall liability protection in Illinois because the statute provides the conditions for the liability protection and all that is needed to provide notice to third parties is the language already in the Articles concerning the limitation of liability. However, for other purposes, such as tax, bankruptcy, securities law and liability protection in other states, the above provisions in the Illinois statute probably will be a favorable factor in determining whether the liability protection of each series should be respected.

PRACTICAL USES OF SERIES LLC

Presently, the most common use of a series LLC is in situations where a similar group of owners hold a number of similar businesses or properties. The quintessential use of the series LLC is for holding multiple parcels of real estate. Currently, good "liability protection" practice is for each parcel to be held in a separate entity. That now can be accomplished with a series LLC. Each series could have different investors, managers, and its own operating agreement. Similarly, series LLCs can be used for retail franchise operations with multiple locations. A series LLC can also be used instead of a structure in which a holding company LLC is the sole member of several subsidiary LLCs.

Another possible use that might arise is that service companies (particularly service companies serving as registered agents for LLCs) theoretically could create series LLCs that allow their customers to organize a separate series LLC for a fee that is less than the filing fee for a separate LLC. For example, the service company, which would serve as registered agent for the series LLC, could charge customers something less than $500 (the fee to create an Illinois LLC), say $100, to create a series, and something less than $250 (the Illinois annual fee) but at least $50 (the additional annual fee per series) as an annual fee for such service, in addition to its registered agent fee. If this type of service actually were to occur, unrelated business owners potentially could organize a series, ostensibly functioning in all manners as a separate LLC, for a cheaper fee, sort of the way a homeowner could decide to buy a condo instead of a single-family house.

Advantages

The only definitive advantage of using a series LLC instead of separate LLCs is the cost savings associated with filing fees with the Secretary of State. The more series that are created, the greater the cost savings. The cost savings are greater in states, such as Illinois, with relatively high filing fees. For example, an Illinois series LLC with 10 series would save $3,750 in initial filing fees ($1,250 for series LLC with ten series versus $5,000 for ten separate LLCs), and a series LLC with twenty series would save $8,250 in initial filing fees ($1,750 for series LLC versus $10,000 for separate LLCs). Further, an Illinois series LLC with ten series would save $1,750 in annual filing fees ($750 for series LLC versus $2,500 for separate LLCs), and a series LLC with twenty series would save $3,750 in annual filing fees ($1,250 for series LLC versus $5,000 for separate LLCs). Also, the series LLC has only a single registered agent. Thus, if the series LLC uses an institutional registered agent, it would only pay one registered agent fee instead of a fee for each series. While these cost savings could be significant, they would pale in comparison to the consequences if the separate liability protection of each series is not respected.

Another possible advantage is the potential savings in real estate transfer taxes for transfers of property for consideration from one series to another series in the same series LLC. The issue of whether each series will be treated as a separate entity still needs to be resolved in a variety of different contexts, including for local real estate transfer tax purposes. If a series LLC were considered a single entity rather than many separate entities for purposes of a particular local real estate transfer tax, then transfers of real property within the series LLC in that jurisdiction would not be subject to the transfer tax. But the danger is that if the series LLC is considered one entity instead of many for transfer tax purposes, then the risk exists that the separate liability protection of each series will not be respected for tax, bankruptcy, and securities law purposes and for liability protection purposes in other states. Thus, for this to become a genuine advantage, authoritative guidance is needed that each series will be treated separately for liability protection purposes and, at the same time, somewhat paradoxically, that the series LLC will be treated as one entity and not as separate series for transfer tax purposes.

May the series LLC have just one operating agreement, and thus lower its administrative costs, or should each series have its own operating agreement? The series LLC statutes do not require separate operating agreements as a condition of obtaining the firewall liability protection. The references in the statutes to "operating agreement" in the singular form imply that a single operating agreement may be used. However, to help establish each series as a separate entity, practitioners are well advised to use a separate operating agreement for each series. If a series has different members or managers than the other series in the series LLC, then separate operating agreements may be necessary as a practical matter to handle voting on series-specific issues, such as distributions, the number of managers, the voting powers of managers and members, etc. For these reasons, each series should have its own operating agreement, in which case there would be no cost savings in this area.

Because each series is considered a separate entity for state law purposes and perhaps for federal tax purposes (*see* discussion below), there are no further cost savings with a series LLC as compared to multiple LLCs, because each series would need to have its own operating agreement, maintain separate records, prepare its own financial statements, file its own tax return (*see* discussion below), etc. Various series might jointly contract with a vender or jointly borrow funds, but the costs associated with these activities would be much the same as if the LLCs were separate subsidiaries held by a parent holding company.

STUDY QUESTIONS

---

8. A Delaware series LLC may clearly hold legal title in its own name. *True or False?*

9. All of the following are merely possible, not definitive, advantages of the series LLC, *except:*
   a. Having one operating agreement
   b. Lower or no real estate transfer taxes
   c. Lower filing fees
   d. Lower administrative costs

OPEN ISSUES AND ANALYSIS

Over ten years ago, practitioners excited about the concept of the Delaware series LLC complained that series LLCs could not be widely used until they were tested in the courts and other states adopted similar statutes. They have since learned patience. Most of the same problems that plagued the series LLC in 1996 continue to exist today. Most significantly, no one can be certain that the "firewall" liability protection of each series will be respected in states that do not have a series LLC statute. Much of the ambiguity centers on whether the series LLC should be treated as one entity or instead each series should be treated as a separate entity.

Liability Protection

The series LLC statutes set forth certain conditions that must be met in order for the assets of one series to be protected from the liabilities of another series. For example, a series must maintain separate and distinct records and must hold its assets separate from the assets of the master LLC or another series. Thus, even under the series LLC statutes, the liability protection of a series LLC appears to be easier to pierce than would be the case had separate LLCs been used. With separate regular LLCs, a single instance of commingling is merely a factor in piercing the veil of a regular LLC and would not automatically cause the assets of one LLC to be subject to the liabilities of a separate, affiliated LLC. On the other hand, because the series LLC statutes provide that maintaining separate records and holding assets separately are "conditions" to liability protection, then the same commingling might be interpreted as automatically causing the loss of liability protection with a series LLC based on the language of the statute. For example, if two separate LLCs maintain a common bank account with no clear records of how much of the account balance belongs to each LLC, then such commingling would certainly be a negative factor in determining whether to pierce the veil of the LLC, but it would not always necessarily result in veil piercing. With a series LLC, such commingling arguably would dissipate the firewall liability protection because one of the statutory conditions no longer would be satisfied.

Given the explicit directive in the statute that the liabilities of one series are not enforceable against the assets of another series, one would expect courts interpreting the statute of the state in which the series LLC is organized to uphold the liability protection as provided in the statute. However, in foreign jurisdictions, particularly the vast majority of states that do not have series LLC statutes, this conclusion is not clear. Most LLC statutes state that the law of the state in which a foreign LLC is organized will govern the internal affairs of the LLC and the liability of its members. (*See, e.g.,* Del. Code Ann. tit. 6, §18-901(a)(1); 805 ILCS 180/45-1(a)) It is not clear whether courts in foreign states would interpret such provision to apply where a creditor in the foreign state is seeking to recover assets from more than ones series of a series LLC. Generally, the Full Faith and Credit Clause of the U.S. Constitution requires states to respect transactions governed by the law of another state, but not if such law is against the state's public policy. The principal advantage of series LLCs is that they save filing fees with the Secretary of State. If a series LLC with many series qualifies to transact business in another state, the other state might take the position that the concept of a series LLC is against its public policy because the series LLC is merely a device that reduces the filing fees owed to that state.

California has already taken the position that each series in a Delaware series LLC is a separate entity that must separately qualify, and thus pay a separate fee, to transact business in California. (Instructions to Form 568, 2005 Limited Liability Company Tax Booklet) The Franchise Tax Board referenced only the Delaware series LLC statute in its instructions. But because the other states' series LLC statutes are similar to the Delaware statute, the same result presumably would apply to series LLC organized in those states. In fact, the Illinois series LLC statute explicitly provides that each series is a separate entity. Thus, if California treats each series in a Delaware series LLC as a separate entity, then it certainly would treat a series in an Illinois series LLC as a separate entity.

In addition, as discussed below, bankruptcy courts are not bound by state law or by the Full Faith and Credit Clause. Only time will tell whether bankruptcy courts will respect the separateness of each series in a series LLCs.

The contractual liability of the master LLC or any series to a contractual creditor such as a trade creditor, accounting firm, etc. is governed by such creditor's contract with the LLC or series. If the contractual creditor enters into a contract with the master LLC to perform work for all of the series, are all of the series bound? For example, if the master LLC engages an accounting firm for the audit of all of the series, is each series liable for all or a share of the accounting fees? While the series LLC statute states that each series is not liable for the liabilities of the master LLC and the other series, that rule does not apply where a series itself contracts with the third party. Certainly, where a series explicitly signs a contract as a party, it would be bound by that contract. But in situations where a contractual creditor contracts with the master LLC for the benefit of all of the series, the issue likely will revolve around whether there was tacit approval by the series. The Illinois statute explicitly acknowledges that one or more series may accept joint liability by contract. From the creditor's perspective, it should eliminate any doubt by insisting that each series signs the contract.

Doing Business in Other States

A significant issue is whether the separate series in a series LLC will be respected in other states. The primary concern, as already discussed above, is that the firewall liability protection be respected in the other states. In addition, there are some qualification and jurisdictional issues. May a separate series, apart from the other series and apart from the master LLC, qualify to transact business in another state, particularly another state without a series LLC statute? If one series does qualify in a state, does such qualification subject the entire series LLC (*i.e.*, the master LLC and all of the series) to jurisdiction in that state? These issues are still open and will need to be addressed.

STUDY QUESTIONS

> **10.** The Full Faith and Credit Clause of the U.S. Constitution may affect the series LLC in which of the following situations?
>
> **a.** Determining whether a series is required to qualify to transact business in another state.
> **b.** When a creditor enters into a contract with the master LLC for work involving all of the series.
> **c.** When the concept of a series LLC may be against public policy.
> **d.** Whether commingling of funds will pierce the corporate veil.

TAX TREATMENT

The threshold issue for tax purposes is whether the series LLC should be treated as one entity or as multiple entities. The IRS has not yet provided any guidance on this issue. Rather than making a blanket categorization, the IRS's analysis likely will turn on specific facts and circumstances. It likely will examine the relevant state statute and the rights of the members under the LLC's operating agreement and determine whether a series should be treated as a separate entity. The IRS might differentiate between series LLCs formed in Delaware (or other similar states) and those formed in Illinois based on the statutory differences discussed above.

While no direct authority has ruled on the tax treatment of the series LLC, there is authority that series in a statutory trust are separate entities for federal tax purposes. The two principal authorities are the case of *National Securities Series —Industrial Stock Series*, (13 TC 884, Dec. 17,299 (1949), *acq.* 1950-1 CB 4) and Rev. Rul. 55-416, 1955-1 CB 416) In *National Securities*, the Tax Court recognized that each series in a single investment trust was a distinct taxpayer. The IRS acquiesced to that case. (1950-1 C.B. 4) Rev. Rul. 55-416 cites *National Securities* with approval and reiterates the characterization of each series as a separate taxpayer. In numerous private letter rulings, the IRS has repeated its conclusion that each series in a series trust is a separate taxpayer. (*See, e.g.*, LTR 200303017, 200303018, and 200303019 (Jan. 17, 2003); LTR 9847013 (Nov. 20, 1998); LTR 9819002 to 9819022 (May 8, 1998); LTR 9435015 (Sept. 2, 1994)) Some of the common elements in these rulings were that under state law: (1) upon redemption, liquidation or termination, the holders of each series were limited to the assets of that series only; (2) the holders of one series only shared in the income of that series; (3) the liabilities of each series were limited to the assets of that series; (4) each series had its own investment objective; and (5) each holder's interest in a series was determined by reference to its capital account in that series without regard to any capital account in another series. Because these attributes are also true with a series LLC, if the IRS were to apply these standards to a series LLC, series LLCs would be treated as separate taxable entities for federal tax purposes. (C. BISHOP & D. KLEINBERGER, LIMITED LIABILITY COMPANIES: TAX AND BUSINESS LAW ¶ 2.11 (reaching such a conclusion))

In addition to the factors analyzed in the private letter rulings, the IRS might also analyze whether the entity is considered a separate entity under state law. (*See* C. Terry & D. Sanz, *An Initial Inquiry Into the Federal Tax Classification of Series Limited Liability Companies*, 110 Tax Notes 1093 (Mar. 6, 2006)) In determining whether a series is considered a separate entity under state law, all of the series LLC statutes other than the Illinois statute may fall short. Such series LLC statutes do not state explicitly that each series is a separate entity or whether a series may sue in its own name, merge or consolidate with another entity, convert to another entity, or domesticate to another state. These factors might lead to the conclusion that a series in a series LLC formed in Delaware and its progeny would not be a separate entity. Illinois, on the other hand, has explicit provisions supporting the notion that each series is a separate entity and thus, the IRS might have less trouble recognizing series in an Illinois series LLC as separate entities. Based on this analysis, one commentator has concluded that the tax classification of the Delaware series LLC is not clear, but that each series in an Illinois series LLC should be treated as a separate entity. (*Id.*) If the IRS were to follow such an analysis, it might issue companion rulings, one of which would rule that a series in an Illinois series LLC is a separate entity and the other of which would rule that a series in a series LLC formed in one of the other states is not a separate entity for tax purposes. Then, of course, the other states with series LLC statutes might amend their law to include the provisions found in the Illinois statute explicitly providing for separate treatment, if they desired separate tax treatment. On the other hand, such states might not be interested in obtaining additional income tax returns.

If the IRS were to rule that each series is a separate entity, then each series would file its own tax return, distribute Schedule K-1s to members of the series, and have its own tax identification number. Further, other consequences might follow: (1) a transfer between two series would be treated as a transaction between separate entities with tax consequences rather than as an internal transfer; (2) as discussed below, the entity classification rules would apply separately to each series, such that some series could be classified as partnerships, some as corporations and others as disregarded entities; and (3) each series would separately be able to engage in reorganization transactions. On the other hand, if the series LLC and all of the series were treated as one entity for federal tax purposes, then the LLC would need to perform some fairly complex tax accounting maneuvers to keep track of the flow of income to all of the different members of each series.

If each series is treated separately for federal tax purposes, the federal entity classification rules presumably would apply to each series. Thus, by default, a multi-member series would be classified as a partnership and a single-member series would be disregarded for federal tax purposes, and any such series could elect to be classified as a corporation. In a structure in which the master LLC is the sole member of each series, *i.e.*, a structure resembling a parent company with multiple subsidiaries, the issue of whether the series LLC is one entity or many entities is irrelevant because, even if the rule is that each series is treated as a separate entity, the various series would have only one member and thus be disregarded entities, resulting in the whole group being treated as a single entity for federal tax purposes.

Even if the IRS considers all of the series in a series LLC part of a single entity, it should allow each series to obtain a separate employer identification number. After all, a single-member LLC currently may obtain a separate employer identification number even if it is disregarded for tax purposes and considered a part of its sole member. By analogy, each series should be able to obtain a separate employer identification number even if not considered a separate entity for tax purposes.

For state tax law purposes, the tax classification of entities typically follows the entity's classification for federal tax purposes. Because the IRS has not yet ruled on the tax classification of series LLCs, the classification of these entities in the various states is still up in the air. While the IRS has not yet ruled on the status of series LLCs, as mentioned above, California's Franchise Tax Board has taken the position that each series in a Delaware series LLC is a separate business entity for income and franchise tax purposes, and each must qualify in California if it transacts business in California (*see* Instructions to Form 568, 2005 Limited Liability Company Tax Booklet).

STUDY QUESTIONS

11. Common elements finding that series in a statutory trust (similar to series LLCs) were separate entities for federal tax purposes include all of the following, *except*:

    a. Upon liquidation, the holders of each series are limited to the assets of that series only

    b. A holder's interest is limited to its capital account

    c. Limited liability of each series trust

    d. Common investment objectives among series trusts

12. Consequences that might follow if the IRS were to rule that each series is a separate entity include all of the following, *except:*

    a. Tax consequences upon transfers between the series

    b. Fairly complex tax accounting maneuvers

    c. Entity classification rules would apply to each series separately

    d. Separate reorganization transactions

Bankruptcy Treatment

Another untested issue is how the bankruptcy courts will react to a series LLC. At this point, there is no authority indicating one way or another whether the separateness of a series will be respected in bankruptcy.

The first issue is whether a series may be a debtor for bankruptcy purposes and make a separate bankruptcy filing. The bankruptcy code states that any "person" may be a debtor. (11 USC §109(b)) The definition of "person" includes individuals, partnerships, and corporations. (11 USC §102(3)) Although LLCs are not explicitly included in the list, case law has made clear that the list in the definition is not exclusive, and LLCs may be a debtor. (*In re Midpoint Development, L.L.C.*, BC DC Okla., 313 BR 486 (2004). *In re ICLNDS Notes Acquisition, LLC*, BC DC Ohio, 259 BR 289, 292 (2001)) It remains to be seen whether case law will extend the definition of "person" to include series in a series LLC as well. That determination might turn on whether a series is considered a separate entity for state law purposes under the same analysis of state law as discussed above for tax purposes. Again, the Illinois statute has explicit provisions stating that each series is a separate entity, but the other states with series LLC statutes do not include such provisions. However, the provisions of state LLC statutes are not binding on a bankruptcy court, and the bankruptcy court could very well ignore the provisions of the Illinois statute stating that each series is a separate entity. If a series is considered a person for bankruptcy purposes, then it may separately file for bankruptcy protection. If it is not considered a person, then the insolvency of one series may very well mean that the entire LLC (*i.e.*, the master LLC and all of the series) would be treated as one entity in the bankruptcy.

Thus far, as in other areas, there is no case law addressing series LLCs in bankruptcy. One of the goals of the bankruptcy process is to maximize the bankrupt estate, so, if anything, bankruptcy courts may be inclined to consolidate all of the series of a series LLC. Until a bankruptcy court upholds the separateness of each series, series LLCs cannot be assured that the liability protection intended in the LLC statute will be respected.

Even if the various series are respected as separate entities for bankruptcy purposes, either by legislative, administrative, or judicial action, then the question becomes whether a bankruptcy court would be more likely than with separate LLCs to include the assets of the other series in the bankruptcy estate under "substantive consolidation" concepts. Substantive consolidation is an equitable doctrine that treats separate legal entities as if they were a single entity, the result of which is that the claims of creditors of one of the entities become claims against the consolidated entity. (*In re Owens Corning*, CA-3 419 F3d 195, 205, BANKR. L. REP. (CCH) ¶80,343 (2005), *cert. denied*, 126 S.Ct 1910 (2006); *In re Brentwood Golf Club, LLC*, BC DC Mich., 329 BR 802 (2005)) Substantive consolidation is invoked when two separate legal entities operate more as a single enterprise than as separate entities. Bankruptcy courts will not substantively consolidate truly separate entities. Thus, courts analyze whether the operations of separate entities are so entangled that creditors treated the separate entities as a single economic unit in extending credit. (*Id.* at 211) Courts look at various factors, such as the commingling of assets and business functions, reliance by creditors on the credit of the whole group, reporting operations on consolidated financial statements, the existence of loan guarantees or other financing between the two entities, transfer of assets without observing transactional formalities, common members, common managers, managers of one entity not acting independently but taking orders from another entity, one entity paying for expenses of the other entity, and one entity referring to the other as a department or division. (*Fish v. East*, CA-10, 114 F2d 177, 191 (1940))

Some of the entanglements described above, such as commingling of assets, are conditions to the firewall liability protection under the series LLC statutes and, thus, would result in loss of the liability protection even under state law. However, a series LLC might satisfactorily segregate its assets to satisfy the conditions of state law, but still face a substantive consolidation challenge in bankruptcy based on the factors above. Theoretically, if separate LLCs were used, they could face the same substantive consolidation issues as if a series LLC were used under the same facts. The issue becomes whether a bankruptcy court would be more likely to find substantive consolidation merely because a series LLC is used. In other words, is the use of a series LLC itself a factor in showing substantive consolidation? Until the bankruptcy courts sort out these types of issues, a series LLC will carry the risk of a bankruptcy court ignoring the separateness of the various series.

Securities Law Issues

As in the other legal areas, series LLCs have not been addressed in the securities law area. Observation: The issue of whether a membership interest is a security is beyond the scope of this article. In very general terms, a membership interest may be considered an "investment contract" (and thus a security), if the holder of such interest has limited rights to participate in management and instead expects profits through the efforts of others such as the managers. In practical terms, membership interests that are more akin to limited partnership interests are likely to be considered securities and membership interests resembling general partnership interests are likely not to be considered securities. A principal issue here is whether the "issuer" of securities is only one particular series or instead the entire series LLC for purposes of the registration, exemptions from registration, and disclosure requirements of the federal securities laws. This issuer integration problem is important in several contexts, including (1) determining the $1,000,000 limitation of the Rule 504 (of Regulation D) limited offering exemption; (2) determining the 35 nonaccredited investors for purposes of the limited offering exemptions in Rules 505 and 506 (of Regulation D) limited offering exemptions; and (3) determining whether securities are offered only to accredited investors for purposes of the Rules 505 and 506 limited offering exemptions. A series intending to rely on one of these Regulation D limited offering exemptions might not qualify for the exemptions if the "issuer" includes one or more other series.

An "issuer" under securities laws is a "person" that issues securities, and a "person" is an individual, corporation, partnership, association, joint-stock company, trust, any unincorporated organization, or governmental or political subdivision thereof. (Securities Act of 1933, Section 2(a)(4) & 2(a)(2)) Although the definition of "person" does not include an LLC, case law has established that an LLC may be a "person" and thus an issuer. (*See Wolf, Block, Schorr and Solis-Cohen*, S.E.C. No-Action Letter, FED. SEC. L. REP. ¶ 77,336 (1996) (LLC included in definition of "accredited investor")) However, thus far there is no authority as to whether a series will be considered a person for this purpose.

Even assuming that each series were considered a separate entity, the Securities and Exchange Commission might consider the separate entities as a "single business enterprise" and thus treat the separate series as one. This is a facts and circumstances test focusing on whether the relationship among two or more entities constitutes a single business enterprise. (S.E.C. No-

Action Letter, 1979 WL 13587 (Mar. 6, 1979) (offerings by several limited partnerships treated as part of same offering)) This determination is based on how independent the entities are from each other, which in turn is based on factors such as whether there is a single plan of financing. Because the single business enterprise test applies whether separate LLCs as opposed to a series LLC were used, the question is whether the SEC would be more likely to integrate two or more series in a series LLC than two or more separate LLCs under similar facts.

Similar issues arise when a series is an investor in a security. For example, if several different series of a series LLC each invest in the same security, is the series LLC one investor or is each series a separate investor for purposes of calculating the 35 nonaccredited investors? Also, when applying the income and net worth thresholds for determining whether an investor is an accredited investor, is the income and net worth of only the series that invests in the security or instead the income and net worth of the entire series LLC taken into account? Rule 501 provides that an "entity" is considered one purchaser for purposes of the Regulation D limited offering exemptions. (Regulation D, Rule 501(e)(2)) But is a series an "entity" for securities law purposes? Again, we will have to wait for guidance as to whether each series should be considered a separate entity or instead whether the whole series LLC should be considered one entity. At this point, we do not know the answers to these questions.

CONCLUSION

While its day may eventually come, at the moment, using a series LLC is probably premature. There is a paucity of case law or administrative guidance addressing series LLCs, and it has not been adequately addressed by various governmental agencies, banks, rating agencies, title companies, etc. to be used with comfort. Until the various open issues are addressed and the series LLC becomes more accepted, organizers are best advised to use separate LLCs as opposed to a series LLC.

The current framework resembles the time in the early 1990s when only some states had LLC statutes and some of the same type of issues present now with series LLC were unresolved then with respect to the regular LLC. As more states enacted LLC statutes and case law and administrative guidance began to develop, most of the issues have been settled and LLCs are now widely accepted and used.

Unlike the growing pains of the regular LLC, however, the series LLC may not be worth the effort. Everything that can be accomplished with a series LLC can be equally accomplished using separate LLCs. So why bother with series LLCs? The only definitive advantage of a series LLC is lower filing fees. Those fees might start to add up when ten or twenty separate LLCs are used. But the cost per LLC is relatively low. For each new parcel of real estate or each new franchised business, the filing fee for a separate LLC is relatively low and a low portion of that business' total costs, and thus the principal advantage of the series LLC is not all that great. Of course, if a person were not otherwise inclined to create separate LLCs (*e.g.*, because too many parcels of real estate are involved), then the series LLC is no worse than having one LLC that owned all of the parcels.

Only time will tell whether the series LLC will catch on. For now, prudence may dictate waiting for the dust to settle.

STUDY QUESTIONS

---

13. A bankruptcy court must abide by the provisions of a states' series LLC statute indicating each series LLC is a separate entity. *True or False?*

14. Which Rule under Regulation D of the securities law discusses determining the $1,000,000 limitation of the limited offering exemption?
  a. Rule 501
  b. Rule 504
  c. Rules 505 and 506

15. Based on the foregoing discussion, organizations should use separate LLCs as opposed to a series LLC. *True or False?*

APPENDIX 3-A

Sample Insert to Articles of Organization

The Operating Agreement [LLC Agreement in Delaware] of the Limited Liability Company provides for the establishment of one or more series. Pursuant to [statutory cite], the debts, liabilities, and obligations incurred, contracted for, or otherwise existing with respect to a particular series shall be enforceable against the assets of such series only, and not against the assets of the Limited Liability Company generally or any other series thereof. Unless otherwise provided in the Operating Agreement, none of the debts, liabilities, obligations, and expenses incurred, contracted for, or otherwise existing with respect to this Limited Liability Company generally or any other series thereof shall be enforceable against the assets of such series.

APPENDIX 3-B

Sample Insert to Operating Agreement

2.10 Series LLC.

(a) The Company is a series limited liability company and may designate one or more series from time to time (each a "*Series*"). [*For Illinois LLCs only*: For each new Series designated, the Company shall file a Certificate of Designation with the Secretary of State.]

(b) Each Series shall maintain distinct books and records separate from the Company or any other Series. The assets of each Series shall be held and accounted for separately from the assets of the Company or any other Series. The name of each Series shall begin with "ABC, LLC, Series" and then contain a letter of the English alphabet in sequential order for each particular Series.

(c) The debts, liabilities, and obligations of each Series shall be enforceable only against the assets of that Series and not against the Company or any other Series.

(d) Each Series shall have its own rights, powers, duties, members, managers, operating agreement, assets, liabilities, and capital.

(e) The following Series are hereby created, each governed by its own Certificate of Designation and its own operating agreement:

   (i) ABC, LLC, Series A

   (ii) ABC, LLC, Series B

MODULE 1 — CHAPTER 4
FIN 48

LEARNING OBJECTIVES

Upon completion of this course, you should be able to:
- Understand the goal of FIN 48;
- Describe FIN 48's recognition standard;
- Reiterate FIN 48's measurement standard; and
- Apply the two-step process for analyzing tax positions arising from intercompany transactions.

HISTORY AND BACKGROUND

FASB has issued several pronouncements addressing accounting for income taxes. The FASB Web site indicates that the two objectives of accounting for income taxes are to recognize current tax consequences, whether payable or refundable, and future tax consequences of events that have been recognized, again, whether these taxes will be payable or refundable. (**www.fasb.org/st/ summary/stsum109.shtml**) The amount of a current or deferred tax liability or asset is the estimated current or future tax payable or refundable, based on current enacted tax law. Often, there are temporary timing differences because of inconsistencies between tax laws and the requirements of financial accounting standards. A deferred tax liability is recognized for temporary differences that will result in taxes payable in future years, while a deferred tax asset is a temporary difference that will result in tax savings in future years. Statement 109 also addresses related issues, such as measurement and consequences of changes in tax laws and rates.

Introduction

FASB Interpretation No. 48 (FIN 48) is an interpretation of FASB Statement No. 109 (SFAS 109), Accounting for Income Taxes generally applicable to years beginning after December 15, 2006. (FIN 48 ¶3 and ¶22) FIN 48 addresses the accounting for uncertainty in income taxes, including state and local income taxes, recognized in an enterprise's financial statements in accordance with FAS 109. (FIN 48 at ¶1) Compliance with state and local income tax laws for enterprises with complex legal structures and operations in numerous jurisdictions can be an extraordinary undertaking. Therefore, it should come as no surprise that complex issues will arise when accounting for uncertain state and local income tax positions in accordance with FIN

48 and FAS 109. The goal of FIN 48 is more consistent reporting of tax positions and it looks to achieve this goal by setting forth separate recognition and measurement standards. Through the use of an example, we will highlight a few of the complex issues an enterprise may face when applying FIN 48 to its state and local income tax positions.

The Interpretation

The beginning of the Interpretation reiterates the current state of "diverse accounting practices ... inconsistency in the criteria used to recognize, derecognize, or measure benefits related to income taxes ... [and] noncomparability in reporting income tax assets and liabilities." Appendix B of the Interpretation includes a helpful summary of certain current practices and describes in greater detail the basis for the FASB's conclusions. The body of the Interpretation addresses a number of issues and identifies covered tax positions, defines the standard for initial and subsequent recognition and derecognition, and describes how the amount of a benefit is measured.

STUDY QUESTION

---

1. What is the goal of FIN 48?
 a. Reporting tax positions consistently
 b. Recognize current tax consequences
 c. Recognize future tax consequences
 d. Define standards for recognition

TAX POSITIONS

The Interpretation applies to all "tax positions" accounted for in accordance with Statement 109. A tax position includes a filing position on a previously filed return and an expected filing position in a future tax return reflected in measuring current or deferred income tax assets and liabilities for interim or annual periods. Significantly, a tax position includes (1) a decision not to file a tax return, (2) an allocation or a shift of income between jurisdictions, (3) the characterization of income or a decision to exclude reporting taxable income in a tax return, and (4) a decision to classify a transaction, entity, or other position in a tax return as tax exempt

The Two-Step Process

FIN 48 utilizes a two-step process for evaluating an enterprise's uncertain tax position taken or expected to be taken in a tax return. (FIN 48 at ¶A2) Before a tax position can be evaluated through this two-step process, the appropriate unit of account must be determined. FIN 48 provides that determining the appropriate unit of account is a matter of judgment based on the individual facts and circumstances of that position evaluated in light of all available evidence. (FIN 48 at ¶5) The determination of the unit of account to be used in applying the provisions of FIN 48 shall consider the manner in which the enterprise prepares and supports its income tax return and the approach the enterprise anticipates the taxing authority will take during an examination. (FIN 48 at ¶5)

After the unit of account for determining what constitutes an individual tax position has been identified, the tax position must then be analyzed under FIN 48's two-step process. The first step of this process is "recognition." (FIN 48 at ¶5 through ¶7) For purposes of this step, an enterprise must determine whether it is more likely than not that a tax position, based on the technical merits, will be sustained upon ultimate resolution in the court of last resort. (FIN 48 at ¶5, ¶6 and ¶A2) If an enterprise is unable to get to a more-likely-than-not level of authority on the technical merits, then a company can take into account widely understood administrative practices for this purpose. (FIN 48 at ¶5, ¶A2 and ¶7(b)) The entire tax benefit for a position is not recognized under FIN 48 when the more-likely-than-not standard is not met. (FIN 48 at ¶10) If a tax position meets the more-likely-than-not recognition threshold, the tax position is evaluated under the second step of the process, "measurement." (FIN 48 at ¶8) For purposes of this step, the tax position is measured to determine the amount of benefit to recognize in the financial statements.

The Recognition Standard

The Interpretation provides that an enterprise should recognize the effects of a tax position "when it is more likely than not, based on the technical merits, that the position will be sustained upon examination." As the standard implies, persons are to presume that the tax position will be examined so the likelihood of an audit is irrelevant. As one might imagine, the key issue is definition of the phrase "more likely than not." The Interpretation assumes the following criteria when assessing the more likely then not standard:

a. the tax position will be examined by the relevant taxing authority and the tax authority has full knowledge of all relevant information.
b. technical merits of the tax position derive from sources of tax law authority and facts and circumstances are applicable to the tax position, including consideration of administrative practices and precedents of the taxing authority, and
c. tax position is evaluated without considering the possibility of offset or aggregation with other positions. (FIN 48 at ¶7)

Helpful material regarding alternative recognition thresholds is found in paragraphs B29 through B33 of Appendix B of the Interpretation. While the "more-likely-than-not" recognition threshold does not require a legal tax opinion, paragraph B34 notes "that a tax opinion can be external evidence supporting a management assertion and that management should decide whether to obtain a tax opinion after evaluating the weight of all available evidence and the uncertainties of the applicability of the relevant statutory or case law. Other evidence, in addition to or instead of a tax opinion, supporting the assertion also could be obtained; the level of evidence that is necessary and appropriate is a matter of judgment that depends on all available information." Thus, the tax opinion of a qualified expert is only one item of evidence that management may consider in reaching its reporting conclusions.

Derecognition

The Interpretation also addresses the consequences when a tax position no longer meets the more-likely-than-not recognition threshold. In this event, the position is "derecognized" by increasing or decreasing a tax liability or a deferred tax asset.

STUDY QUESTIONS

2. What must a taxpayer do before beginning the two-step process?
   a. Determine a more-likely-than-not tax position
   b. Measure the tax position
   c. Decide whether to file a tax return
   d. Determine an appropriate unit of account

3. All of the following are true statements about the more-likely-than-not recognition threshold are assumed, *except:*
   a. The tax position will be examined by the relevant tax authority.
   b. The enterprise has obtained a legal tax opinion with regard to its tax position.
   c. The tax position is evaluated without considering offset with other tax positions.
   d. The technical merits of the tax position derive from sources of tax law authority.

FIN 48 APPLICATION

The following example highlights some of the key issues that an enterprise may face when applying FIN 48 to its state income tax positions.

Company A is a retailer that has income tax nexus with all states and files income tax returns in the appropriate jurisdictions. Company A has a subsidiary, Company B, that manages Company A's intangibles. Company

A and Company B also have various intercompany transactions related to management services that Company B provides to Company A. Company B was incorporated in a state without an income tax, and does not file state income tax returns in any state. Both Companies A and B have been operating at a profit for the last 20 years.

FIN 48 provides that the term "tax position" encompasses a decision by an enterprise not to file a tax return. (FIN 48 at ¶4(a)) Therefore, Company B's decision in the above example not to file state income tax returns in any state is a tax position in each state in which a tax return was not filed. The unit of account for analyzing each tax position under FIN 48 will vary from state to state based, in part, on the approach the enterprise anticipates the taxing authority will take during an examination. (FIN 48 at ¶5) In other words, the states may use various approaches to attempt to tax Company B's income. We will now focus on four possible approaches and how the unit of account related to Company B's non-filing position may vary.

Economic Nexus Approach

A state taxing authority may assert that Company B has economic nexus with their state based on a statute, regulation, case or other applicable authority. If an economic nexus approach is expected to be taken by the state, is it possible for Company B to reach a more-likely-than-not level of authority that it will prevail? FIN 48 provides that for purposes of determining whether or not the more-likely-than-not recognition threshold is met, it is assumed that the taxpayer will litigate the nexus issue to the court of last resort. (FIN 48 at ¶A2) In the case of a nexus determination, as with other constitutional issues, the court of last resort is the U.S. Supreme Court. Is it possible to be more than 50 percent certain how the U.S. Supreme Court will decide an issue? If not, Company B would be required to accrue a FIN 48 liability for the direct taxation of its income in all economic nexus states, assuming there is not an overriding, widely understood administrative practice in the state that would change the conclusion. This also assumes that there are no other tax positions, such as those related to apportionment factor determinations, which would impact this conclusion.

Forced Combination Approach

A state taxing authority may attempt to force combination of Company A and Company B. If Company B cannot reach the more-likely-than-not recognition threshold that it can preclude forced combination, then the companies would also be required to accrue a FIN 48 liability. However, for purposes of determining the liability, additional analysis would be required, as the tax liability under a forced combination may be different than it would be if B's income were taxed directly by the state.

Expense Adjustment Approach

A state taxing authority may attack the transactions between the two companies in an attempt to reduce the expense in Company A. The intercompany transactions between Company A and Company B may give rise to uncertain tax positions if they are not supported by a valuation or a current transfer pricing study. What if a transfer pricing study is in place, but it is based on 10-year-old comparables and there has been a significant change in facts and circumstances? In both circumstances, this may give rise to an uncertain tax position due to potential state income tax exposure for the entity whose taxable income is understated.

Income Reallocation Approach

Finally, a state taxing authority may look to a more general statutory or regulatory authority to reallocate income between the two related entities to properly reflect the income related to the entity's activity in the state. If it is believed that a state will take this approach, and B does not believe it is more likely than not that it will prevail, then it must accrue a liability based upon the manner in which it believes the state will reallocate income.

The Look-Back Issue

What if, after determining the unit of account to address the potential attack on Company B's income (or Company A's expenses), it is not more likely than not that the enterprise's non-filing position will be sustained upon examination in a particular state? In some states, the decision not to file a state tax return may never start the statute of limitations. Under these circumstances, is Company B required to look back 20 years? FIN 48 provides that in determining a state income tax provision, a company can consider widely understood practices and precedents of a particular state to determine the look-back period. (FIN 48 at ¶7(b)) What if the practice or precedent in State X is to analyze each taxpayer's facts and circumstances on a case-by-case basis to determine the appropriate look-back periods? What is the best way to document this practice or precedent? These questions need to be addressed to determine whether the more-likely-than-not standard for recognition has been met. A 20-year liability plus growing interest and penalties can quickly become an extraordinary amount, even though it is sometimes the case that a state will limit its look-back period to significantly less than 20 years.

STUDY QUESTIONS

---

4. All of the following are approaches a taxing authority may use when attempting to tax Company B's income, *except:*

   a. Income Reallocation Approach
   b. Forced Combination Approach
   c. Look-Back Approach
   d. Economic Nexus Approach

5. Which approach used by a state to attempt to tax Company B's income would require Company A and Company B to support their tax position with a current transfer pricing study?

   a. Expense Adjustment Approach
   b. Forced Combination Approach
   c. Economic Nexus Approach
   d. Income Reallocation Approach

THE MEASUREMENT STANDARD

Regarding any of the tax positions discussed in the example above, what if the companies determine it is more likely than not that a tax position will be sustained upon examination in a particular state? The companies would then evaluate the tax position under the second step of the process, measurement. (FIN 48 at ¶8) For purpose of measurement, the companies must consider the amounts and probabilities of the outcomes that could be realized upon ultimate settlement to determine the tax benefit to be recognized.(FIN 48 at ¶8) Therefore, it is possible that a company can reach the more-likely-than-not recognition threshold on the same state income tax position covering several states, but the relative "measured" tax benefit may vary in each of those states because the states may approach an ultimate plan of settlement differently.

CONCLUSION

There is no doubt that management will look more often to tax practitioners for opinions to support management assertions regarding tax positions in financial statements. Over time, the meaning of the relevant terms and standards may become clearer.

Through the foregoing example, we have only scratched the surface of the complex issues that a business might face when applying FIN 48 to its state and local income tax positions. This chapter highlights the need for an enterprise to consider whether it has the resources in place to identify and analyze material state income tax positions for purposes of FIN 48.

CPE NOTE: When you have completed your study and review of chapters 1-4, which comprise this Module, you may wish to take the Quizzer for the Module.

For your convenience, you can also take this Quizzer online at **www. cchtestingcenter.com.**

MODULE 2: OTHER CURRENT STATE TAX ISSUES — CHAPTER 5

State Tax Appeals Process

This chapter examines current state tax appeals processes and discusses how those processes can be made more fair and efficient.

LEARNING OBJECTIVES

Upon completion of this chapter, you should be able to:

- Identify states' arguments in favor of requiring prepayment of assessments;
- Enumerate the elements of a fair tax tribunal;
- Describe the current status of some states' tax resolution process; and
- Understand the Model Act and its suggestions for a fair tax appeals process.

INTRODUCTION

Taxes are a necessary societal evil; however, the governmental processes to secure collection of those taxes should be fair and transparent. This publication identifies and addresses the elements in state tax appeals systems that are fundamental to achieving that goal:

- Availability of prepayment/prebonding review of assessments
- Availability of an impartial reviewing forum
- A reviewing forum staffed by well-qualified, well-compensated and politically independent individuals
- A reviewing forum that promptly resolves matters before it
- A reviewing forum whose rules are clear and consistent
- A transparent appellate process with rendered published decisions
- An appellate process that gives deference to the independent fact-finder
- Availability of confidentiality in appropriate situations
- Availability to all parties of the right to appeal adverse decisions

The chapter provides an outline of counterpoints that addresses certain of these goals from the vantage point of state officials.

In recent years, many states have taken to heart concerns regarding the appeals process and have addressed those concerns by restructuring their systems for review of assessments of taxpayers. This chapter recounts a few examples of state successes as well as the struggles that one state—California—has faced in seeking improvements to its tax appeals system.

Although a fair tax appeals process is a critical element of a tax system, it is not its only element. Tax laws and their interpretation and administration are also required for an optimal tax system to exist.

The American Bar Association's State and Local Tax Committee has been at the forefront of the effort to ensure that all states have tax appeals processes that incorporate the desirable elements of such processes, and that committee has drafted a Model Act that incorporates those elements. A copy of the draft Model Act is provided in this chapter.

Finally, a survey of states' tax appeals systems is included (Exhibit A), along with the request that all states consider their current tax systems, isolate problem areas, and seek improvement. It's the right thing to do.

COUNTERPOINT: WHY PAY-TO-PLAY AND INTERNAL HEARING SYSTEMS ARE APPROPRIATE

Pay-to-Play and/or Bond-to-Play

The following reflect the vantage point of state tax officials as to why pay-to-play and/or bond-to-play is appropriate:

- States need the money and should be allowed to collect it upon the auditor's assertion. If the auditor is ultimately incorrect, the money can be refunded to the taxpayer, usually with interest. Therefore, the taxpayer is not harmed and the state immediately receives the money the auditor says is due.
- A large corporation can afford to pay a few million dollars based solely on an auditor's assertion. If the auditor is wrong, the corporation will receive a refund. Therefore, no harm, no foul.
- If a taxpayer does not want to pay, it can simply post a bond. A bond is not unaffordable for a large corporation.
- During the pendency of the review of the assessment, the taxpayer may have business setbacks, which might prevent the ultimate recovery of the assessed amount.
- Pay-to-play and/or bond-to-play will ensure that the taxpayer will mount its best defense to an assessment.

Internal Hearing Systems

Internal hearing systems are appropriate because:

- Who better to determine whether the auditor is correct than his or her supervisor? A person who regularly supervises the auditor knows when the auditor is overreaching and is therefore qualified to determine whether a taxpayer's protest is valid.
- An internal hearing officer has generally spent many years working for the tax department. Therefore, the person will be knowledgeable of the state's tax law, which is important when the application of technical tax laws is at issue.

- It is not a problem if the hearing officer is a little biased in favor of the tax department because many taxpayers are represented by qualified attorneys and accountants, which levels the playing field.
- Internal hearing officers are privy to internal tax department materials and policies, which may be of aid in reaching the "right" determination.
- Internal hearing officers have access to the tax department personnel involved in the issuance of the assessment and can discuss questions regarding the basis for the assessment.

STUDY QUESTION

> 1. Based on the counterpoints, "pay-to-play" and/or "bond-to-play" can be justified for the following reason:
>   **a.** A large corporation cannot afford to pay a few million dollars based solely on an auditor's assertion.
>   **b.** Pay-to-play and/or bond-to-play will ensure that the taxpayer will mount its best defense to an assessment.
>   **c.** A taxpayer's business setbacks during the appeals process will result in the loss of revenues to the state.
>   **d.** None of the above reflects the justification.

INTRODUCTION TO THE TAX APPEALS PROCESS

Taxes are the lifeblood of governments, and it is essential that the tax collection process be administered fairly and expeditiously. The words of Oliver Wendell Holmes inscribed at the entrance of the IRS building in Washington advise us that "Taxes are what we pay for a civilized society." However, as he also stated, "It is reasonable that a man who denies the legality of a tax should have a clear and certain remedy."

State Tax Appeals Systems

Over time, state appeals systems have evolved from informal, internal review systems to sophisticated tax court debates. Given that corporate and individual tax burdens have shifted away from the federal government to states in recent years, the gradual movement toward fairer and more efficient state tax appeals systems is a welcome change.

However, the changes have been slow in coming, and many more states need to take a critical look at whether their appeals systems are fair and efficient. As Justice Jackson recognized, "[I]t is very well to say that those who deal with the Government should turn square corners. But there is no reason why the square corners should constitute a one-way street."

Elements Necessary for Fair and Effective Tax Appeals Systems

■ Fair and effective tax appeals systems share, at a minimum, the following attributes:
■ Prepayment/prebonding review of assessments
■ Impartiality of the reviewing forum in form and substance
■ A reviewing forum staffed by qualified, appropriately compensated, tax professionals appointed without regard to their political affiliation
■ Resolutions that are prompt
■ Governing rules that are clear and consistent
■ Be a transparent process issuing decisions that are made public
■ Deference to the fact-finder
■ Confidentiality afforded in appropriate situations
■ The right of all parties to appeal adverse decisions.

Prepayment/Prebonding Review of Assessments Should Be Available. Unless there is a clear risk of a taxpayer fleeing the jurisdiction, divesting its assets, or becoming insolvent, a taxpayer should be afforded the right to have its appeal heard by, and the record made before, an independent forum prior to the payment of the contested assessment or the posting of a bond. Indonesia's establishment of an independent, prepayment Tax Court was motivated by the recognition by "most tax scholars" that failure to provide a prepayment remedy "amounted to a human rights violation."

The majority of states do not require that taxpayers "pay-to-play;" that is, require that they either pay the tax or post a bond as a precondition to challenging an assessment. However, in some jurisdictions, although taxpayers are not required to pay during the pendency of the administrative review process, once the taxpayer is in court, the pay-to-play requirement kicks in. Pay-to-play and bond-to-play rules should be rejected.

Reviewing Forum Should Be Impartial. One critical element of any fair and effective reviewing tribunal is that it be impartial, *i.e.,* taxpayers should have the ability to make their record and have decisions rendered by independent hearing officers. Further, decisions should be issued regardless of any potential financial impact, and the individuals hearing the cases should be instructed that they are not there to protect the revenue but to reach fair, impartial conclusions based on the evidence presented, consistent with the law.

Practitioners are familiar with the tactic employed by many states of "reminding" the reviewing forum of the negative financial impact to the state that a taxpayer-favorable decision would cause. Although painting an oral picture of starving, uneducated children can, and should, stir the heart, that picture should play no part in ensuring that tax laws are properly interpreted and constitutional. Indeed, the California State Board of Equalization considered amending its briefing rules to prohibit revenue estimates or statements regarding revenue impact. Certain board members expressed their opinion that revenue impact should play no part in deciding a case, but the regulation was not amended.

In response to legislative attempts to provide impartial review in tax disputes, one state comptroller recently suggested that moving administrative law judges from the tax agency to a general administrative agency would require lowering revenue estimates, giving credence to the impression that internal processes are biased.

If independence and impartiality are truly elements of an appeals system, reviewing personnel should be barred from consideration of the revenue implications of the issues they are deciding.

Reviewing Forum Should Be Staffed by Well-Qualified, Well-Compensated, Politically Independent Individuals. The personnel problems that have plagued tax collection throughout history are illuminating and should be given due consideration in the formation of any appeals agency. Inexperience, low pay, high turnover and corruption can be the death knell of any tax appeals agency.

In ancient Egypt, special agents were assigned to be vigilant for evidence of corruption within the revenue collection bureau manned by "scribes," as the tax collectors were called. When the pharaoh Haremhab discovered that these agents themselves were corrupt, he enacted laws to address the problem. A scribe found to have cheated a taxpayer had his nose cut off and was banished. Another pharaoh dealt with corruption by increasing the salaries of scribes.

The ancient Greeks and Romans often used men of note and integrity as tax assessors so their admirable habits purportedly "rubbed off" on taxpayers. Appointing individuals who are not fully tax compliant to administer the process of review can cause taxpayers to likewise flout the law; a farmer cannot have the fox guarding the chicken coop.

Partisan politics should play no part in the appointment process, and tax appeals positions should not be awarded as part of a political patronage system. Such appointments demean the tax appeals process. Certain states explicitly prohibit current appeals tribunal personnel, from running for public office or from serving on a committee of a political party; others restrict the number of tribunal members that can be from the same political party.

Many states specify the qualifications necessary for appointment, requiring federal or state tax expertise; often a minimum number of years of such experience is needed. West Virginia requires that the chief administrative law judge be appointed by the Governor from a list of three qualified nominees submitted by the Board of Governors of the West Virginia State Bar.

Although pay varies greatly depending upon appellate system and jurisdiction, in order to employ well-qualified individuals, the reviewing personnel must be fairly and reasonably compensated. In Idaho, members of the Board of Tax Appeals are paid $200 per day, and members of the New York City Tax Appeals Tribunal are paid at the prevailing rate of civil court judges, currently $126,600. The Chair of the Massachusetts Appellate Tax Board receives 75 percent of the salary of the chief administrative justice of the trial court, and the board's other members receive 75 percent of the salary received by an associate justice of the trial court.

The stature of the appeals forum is in large part dictated by the prominence of its members, so attracting the best and the brightest–regardless of party affiliation–serves the interests of all parties and should be a significant factor in the formation of any tax appeals system.

STUDY QUESTIONS

2. Based on the text, what is one of the most critical elements of a fair and effective reviewing tribunal?
   a. Well compensated tax professionals
   b. Judicial experience
   c. Pay –to-play required
   d. Impartiality

3. With respect to compensating members of the appeals forums, which of the following compensation approaches is advocated here?
   a. They should be paid consistent with members of appeals forums in other jurisdictions
   b. They should be paid the same salary as judges sitting in the jurisdiction's highest court
   c. The pay should be sufficient to attract qualified members
   d. All members of the reviewing forum should receive the same compensation

4. All of the following statements pertain to appointing tax professionals to the reviewing forum **except:**
   a. Partisan politics should play no part in the appointment process.
   b. The appointees should be fairly and reasonably compensated.
   c. Appointees should be fully tax compliant.
   d. Appointees should be willing to protect the state's revenue.

Resolutions Should Be Promptly Rendered. Ideally, a tax appeals system should afford parties the ability to settle cases without the need for a hearing. If a hearing is necessary, it should be promptly scheduled, and decisions should be issued expeditiously. The old adage, attributed to William Gladstone, should be remembered: "Justice delayed is justice denied." Mr. Gladstone's notion, which can be traced to paragraph 40 of the Magna Carta, written by King John's chancery in 1215, mandated that: "To no one will we sell, to no one will we refuse or delay, right or justice."

Some tax tribunals have rules governing the timing for issuance of decisions. For example, the Massachusetts Appellate Tax Board must issue decisions within three to six months from the close of the record, and the New York State and New York City Tax Appeals Tribunals provide for the issuance of findings of fact and conclusions and decisions within six months.

Practically speaking, however, taxpayers have little, if any, recourse should the reviewing tribunal fail to issue its decision within the "mandated" time, and courts have been loathe to enforce "mandatory" time limits, finding instead that the language was merely directory. One of the few options available for forcing a tribunal to issue an overdue decision, commencing an action for *mandamus* against the tardy tribunal to force the issuance of its decision, would surely be unpopular with the tribunal and would be considered a tactical error by most practitioners.

Thus, an important component of an appeals system is that a finite time for the issuance of decisions be provided, along with a "reward" to the taxpayer (perhaps an interest abatement or partial abatement) for tardy decisions. The issuance of decisions on a timely basis, moreover, affords the parties the same respect that most reviewing bodies require of those who appear before them.

Governing Rules Should Be Clear and Consistent. Tax laws have become increasingly complex. For example, the 1974 CCH standard federal tax reporter contained 19,500 pages; in 2005 it contained more than three times that amount: 61,722 pages. Given the complexities of the laws themselves, it becomes incumbent for a state to not further complicate matters by enacting onerous, confusing, or conflicting procedural rules.

Taxpayers should not be left to ponder about the practical procedures for commencing, litigating, or appealing cases brought before the tribunal. Barring any substantial reason for a distinction (*e.g.,* property taxes), rules should be consistent regardless of the nature or type of tax involved.

Appeals Process Should Be Transparent, and Decisions Should Be Published. In addition to having clear and consistent rules, the process itself should be transparent, that is, what you see is what you get. In *Ballard v. Commissioner* (125 S. Ct. 1270 (2005)), the U.S. Supreme Court reminded the U.S. Tax Court—a reminder that should, likewise, apply to all administrative and judicial forums that hear tax matters—that a fair, transparent procedure is critical to sound tax administration and determination of substantive rights.

In *Ballard,* the U.S. Supreme Court held that the Tax Court's rules do not authorize the Tax Court's concealment of the report issued by a special trial judge (STJ) and the collaborative process that results in the issuance of a single decision of the Tax Court judge, which invariably states that it "agrees with and adopts" the opinion of the STJ. The Supreme Court found that the Tax Court's procedure "[i]n comparison to the nearly universal practice of transparency in forums in which one official conducts the trial (and, thus, sees and hears the witnesses), and another official subsequently renders the final decision, the Tax Court's practice is anomalous."

Deference Should Be Given to the Independent Fact-Finder. As the U.S. Supreme Court has recognized, "Only the trial judge can be aware of the variations of demeanor and tone of voice that bear so heavily on the listener's understanding of and belief in what is said." Thus, if an explicit finding of credibility is made, due process concerns require that a reviewing court give substantial deference to such findings, and reversals of credibility determinations—should they occur at all—should be subject to heightened scrutiny of any reviewing court. No deference should be accorded to internal hearing officers whose records are made before them.

Confidentiality Should Be Available in Appropriate Situations. Individual taxpayers should not have to relinquish their right to privacy in order to challenge tax assessments. Despite human nature's prurient element in most of us, which urges us to enjoy reading a juicy tax decision chock-full of the seamier side of people's lives, tax decisions can and should be rendered without having to display the individual's intimate personal details. Revealing such details only serves as an effective bar to seeking review by those of us who might like to keep our private lives private.

Examples abound, often in connection with residency determinations for personal income tax purposes. Do we really need to know about someone's sexual preferences; extramarital activities; nature, types and amounts of personal income and expenditures; relationships with spouses and children; health issues; and substance abuse habits? Having such details splayed across a decision only demeans the process. Even though a record may need to be made with regard to such personal details, surely decisions can be rendered in a redacted format without compromising the review process.

When the first federal income tax was enacted in 1862, it contained a provision for the "advertisement in some public newspaper" and posting of lists of taxpayers and their assessments. Although the position of some newspapers waffled regarding publishing such information, by the end of the Civil War, such information was routinely published.

In 1866, Congress considered repealing the publication provision, but such a proposal was rejected because publication was viewed by many as preventing tax fraud by allowing "taxpayer surveillance of neighbors." Representative (later President) Garfield, while continuing to support public access to tax return information, argued for repeal of the provision allowing for publication of tax return information in newspapers: "There is no reason in the world, unless the public interest require, that the private affairs of individuals should be brought out and paraded in the public papers."

In 1870, responding to increased criticism of publishing tax return information, which some called "offensive and objectionable," Congress prohibited newspaper publication of the list of assessments. The 1862 tax was later found to be unconstitutional, and all tax returns were burned.

Congress has continued to grapple with the two countermanding concerns with respect to the secrecy of personal income tax information: keeping taxpayers honest versus the lack of honest disclosure if income tax information is publicized. However, taxpayers should not be forced to disclose embarrassing or sensitive private facts, particularly if such facts will find themselves in the public domain. Appeals tribunals should provide for sealing records and redacting published decisions in appropriate circumstances.

All Parties Should Have the Right to Appeal Adverse Decisions. While the appeals process in most states provides the losing party—the taxpayer or the state—the right to seek review, there are some exceptions. New York State and New York City, for example, are not permitted to appeal adverse determinations by their respective tribunals. When the tribunal statutes were enacted, the business community contended that if a taxpayer prevailed after several levels of review, including independent review, it should not be required to expend additional resources for yet another layer of independent review. New York City vigorously sought the right to appeal, its then mayor saying that it is a:

> ...Fundamental tenet of fairness in the judicial system. Every person —taxpayer and tax collector — is entitled to a day in court. The right to appeal provides necessary 'checks and balances' and improves the Tribunal's jurisprudence, since there is a greater incentive to produce the best possible decision if that decision is subject to review. Tribunal members are human; they will make mistakes. Giving both parties the ability to appeal will preserve the Tribunal's impartiality, promote accountability and minimize mistakes.

STUDY QUESTIONS

---

5. Based on the material above, in which state is the tax collector prohibited from appealing an adverse tax decision?
   a. New York
   b. Massachusetts
   c. California
   d. West Virginia

6. All of the following statements are true *except:*
   a. Procedural rules should be clear and consistent.
   b. Confidentiality is not entirely inconsistent with a transparent appeals process.
   c. Deference should be given to the independent fact-finder.
   d. Mandatory timelines for rendering decisions are absolute.

LAUDATORY ATTEMPTS TO IMPROVE STATES' APPEALS PROCESSES

States have been moving in the right direction, *e.g.,* forming independent tribunals and tax courts and eliminating pay-to-play and bond-to-play provisions, but changes are often years in the making. A few examples of the many success stories follow.

New York State and New York City. New York State and New York City revamped their tax appeals processes in 1986 and 1989, respectively, after years of lobbying efforts by New York's tax community, recommendations of several commissions, and failed legislative attempts. Not only did the New York State and City tribunals become independent from the New York State and City tax departments, they became physically separated from the departments whose assessments they would be reviewing. The State Tax Commission and New York City Hearings Bureau were disbanded.

In advocating for the creation of a body to independently adjudicate tax disputes with New York City in place of New York City's Department of Finance's internal Bureau of Hearings, one bar association report noted that the Bureau of Hearings rendered decisions affirming in whole or in part the Department of Finance's deficiency assessments in more than 97 percent of the cases in each of three of the four years evaluated (in the other year, the affirmation rate was 91.2 percent). Moreover, no refunds were granted in three of the four years.

After the formation of New York City's Tax Appeals Tribunal, its "greater independence" was statistically confirmed.

West Virginia. In 1997, then West Virginia Governor Cecil Underwood created the Commission on Fair Taxation. He charged the commission with the task of reviewing West Virginia's tax system "to determine whether it adequately embodies the principles and values" of its constituents.

After an evaluation of the state's constituents' values, the commission determined that one of the state's goals should be to have "[a] state tax appeal system that provides for both informal administrative and independent review of disputes." Like its 1980s predecessor, the commission found that the "current system for administrative review of state tax disputes suffers from the appearance of bias and lack of independence," and it recommended the formation of an independent board of tax appeals.

In 2002, an Office of Tax Appeals (OTA) was created. The OTA's rules were modeled after those of the U.S. Tax Court.

TRANSITIONS IN PROCESS

Change is rarely easy. However, as the earlier success stories establish, the formation of independent tax appeals tribunals has been a boon to taxpayers and taxing authorities alike. But as California's efforts to institute changes show, the road is fraught with obstacles.

California. Since at least 1979, the California State Assembly and California State Senate have entertained bills to establish an administrative body solely to hear tax appeals. At least two types of adjudicatory bodies have been proposed in both the Assembly and Senate: a Board of Tax Appeals and a California Tax Court. Each time a bill establishing a board or tax court has been introduced, it has been rejected.

Bills proposing to enact a Board of Tax Appeals would have established a seven-member board, with members appointed by the governor but subject to confirmation by the Senate. Each appointee would serve a six-year term with the initial appointees serving terms of two, four and six years, as determined by the governor. Taxpayers disputing taxes assessed by the California Franchise Tax Board (FTB) could directly appeal the assessment to the Board of Tax Appeals rather than to the California State Board of Equalization (BOE). Either the FTB or the taxpayer would then be able to appeal the determination of the Board of Tax Appeals to either a California superior court or the California courts of appeal. The courts of appeal could either reject or hear the appeal. Appeals from cases that the courts of appeal chose not to hear could, instead, be heard in superior court.

Bills proposing to enact a California Tax Court would have allowed for the appointment of five judges, to be selected by the governor and subject to confirmation by the Senate. Each member would be appointed to a 12-year term, except for the initial appointees who would serve terms of four, six, eight, 10 and 12 years, respectively, as appointed by the governor. Legislation that died in the Senate at the end of the 2004 legislative session, stated that, for corporate income tax appeals, the California Tax Court would only hear appeals involving deficiency assessments. If a corporate income taxpayer were claiming a refund, the BOE would hear the appeal.

Opponents of the bill to enact a California Tax Court argued that the bill created forum shopping. In reality, the bill would have created a better way to administer tax appeals in California.

Because no further steps have been taken to create a California Tax Court, California taxpayers that have received assessments from the FTB are forced to comply with the processes that currently exist. From the onset of the appellate process, taxpayers are faced with an uphill challenge. A taxpayer's first attempt at defending its filing position generally takes place with an FTB protest hearing officer, whose job is to determine whether the FTB auditor's findings are correct or the taxpayer correctly determined its tax liabilities, if any, to the state.

The taxpayer then appeals to the BOE. The BOE consists of four elected members, each representing one of four equalization districts, and the state controller—an elected official and *ex officio* member who also serves as an officer of the FTB. Not only does the state controller "cross-pollinate" the FTB and BOE, but the chairman of the BOE also serves as a member of the FTB. The third member of the FTB is the director of finance.

If a taxpayer loses its protest and loses its BOE appeal, the taxpayer is forced to pay the total tax assessed by the FTB before it may even enter an independent forum. Such a process should be reformed. The creation of a California Tax Court without pay-to-play or bond-to-play would improve California's tax appeals process.

STUDY QUESTION

---

7. Which jurisdiction created the Office of Tax Appeals in 2002?
   a. New York State
   b. West Virginia
   c. California
   d. New York City

THE TAX APPEALS PROCESS SHOULD OPERATE AS PART OF A FAIR TAX SYSTEM

The tax appeals process is just one element of a state's tax system. In order for a state's tax system to be successful, all of the system's elements—laws, interpretations, administration and appeals process—must be fair. The Council on State Taxation has identified five elements that, at a minimum, should be present in a state's tax administration process:

1. Even-handed statutes of limitation
2. Equalized interest rates
3. Adequate time to file a protest
4. Automatic extension of state return filing dates beyond the federal due date
5. Whether federal audit changes open the entire state return to audit

The effectiveness of even a stellar tax appeals forum is rendered moot if the department of revenue refuses to abide by the forum's decisions, or if the legislature bars refunds to taxpayers whom the forum has determined are entitled to refunds. Nonetheless, time and again, taxpayers have had their hard-won victories marginalized by the failure of states to issue refunds, even in instances where the tax was declared unconstitutional.

For example, Alabama did not issue refunds after its foreign franchise tax was declared unconstitutional in *South Central Bell* (SCt, 526 US 160 (March 23, 1999)). Of the $142 million refund sought by South Central Bell, it ended up settling for future tax credits having a present value of $26 million, that is, a 19 percent settlement.

Similarly, Kentucky did not like the revenue implications of its loss in *GTE v. Revenue Cabinet* (Ky. 889 S.W.2d 788 (Dec. 22, 1994)). So, in 2000, it enacted retroactive legislation prohibiting corporate tax refunds based on the filing of unitary business tax returns after December 22, 1994. Such action was upheld by the Kentucky court in *Johnson Controls* (Ky. Ct. App. No. 2004-CA-001566-MR (May 5, 2006)).

Texas tried another tactic: refunds exceeding $250,000 would not be paid without a specific legislative appropriation. Enactment of retroactive legislative changes under the guise of "clarification" to overrule unfavorable judicial decisions is also offensive and is repugnant to the separation-of-powers doctrine.

It is imperative for all participants in the tax appeals process—taxpayers, tax departments and legislators—to play fair.

LEGISLATIVE MODEL

The American Bar Association's State and Local Tax Committee has drafted and approved a *Model State Administrative Tax Tribunal Act* (the Model Act) that incorporates the desirable elements for a fair tax tribunal.

The Model Act would guarantee that every taxpayer who receives a state tax assessment receives a de novo hearing of record, before paying the tax, from a competent body with tax expertise that is completely independent from the tax collecting revenue department. The four main goals of the Model Act can be remembered by a somewhat cheesy acronym —BRIE: B(efore payment), a taxpayer who receives a tax assessment must be able to make a R(ecord) before an I(ndependent body) that has E(xpertise) in tax matters.

The Model Act reflects the input of a wide variety of knowledgeable sources, including the American Bar Association's 1971 Model State Tax Court Act and state statutes and regulations governing the nation's most successful, existing state tax tribunals and tax courts. The Act also draws upon academic literature reflecting modern thinking on the operation of state tax dispute resolution systems, as well as the practical experience of numerous state tax practitioners from around the country.

The Model Act contains a detailed commentary that explains the Act's provisions and their rationale. A copy of the final draft of the Model Act is included in this chapter.

STUDY QUESTIONS

---

8. Which state did not issue refunds after its foreign franchise tax was declared unconstitutional?

    a. Alabama
    b. California
    c. Kentucky
    d. Texas

9. Which organization has identified five elements that should be present in a state's tax administration process?

    a. Council on State Taxation
    b. California's State Board of Equalization
    c. State and Local Tax Committee
    d. Joint Committee on Taxation

THE MODEL ACT—EXPLANATION

Summary

In many states, a taxpayer who desires to contest the state tax authority's determination of a tax liability, or denial of a refund claim, faces several obstacles that seriously undermine the public's perception of the fairness of tax decisions made by the state. In a number of states, a taxpayer who disagrees with a state tax determination must present his legal challenge and make his factual record to a hearing officer who is employed by the same tax agency that made the determination in issue. In such states, such an internal hearing is the first and last opportunity the taxpayer has to present his case to a person who is knowledgeable about taxes. Moreover, the standard for judicial review of the internal hearing officer's factual determinations is often extremely onerous, *e.g.*, the hearing officer's findings must be upheld by a reviewing court unless "arbitrary and capricious," "without rational basis," "clearly erroneous," or "against the manifest weight of the evidence in the record." No matter how conscientious and fair the particular hearing officer, the hearing officer's status as an employee and agent of the tax collector creates an unavoidable perception of bias.

In some states, the taxpayer must pay part or all of the asserted liability for tax, interest and penalty before the taxpayer can challenge the state's tax determination before a court or administrative tribunal that is independent from the state taxing agency that made the determination (pay-to-play). In other states, the taxpayer must post a bond—which can be very expensive—as a condition to challenging the assessment (bond-to-play). By imposing a substantial cost upon the exercise of the taxpayer's right to an initial hearing before an independent body, pay-to-play and bond-to-play provisions discourage taxpayers—particularly smaller taxpayers—from challenging decisions that are not clearly supported by controlling law or by the taxpayer's facts.

Relevant Publications

Comprehensive surveys of the tax appeal regimes in the various states and their salient characteristics may be found in Ocasal and Federation of Tax Administrators, *State Tax Appeal Systems*, 1700 Tax Management Portfolio (BNA), and Publication RR-144, *State Tax Appeal Systems*, Federation of Tax Administrators (1994). An analysis of the characteristics and advantages of the various types of independent judicial and administrative state tax courts and tribunals now in existence is set forth in Coffin, *The Case for a State Tax Court*, 8 State and Local Tax Lawyer 68ff. (2003). The existing dispute resolution systems in the various states are critiqued from the point of view of larger, multistate business taxpayers in Lindholm and Kranz, *Best and Worst of State Tax Administration: COST Scorecard on Appeals, Procedural Requirements*, Tax Management Multistate Tax Report, Vol. 11, No. 3, at 137-152 (BNA, March 26, 2004).

The Model Act

Basic fairness demands that a taxpayer be allowed to make his case against an assertion of tax liability before an independent adjudicatory body with tax expertise. And, except in unusual situations, a taxpayer challenging a tax determination should not be required to pay the amount in dispute or post a bond as a condition to receiving an initial hearing before an unbiased, adjudicatory body.

To address these instances of unfairness, and to make available to taxpayers in all states the best practices of the independent state tax courts and tribunals that now exist, the Committee on State and Local Taxation of the American Bar Association's Section of Taxation proposes the following Model State Administrative Tax Tribunal Act (the Model Act) for consideration by the states. Drafted by the Committee's Administrative Tribunal Task Force, the Model Act would establish within the executive branch of government a tax tribunal with virtually the same powers as a state trial court of general jurisdiction, but with its subject matter jurisdiction limited to taxes.

The new tax tribunal would assume jurisdiction over most or all of the taxes collected by the state's revenue department, and would do away with the need for the state to maintain a formal hearing system within the department. In recognition of the fact that only a small percentage of tax disputes should be litigated, the Act includes a provision whereby the state affords every taxpayer a realistic opportunity to resolve a dispute with the revenue department on an informal basis, without the obligation to hire professional tax representatives, before the taxpayer is given the option to commence a proceeding in the new tribunal.

The taxpayer may invoke the tax tribunal's jurisdiction after receiving an adverse determination from the department of revenue. The tribunal's proceedings would be *de novo* and without a jury. The tribunal would include both a regular and a small claims division. The taxpayer or the department could appeal a tax tribunal decision, except a decision of the tribunal's small claims division, in the same manner as an appeal from a decision of the state's trial court of general jurisdiction.

How the Model Act Relates to Prior State Tax Court Proposals

In 1957, the American Bar Association (ABA) sponsored a study of state tax courts. The ABA study prompted the National Conference of Commissioners on Uniform State Laws to promulgate a Model State Tax Court Act, which was designed to provide a model for state legislatures to use in establishing such a court.

Subsequently, the ABA itself endorsed a revised model act (Revised Model State Tax Court Act 1971-12) drafted by the Section of Taxation's Committee on State and Local Taxes, which clarified some of the ambiguities of the 1957 Model Act and placed the proposed court in the state's judicial system.

After studying the Revised Model State Tax Court Act 1971-12; the independent tax court and tribunal statutes enacted by various states, including Maryland, Massachusetts, New Jersey, New York and West Virginia; the literature reflecting modern thinking on the operation of state tax tribunals; and the practical knowledge of attorneys with extensive state tax litigation experience; the Section of Taxation's Committee on State and Local Taxes has prepared the Model State Administrative Tax Tribunal Act, which would establish a tax tribunal within the executive branch of government with plenary jurisdiction over tax matters.

The Model Act uses the terms "[general trial]" and "[statute]" to indicate to the draftsman that reference to local usage and statutes must be inserted at this point. Other insertions are suggested by the use of material in brackets. A detailed commentary follows the Model Act's text.

STUDY QUESTIONS

10. Based on the material quoted here from the Model Act, which of the following publications contains a critique of existing dispute resolution systems from the point of view of larger business taxpayers?

    a. State and Local Tax Lawyer
    b. Committee on State and Local Taxation
    c. Tax Management Portfolio (BNA)
    d. Tax Management Multistate Tax Report

11. Which group drafted the first Model State Tax Court Act?

    a. Committee on State and Local Taxation
    b. National Conference of Commissioners
    c. Federation of Tax Administrators
    d. Joint Committee on Taxation

MODEL STATE ADMINISTRATIVE TAX TRIBUNAL ACT

Section 1. Statement of Purpose

To increase public confidence in the fairness of the state tax system, the state shall provide an independent agency with tax expertise to resolve disputes between the [department of revenue] and taxpayers, prior to requiring the payment of the amounts in issue or the posting of a bond, but after the taxpayer has had a full opportunity to attempt settlement with the [department of revenue] based, among other things, on the hazards of litigation. By establishing an independent tax tribunal within the executive branch of government, this Act provides taxpayers with a means of resolving controversies that ensures both the appearance and the reality of due process and fundamental fairness.

The tax tribunal shall provide hearings in all tax matters except those specified by statute, and render decisions and orders relating thereto. A tax tribunal hearing shall be commenced by the filing of a petition protesting a tax determination made by the [department of revenue], including any determination that cancels, revokes, suspends or denies an application for a license, permit or registration. A final decision of the tax tribunal shall have the same force and effect as, and shall be subject to appeal (except in the case of small claims) in the same manner as, a final decision of a state trial court.

It is the intent of the [General Assembly] that this Act foster the settlement or other resolution of tax disputes to the extent possible and, in cases in which litigation is necessary, to provide the people of this state with a fair, independent, pre-payment procedure to determine a dispute with the

[Department of Revenue]. The Act shall be interpreted and construed in accordance with, and in furtherance of, this intent.

Section 1 Commentary

This section declares the legislature's purposes in creating an independent administrative tax tribunal. Portions of this section were taken from the legislation that established the West Virginia Office of Tax Appeals, the statement of purpose from the legislation establishing the New York State Division of Tax Appeals, and provisions of the South Carolina Revenue Procedures Act.

Section 2. Tax Tribunal: Establishment

a) A tax tribunal is hereby established in the executive branch of government. The tribunal is referred to in this Act as the "Tax Tribunal."

b) The Tax Tribunal shall be separate from and independent of the authority of the [commissioner of revenue] and the [Department of Revenue].

c) The Tax Tribunal shall have a seal.

d) The Tax Tribunal shall be created and exist on and after January 1, 200_, but the judge[s] thereof may be appointed prior thereto and may then take any action that is necessary to enable the judge[s] properly to exercise after that date the duties, functions and powers given the Tax Tribunal under this Act.

Section 2 Commentary

The Model Act places the Tax Tribunal in the executive branch, while simultaneously ensuring that the tribunal is separate from and independent of the commissioner of revenue and the department of revenue.

The Model Act establishes a Tax Tribunal in the executive branch, rather than the judicial branch, for several reasons. First, a number of state constitutions either do not permit the legislature to establish a specialized court within the judicial branch without an amendment to the state constitution or require judicial branch judges to be elected in a manner that makes it difficult or impossible to ensure that the court has tax expertise.

Second, experience over the last 20 years demonstrates that executive-branch state tax tribunals can efficiently achieve the Model Act's principal goals of providing every taxpayer faced with a tax dispute a pre-payment opportunity to make his factual record before an independent forum of tax experts. Executive-branch tribunals in states such as Maryland, Massachusetts, Michigan and New York have operated successfully for a number of years and have earned a reputation for fairness and tax expertise.

A specialized judicial branch court would have advantages over the executive branch tribunal contemplated by the Model Act, *i.e.,* a judicial court would have greater institutional independence and the power to invalidate facially unconstitutional tax statutes. Accordingly, a state considering reform of its tax appeals system should explore the alternative of accomplishing the Model Act's goals by establishing a specialized tax court in the judicial branch. If that alternative is chosen, Sections 7 through 19 contain important and useful provisions that should be considered for enactment by the legislature or adoption by the new court as rules.

Subsection (d) permits the first judge (or judges) to establish the Tax Tribunal before the tribunal actually has jurisdiction to hear cases.

Section 3. Judges: Number, Appointment, Term of Office, Removal

a) The Tax Tribunal shall consist of at least one full-time judge. If there is more than one judge, each shall exercise the powers of the Tax Tribunal.

b) The judge[s] of the Tax Tribunal shall be appointed by the Governor, with the advice and consent of the Senate, for a term of 10 years. If the Tribunal has more than one judge, the judges initially appointed should be given terms of different lengths not exceeding 10 years, so that all judges' terms do not expire in the same year.

c) The [Each] judge of the Tax Tribunal shall receive an annual salary no less than that provided for [general trial] court judges under [statute], which salary shall not be diminished during the judge's term of appointment.

d) Once appointed and confirmed, the [each] judge shall continue in office until his or her term expires and until a successor has been appointed and confirmed.

e) A vacancy in the Tax Tribunal occurring otherwise than by expiration of term shall be filled for the unexpired term in the same manner as an original appointment.

f) If more than one judge is appointed, the Governor shall designate one of the members as chief judge, in this chapter referred to as the "Chief Judge." The Chief Judge shall be the executive of the Tax Tribunal, shall have sole charge of the administration of the Tax Tribunal and shall apportion among the judges all causes, matters and proceedings coming before the Tax Tribunal. The individual designated as Chief Judge shall serve in that capacity during the pleasure of the Governor.

g) The Governor may remove a judge, after notice and an opportunity to be heard, for neglect of duty, inability to perform duties, malfeasance in office, or other good cause, with the advice and consent of the Senate.

h) Whenever the Tax Tribunal trial docket or business becomes congested, or the [any] judge of the Tax Tribunal is absent, is disqualified or for any other reason is unable to perform his or her duties as judge, and it appears to the

Governor that it is advisable that the services of an additional judge or judges be provided, the Governor may appoint a judge, or judges, *pro tempore* of the Tax Tribunal. Any person appointed judge *pro tempore* of the Tax Tribunal shall have the qualifications set forth in subsections (a) and (b) of Section 4 of this Act and shall be entitled to serve for a period no longer than six months.

i) A judge may disqualify himself or herself on his or her own motion in any matter, and may be disqualified for any of the causes specified in [judicial disqualification statute].

Section 3 Commentary

The number of judges needed by a state necessarily depends upon the volume of cases in the state. To provide flexibility, the Act provides that there will be at least one judge. If there is more than one judge, the number should be uneven, to avoid tied *en banc* decisions. This and succeeding sections are written to apply in states having only one judge. In brackets are the changes necessary to accommodate states having more than a single judge. If the tribunal will have more than one judge, the statute should provide for staggered terms for the judges that are first appointed.

Consistent with the practice in many states, the Act provides that judge(s) shall be appointed by the governor with the consent of the Senate.

Subsections (b)'s and (c)'s requirements that each judge serve a 10-year term and receive at least the same annual salary as a state [general trial] court judge are intended to ensure that the position of Tax Tribunal judge will have sufficient prestige, freedom from political pressure, and job security to attract and retain experienced and knowledgeable tax experts.

Subsection (f) provides for a chief judge when more than one judge is serving.

Subsection (h) allows the appointment of *pro tempore* judges to deal with temporary circumstances affecting the tribunal's ability to efficiently process its docket.

Section 4. Judges: Qualifications, Prohibition Against Other Gainful Employment

a) The [Each] judge of the Tax Tribunal shall be a citizen of the United States and, during the period of his or her service, a resident of this state. No person shall be appointed as a judge unless at the time of appointment the individual has substantial knowledge of the tax law and substantial experience making the record in a tax case suitable for judicial review.

b) Before entering upon the duties of office, the [each] judge shall take and subscribe to an oath or affirmation that he or she will faithfully discharge the duties of the office, and such oath shall be filed in the office of the Secretary of State.

c) The [Each] judge shall devote his or her full time during business hours to the duties of his or her office. A judge shall not engage in any other gainful employment or business, nor hold another office or position of profit in a government of this state, any other state or the United States. Notwithstanding the foregoing provisions, a judge may own passive interests in business entities and earn income from incidental teaching or scholarly activities.

Section 4

A judge of the tribunal should have substantial knowledge of the tax laws of the state and substantial experience making a tax case record suitable for review through the court system. In states with a tax certification program, such as Louisiana and its Board Certified Tax Specialist program, consideration should be given to adding such a requirement to the qualifications of a Tax Tribunal judge. Consideration should also be given to including a provision authorizing the governor to request a list of qualified, potential judges from the governing boards of appropriate professional organizations.

Subsection (c) prohibits a judge from engaging in other employment during the time the person is serving as a judge, except for passive ownership of business interests and incidental teaching or scholarly pursuits.

In jurisdictions in which the number of tax cases does not justify the employment of a full-time Tax Tribunal judge, consideration should be given to providing for a part-time judge and allowing the individual to engage in other employment so long as such other employment does not conflict with his or her employment as a Tax Tribunal judge. In such a situation, subsection (a) of Section 3 should be amended to delete the "full-time" requirement and subsection (c) of Section 4 should be replaced with a conflict-avoidance provision similar to subsection (c) of Section 6.

Section 5. Principal Office: Locations, Facilities

a) The Tax Tribunal's principal office shall be located in [the state capital or other city].

b) The Tax Tribunal shall conduct hearings at its principal office. The Tax Tribunal may also hold hearings at any place within the state, with a view toward securing to taxpayers a reasonable opportunity to appear before the Tax Tribunal with as little inconvenience and expense as practicable.

c) The principal office of the Tax Tribunal shall be located in a building that is separate and apart from the building in which the [department of revenue] is located. When the Tax Tribunal holds hearings outside of its principal office, it shall do so in a location that is physically separated from facilities regularly occupied by the [Department of Revenue].

d) The state shall provide hearing rooms, chambers and offices for the Tax Tribunal at its principal office and shall arrange for hearing rooms, chambers and offices or other appropriate facilities when hearings are held elsewhere.

Section 5 Commentary

This section provides that hearings will take place at the principal office of the tribunal as well as at other locations throughout the state.

Inasmuch as the appearance of independence is extremely important, Section 5 also provides that the principal office of the tribunal will be located in a building that is separate and apart from the building in which the department of revenue is located.

Similarly, when the tribunal is holding hearings away from its principal office, it should do so in a location that is physically separate from any location regularly occupied by the department of revenue. When the New York State Legislature created the Division of Tax Appeals, it located the Division of Tax Appeals in Troy, N.Y. while the Department of Taxation and Finance was (and is) located in Albany, N.Y. This furthered the separation of the two bodies.

Section 6. Appointment of Clerk and Reporter, Expenditures of the Tax Tribunal

a) The Tax Tribunal shall appoint a clerk and a reporter, and may appoint such other employees and make such other expenditures, including expenditures for library, publications and equipment, as are necessary to permit it to efficiently execute its functions.

b) The reporter shall be subject to the provisions of [court reporter statutes] as if appointed by a judge of the [general trial] court, except where such provisions are in conflict with this Act.

c) No employee of the Tax Tribunal shall act as attorney, representative or accountant for others in a matter involving any tax imposed or levied by this state.

d) An employee of the Tax Tribunal may be removed by the judge [Chief Judge], after notice and an opportunity to be heard, for neglect of duty, inability to perform duties, malfeasance in office, or for other good cause.

e) In addition to the services of the official reporter, the Tax Tribunal may contract the reporting of its proceedings and, in the contract, fix the terms and conditions under which transcripts will be supplied by the contractor to the Tax Tribunal and to other persons and agencies.

Section 6 Commentary

Subsection (c) prohibits an employee of the tribunal from acting as an attorney, representative or accountant for others in a matter involving any tax imposed or levied by the state. This prohibition would not prohibit the employee from performing such activities on his or her own behalf. Consideration should be given to allowing the employee to perform such activities on behalf of family members and/or on behalf of others so long as the employee is not paid for such services (for example, on a *pro bono* basis).

Subsection (d) may have to be conformed to meet an individual state's civil service laws.

STUDY QUESTIONS

12. The Model Act would require taxpayers to pay the amounts in issue or post a bond prior to resolving issues before the independent tax tribunal. ***True or False?***

13. Based on the Model Act, in which branch of government will the Tax Tribunal be established?

   a. Judicial
   b. Executive
   c. Legislative
   d. No single branch will be responsible for establishing the tribunal; authority will be shared.

Section 7. Jurisdiction of the Tax Tribunal

a) Except as permitted by Section 15 of this Act relating to judicial review and by [other state law, such as the state constitution, a statute or case law], the Tax Tribunal shall be the sole, exclusive and final authority for the hearing and determination of questions of law and fact arising under the tax laws of this state. For purposes of this section, the following statutes are not tax laws of this state, except to the extent that they preclude the imposition of other taxes: [Any laws regulating the payment of taxes or assessments over which it is not intended the Tax Tribunal shall have jurisdiction, *e.g.*, Workman's Compensation Laws, Racing Taxes, and Commodities Assessments].

b) Except as permitted by Section 15 of this Act relating to judicial review and by [other state law, such as the state constitution, a statute, or case law], no person shall contest any matter within the jurisdiction of the Tax Tribunal in any action, suit or proceeding in the [general trial] court or any other court of the state. If a person attempts to do so, then such action, suit or proceeding shall be dismissed without prejudice. The improper commencement of any action, suit or proceeding will not extend the time period for commencing a proceeding in the Tax Tribunal.

c) Except in cases involving the denial of a claim for refund and except as provided in [state statute regarding jeopardy assessments], the taxpayer shall have the right to have his case heard by the Tax Tribunal prior to the payment of any of the amounts asserted as due by the [epartment of revenue] and prior to the posting of any bond.

d) If, with or after the filing of a timely petition, the taxpayer pays all or part of the tax or other amount in issue before the Tax Tribunal has rendered a decision, the Tax Tribunal shall treat the taxpayer's petition as a protest of a denial of a claim for refund of the amount so paid.

e) The Tax Tribunal shall decide questions regarding the constitutionality of the application of statutes to the taxpayer and the constitutionality of regulations promulgated by the [department of revenue], but shall not have the power to declare a statute unconstitutional on its face. A taxpayer desiring to challenge the constitutionality of a statute on its face may, at the taxpayer's election, do so by one of the following methods:

1) commence a declaratory action in the [general trial] courts of this state with respect to the constitutional challenge, and file a petition in the Tax Tribunal with respect to the remainder of the matter, which proceeding shall be stayed by the Tax Tribunal pending final resolution of the constitutional challenge;

2) file a petition with the Tax Tribunal with respect to issues other than the constitutional challenge, in which the taxpayer preserves the constitutional challenge until the entire matter, including the constitutional challenge and the facts related to the constitutional challenge, is presented to the appellate court; or

3) bifurcate the matter by commencing a declaratory action in the [general trial] court with respect to the facial constitutional challenge and by filing a petition with the Tax Tribunal with respect to the remainder of the issues.

Section 7 Commentary

Subsections (a) and (b) grant to the tribunal jurisdiction in all cases involving "questions of law and fact arising under the tax laws of this state," except tax laws specifically excluded. Under this language, the tribunal has jurisdiction in all tax cases, unless the legislature affirmatively removes that jurisdiction. While some states may include, for example, property taxes within the jurisdiction of the tribunal, it is likely that many states will exclude such taxes from the tribunal's jurisdiction.

Subsection (a) does not grant jurisdiction over tax collection actions initiated by the state, which must be brought in the regular courts. Since the tax liability in such cases has been finalized and cannot be contested by the taxpayer, there are generally no "questions of law and fact arising under the tax laws of this state" to be determined. If collection action authority is treated in the state's tax laws, such provisions may need to be amended to make clear that they are not affected by enactment of the Model Act.

Serious consideration should be given to including within the jurisdiction of the tribunal disputes involving taxes imposed by local jurisdictions. Inclusion of local tax disputes before the tribunal will help ensure consistency in interpretations of similarly worded statutes.

Consideration should also be given to allowing the tribunal to hear cases involving other state statutes for which the tribunal judges have an appropriate background. This would allow full utilization of the tribunal in states in which there are not many tax cases in a particular year.

The subsection (b) exceptions to exclusive jurisdiction refer primarily to situations in which the state constitution or statutes give jurisdiction over specific matters to the state supreme court or other courts. The subsection also makes clear that an action within the jurisdiction of the Tax Tribunal that is improperly commenced in another forum shall be dismissed, but without prejudice to re-file in the Tax Tribunal; however, the time period for commencing an action in the Tax Tribunal shall not be extended.

Some states currently allow refund actions or suits to recover taxes paid under protest to be brought in the regular courts. Unless existing law is changed, subsections (a) and (b) will cause the regular courts and the Tax Tribunal to have simultaneous jurisdiction over such matters.

Subsection (c) makes clear that a taxpayer need not pay, nor post a bond for, any amount asserted to be due by the department of revenue prior to being allowed to challenge the assertion before the new tribunal, *i.e.,* no pay-to-play or bond-to-play as a condition to having the case heard by the tribunal. The Model Act does not preclude the state from conditioning appeal from a decision of the tribunal upon prepayment or a bond, assuming that is the rule with respect to appeals from state trial courts of general jurisdiction.

If the tribunal's jurisdiction extends to property taxes, relaxation of subsection (c)'s no-prepayment rule may be appropriate, since a single taxpayer's tax liability may constitute a substantial part of a local jurisdiction's annual revenue. For example, the state could condition the taxpayer's petition with respect to a property tax dispute upon prepayment of the portion of the tax or other liability not genuinely in dispute. In the case of non-property taxes, the tax or other liability disputed by a single taxpayer is rarely material to the state's finances, the amount in dispute is often difficult to determine, and deficiency interest provisions are usually adequate to protect the taxing authority's interest.

Subsection (d) allows the taxpayer to pay all or a portion of the asserted deficiency prior to the Tax Tribunal's rendering of a decision, without thereby mooting the case and requiring the taxpayer to commence a new proceeding by filing a claim for refund of the amount paid. This provision is modeled on §19335 of the California Revenue and Taxation Code.

Subsection (e) acknowledges that the tribunal will not have the power to rule on the constitutionality of a statute on its face, as this power is thought to be the sole province of the judicial branch of government. The Model Act does, however, authorize the Tax Tribunal to decide the constitutionality of a statute as applied to a particular taxpayer, as well as the constitutionality of a regulation, both on its face and as applied to a particular taxpayer.

In the case of a challenge to the constitutionality of a statute on its face, subsection (e) provides that the taxpayer may proceed, at its election, in one of three ways. First, the taxpayer may commence a declaratory action in the state trial court with respect to the constitutional challenge and have the remaining issues in the Tax Tribunal stayed pending final resolution of the constitutional challenge. This would be the approach likely taken if the other issues are contingent upon the constitutionality of the statute.

As a second option, the taxpayer could file a petition in the new administrative tribunal, which would adjudicate all issues other than the constitutional challenge. The tribunal's decision could then be appealed to the appropriate appellate court, at which time the taxpayer would also present the constitutional issue to the appellate court. This option would likely be taken when the other issues are unrelated to the constitutional challenge and their prompt resolution is more significant to the taxpayer.

The final option would be for the taxpayer to bifurcate the case, with the constitutional challenge proceeding directly through the judicial system and the remaining issues proceeding through the Tax Tribunal and, if necessary, to the appellate courts. This option would likely be used if the constitutional issue were separate and distinct from the remaining issues. Also, this option would allow the facial challenge to be handled by the judicial branch, while avoiding any prejudice to the taxpayer that might be occasioned by delaying presentation of the taxpayer's case to the administrative Tax Tribunal, *e.g.*, loss of witnesses or other evidence.

In some jurisdictions, the legislature acts on regulations in addition to enacting statutes. In such a jurisdiction, subsection (e) may need to be modified to provide that the tribunal can only rule on the constitutionality of a regulation as applied to a particular taxpayer. In those situations, similar conforming changes will need to be made to the remainder of subsection (e).

Section 8. Opportunity to Resolve Tax Disputes Informally Prior to Commencing a Proceeding in the Tax Tribunal

a) Before the [department of revenue] finalizes a determination that triggers a taxpayer's right to commence a proceeding in the Tax Tribunal under Section 9 of this Act, the [epartment of revenue] shall provide to the taxpayer, including for purposes of this section any person asserted by the [department of revenue] to be a taxpayer, the option to obtain review of the audit function's proposed determination by an independent administrative appeals function. An independent administrative appeals function means a program of holding conferences and negotiating settlements that is designed to resolve the vast majority of tax controversies without litigation on a basis that is fair and impartial to the state and the taxpayer and that enhances voluntary compliance and public confidence in the integrity and efficiency of the [department of revenue].

b) The independent administrative appeals function to be maintained or established by the [department of revenue] shall have all of the following characteristics:

1) Appeals personnel shall exercise independent judgment with the objective of settling as many disputed issues as possible without litigation.

2) Appeals personnel shall have expertise in, and extensive experience with, the state's tax laws.

3) Appeals personnel shall concede or settle individual issues based on the facts and the law, including the hazards of litigation, and an issue specifically conceded or settled by appeals personnel shall not thereafter be contested by the taxpayer or the [department of revenue].

4) Appeals conferences shall be conducted in an informal manner.

5) Appeals conferences shall be conducted, at the taxpayer's option, by correspondence, by telephone or in person.

6) Appeals personnel shall consider argument as to the applicability of the tax laws; settlement proposals and counterproposals; and new evidence in support of the taxpayer's position, provided that, if the new evidence is substantial and should have been presented at the time of audit, appeals personnel may request the audit function to examine the evidence and to make a recommendation as to the effect of the evidence on the related issue.

7) The taxpayer shall have the right to bring witnesses to an in-person conference.

8) The taxpayer may participate in appeals conferences without representation; may be represented by an officer, employee, partner or member of the taxpayer; or may be represented by a third-party representative.

9) Appeals personnel shall not engage in *ex parte* communications with [department of revenue] employees to the extent that such communications appear to compromise the independence of the appeals function. Consistent with this rule, appeals personnel may on an *ex parte* basis (a) ask questions that involve ministerial, administrative or procedural matters and that do not address the substance of the issues or positions

taken in the case, and (b) seek legal advice on an issue from a [department of revenue] attorney who was not involved in providing advice on that issue to the employees who made the determination being reviewed. In all other cases, appeals personnel shall allow the taxpayer to participate in any communications with [department of revenue] employees.

10) Appeals decisions and agreements shall not be considered as precedent.

11) A taxpayer's decision to forego appeals consideration shall not constitute a failure to exhaust administrative remedies, nor shall a taxpayer's decision to request appeals consideration with respect to a determination preclude the taxpayer from commencing a proceeding in the Tax Tribunal with respect to any issue not resolved by settlement or concession.

12) The [department of revenue] may promulgate emergency and other rules governing the operation of the independent administrative appeals function, including, without limitation, a rule allowing the [department of revenue] to finalize its determination if the taxpayer fails to timely request or pursue appeals consideration or a rule allowing the [department of revenue] to publicly designate specific issues that appeals personnel may not compromise.

Section 8 Commentary

This section is designed to ensure that a taxpayer faced with a tax determination will have a realistic opportunity to resolve the dispute, without litigation, through informal conferences with experienced state tax officials charged with the duty of exercising independent judgment, *i.e.,* independent of the judgment of the auditor and other tax enforcement personnel who made the determination. No litigation forum, however independent—including the new Tax Tribunal—can or should be the vehicle for resolving most legitimate tax disputes: litigation is simply too legalistic, too time-consuming, and too expensive.

The independent administrative appeals function contemplated by this section is consciously modeled on the appeals function within the IRS, and reflects the best practices of conference/appeals/settlement functions already operating in states such as California, Illinois and New York.

Virtually every state currently provides one or more opportunities for the taxpayer to meet with senior revenue department personnel to discuss and resolve a proposed audit determination before litigation, *i.e.*, before the taxpayer is required to make the record that may ultimately be reviewed by the state's courts.

As contemplated by this section, in some states, the administrative appeals function is formally separated from the audit function. In New York State, for example, before commencing litigation before the Division of

Tax Appeals, the taxpayer may, at his option, obtain review of the proposed determination in the Department's Bureau of Conciliation and Mediation Services. In California, the taxpayer can propose settlement of a proposed audit determination to the revenue department's Settlement Bureau. In Illinois, the taxpayer may discuss proposed audit determinations and settle cases, on a hazards-of-litigation basis, within the revenue department's Informal Conference Board. In other states, there is no separate administrative appeals function, but taxpayers are nonetheless routinely given the opportunity to meet with senior department officials and to persuade them that the proposed audit determination should be modified or conceded.

The new Tax Tribunal is not intended to replace or downgrade existing pre-litigation review and settlement mechanisms, but rather to provide a forum for the hearing of record in the minority of cases that cannot be resolved informally within the department. Even if, for budgetary or other reasons, a state adopting the Model Act decides not to create an administrative appeals function within the department of revenue that is separate from the audit/tax enforcement function, as contemplated by this section, the department should strengthen existing mechanisms by modifying them to incorporate, to the extent possible, the characteristics of an independent administrative appeals function enumerated in this section.

STUDY QUESTIONS

14. The Model Act does not give jurisdiction over tax collection to the tax tribunal. *True or False?*

15. If a taxpayer challenges the constitutionality of a tax statute on its face, the taxpayer may exercise any one of the following options *except:*
   a. File a petition with the tax tribunal to adjudicate all tax issues
   b. Bifurcate the tax case between the constitutional and nonconstitutional issues, with the nonconstitutional issues being heard by the tax tribunal
   c. File a petition with the state court to adjudicate the entire case
   d. Commence a declaratory action in the state court

Section 9. Pleadings

a) A taxpayer may commence a proceeding in the Tax Tribunal by filing a petition protesting the [department of revenue]'s determination imposing a liability for tax, penalty or interest; denying a refund or credit application; canceling, revoking, suspending or denying an application for a license, permit or registration; or taking any other action that gives a person the right to a hearing under the law. The petition shall be filed in the Tax Tribunal no later than 90 days after receipt of the [department of revenue]'s written notice of such determination. For purposes of this Act, the term "taxpayer" includes a person (1) who is challenging the state's jurisdiction over the person, and (2) who has standing to challenge the validity or applicability of the tax.

b) The [department of revenue] shall file its answer in the Tax Tribunal no later than 75 days after its receipt of the Tax Tribunal's notification that the taxpayer has filed a petition in proper form. Upon written request, the Tax Tribunal may grant up to 15 additional days to file an answer. The [department of revenue] shall serve a copy on the taxpayer's representative or, if the taxpayer is not represented, on the taxpayer, and shall file proof of such service with the answer. Material facts alleged in the petition, if not expressly admitted or denied in the answer, shall be deemed admitted. If the [department of revenue] fails to answer within the prescribed time, all material facts alleged in the petition shall be deemed admitted.

c) The taxpayer may file a reply in the Tax Tribunal within 30 days after receipt of the answer. The taxpayer shall serve a copy on the authorized representative of the [department of revenue] and shall file proof of such service with the reply. If the taxpayer fails to reply within the prescribed time, all material facts alleged in the answer shall be deemed denied. When a reply has been filed, or, if no reply has been filed, then 30 days after the filing of the answer, the controversy shall be deemed at issue and will be scheduled for hearing.

d) Either party may amend a pleading once without leave at any time before the period for responding to it expires. After such time, a pleading may be amended only with the written consent of the adverse party or with the permission of the Tax Tribunal. The Tax Tribunal shall freely grant consent to amend upon such terms as may be just. Except as otherwise ordered by the Tax Tribunal, there shall be an answer or reply to an amended pleading if an answer or reply is required to the pleading being amended. Filing of the answer, or, if the answer has already been filed, the amended answer, shall be made no later than 75 days after filing of the amended petition. Filing of the reply or, if the reply has already been filed, the amended reply, shall be made within 30 days after filing of the amended answer. The taxpayer may not amend a petition after expiration of the time for filing a petition, if such amendment would have the effect of conferring jurisdiction on the Tax Tribunal over a matter that would otherwise not come within its jurisdiction. An amendment of a pleading shall relate back to the time of filing of the original pleading, unless the Tax Tribunal shall order otherwise either on motion of a party or on the Tax Tribunal's own initiative.

Section 9 Commentary

This section provides that a proceeding is commenced by the filing of a petition by the taxpayer. Even though the term "taxpayer" does not accurately describe a person contesting jurisdiction over his person, the Model Act uses the term taxpayer for administrative convenience.

Subsection (a) provides that the taxpayer commences an action in the tribunal by filing a petition within 90 days from the date of receipt of notice of the determination being protested. This 90-day period is sufficient for a person to review the department of revenue's position and prepare a proper petition. If the state's current deadline for protesting a determination is different, either the current provision will need to be amended or the time period in subsection (a) conformed to the current provision.

Subsection (b) requires the department of revenue to file an answer within 75 days (which can be extended to a total of 90 days) after the petition is acknowledged by the tribunal to be in proper form. Since the tribunal receives the petition, reviews it for facial adequacy, and delivers a copy to the department, the taxpayer need not serve the petition on the department. If the department fails to answer within the prescribed time, then all material facts alleged in the petition are deemed admitted. This procedure is similar to that followed in the New York State Division of Tax Appeals.

Subsection (c) provides that the taxpayer may, but is not required to, file a reply within 30 days after service of the answer. If the taxpayer fails to reply within the prescribed time, then all material facts alleged in the answer are deemed denied.

The distinction between the consequence of the department's failure to timely answer and the taxpayer's failure to timely reply is intentional. Since the department issued the determination in issue and the taxpayer has the burden of proof, the taxpayer is entitled to learn the department's position on the taxpayer's factual assertions and it is reasonable to hold the department accountable for failing to respond to the taxpayer. In other words, the Act in effect requires the department to answer the petition in a timely manner. On the other hand, it is often unclear whether a reply from the taxpayer is necessary and in many cases the taxpayer is not represented. To avoid unintended dismissals of the petition based on procedural foot faults, the Act does not require a reply be filed and deems all material allegations of facts set forth in the answer to be denied.

Section 10. Fees

a) Upon filing a petition, the taxpayer shall pay to the clerk a fee in the amount of $_____, except that, in case of a petition filed in the Small Claims Division as provided in Section 14 of this Act, the fee shall be $_____. A similar fee shall be paid by other parties making an appearance in the proceeding, except that no fee shall be charged to a government body or government official appearing in a representative capacity.

b) The Tax Tribunal may fix a fee, not in excess of the fees charged and collected by the clerks of the [general trial] courts, for comparing, or for preparing and comparing, a transcript of the record, or for copying any record, entry or other paper and the comparison and certification thereof.

Section 10 Commentary

This section provides that a fee will be charged to the taxpayer for filing a petition. Although the Act provides that one fixed fee will be charged for filing a petition with the tribunal and another for filing a petition with the Small Claims Division, a state could instead base the fee on the amount in dispute. The Massachusetts Appellate Tax Board, for example, currently bases its fee on the amount of tax in dispute, subject to a maximum fee.

Section 11. Discovery and Stipulation

a) The parties to a proceeding shall make every effort to achieve discovery by informal consultation or communication, before invoking the discovery mechanisms authorized by this section.

b) The parties to a proceeding shall stipulate all relevant and non-privileged matters to the fullest extent to which complete or qualified agreement can or fairly should be reached. Neither the existence nor the use of the discovery mechanisms authorized by this section shall excuse failure to comply with this provision.

c) Subject to reasonable limitations prescribed by the Tax Tribunal, a party may obtain discovery by written interrogatories; requests for the production of returns, books, papers, documents, correspondence or other evidence; depositions of parties, non-party witnesses and experts; and requests for admissions. The Tax Tribunal may provide for other forms of discovery.

d) The [A] judge or the clerk of the Tax Tribunal, on the request of any party to the proceeding, shall issue subpoenas requiring the attendance of witnesses and giving of testimony and subpoenas *duces tecum* requiring the production of evidence or things.

e) Any employee of the Tax Tribunal designated in writing for the purpose by the judge [chief judge] may administer oaths.

f) Any witness subpoenaed or whose deposition is taken shall receive the same fees and mileage as a witness in a [general trial] court of this state.

g) The Tax Tribunal may enforce its orders on discovery and other procedural issues, among other means, by deciding issues wholly or partly against the offending party.

Section 11 Commentary

Subsection (a) of this section, which is based on Rule 70(a)(1) of the U.S. Tax Court's Rules of Practice and Procedure, requires the parties to use informal means of discovery before resorting to the formal discovery mechanisms authorized by this section.

Subsection (b) requires the parties to stipulate the facts to the fullest extent possible. Modeled on U.S. Tax Court Rule 91, this provision is intended to ensure the fair and expeditious resolution of disputed issues. Under this rule, no party, including the revenue department, shall refuse to stipulate to a fact, document or piece of evidence that is not fairly the subject of a genuine dispute. The tribunal may wish to adopt further rules to ensure compliance with this provision.

Subsection (c) specifically allows written interrogatories, requests for production of evidence, depositions and requests for admission to be used by either party to accomplish discovery, based on U.S. Tax Court Rules 70-76, 81-84 and 90. Subsection (c) also allows the tribunal to provide reasonable limitations on the use of these discovery mechanisms, either by rule or by order in a particular proceeding, as well as to permit other forms of discovery.

Section 11 allows both the taxpayer and the revenue department to conduct discovery. A taxpayer should not be required to prepare for a trial challenging an assessment of tax without an opportunity to learn the department's position before the trial begins.

Some may argue that the department should not be allowed discovery at trial, since the department has already conducted an audit, *i.e.,* that the department should not be able to force the taxpayer to undergo a second "audit" as the price of contesting the resulting assessment. Although this argument was considered, it was ultimately decided that discovery by the department should be permitted.

Allowing discovery by the department is justified by fairness, current practice in many states, and practical considerations. Discovery by the department is appropriate in cases in which facts with key legal importance to the taxpayer's liability have not been developed by the audit staff. While auditors can interview employees and officers or the individual taxpayer, such interviews are quite different from trial depositions. Moreover, when expert witnesses are used by a party, the other party (be it the department or the taxpayer) should be able to discover information concerning such testimony and to receive a copy of any report prior to the time the individual is called as a witness.

Many states' administrative hearing regimes already permit discovery by the department, so that allowing it does not expand the department's powers in those states.

The practical effect of not allowing such discovery would be to intensify the scrutiny given by the audit staff to all taxpayers—since the audit staff and the department's representatives cannot be sure which matters will eventually go to trial. By contrast, experience demonstrates that departments that are permitted to conduct discovery at trial rarely abuse the discovery process. If this were to occur, the tribunal should step in to prevent abuse.

STUDY QUESTION

> **16.** Under the Model Act, when the taxpayer commences a proceeding before the Tax Tribunal, how many days after receiving the department of revenue's notice of determination does the taxpayer have to file a petition?
>
> **a.** 90
> **b.** 30
> **c.** 75
> **d.** 15

Section 12. Hearings

a) Proceedings before the Tax Tribunal shall be tried *de novo* and, to the extent permissible under the constitution, without a jury.

b) Except as set forth in this Act or otherwise precluded by law, the Tax Tribunal shall take evidence, conduct hearings and issue final and interlocutory decisions.

c) Hearings shall be open to the public and shall be conducted in accordance with such rules of practice and procedure as the Tax Tribunal may promulgate. Notwithstanding the foregoing, on motion of either party the Tax Tribunal shall issue a protective order or an order closing part or all of the hearing to the public, if the party shows good cause to protect certain information from being disclosed to the public.

d) The Tax Tribunal shall not be bound by the rules of evidence applicable to civil cases in the [general trial] courts of this state. The Tax Tribunal shall admit relevant evidence, including hearsay, if it is probative of a material fact in controversy. The Tax Tribunal shall exclude irrelevant and unduly repetitious evidence. Notwithstanding the foregoing, the rules of privilege recognized by law shall apply.

e) Testimony may be given only on oath or affirmation.

f) The petition and other pleadings in the proceeding shall be deemed to conform to the proof presented at the hearing, unless a party satisfies the Tax Tribunal that presentation of the evidence would unfairly prejudice the party in maintaining its position on the merits, or unless deeming the taxpayer's petition to conform to the proof would confer jurisdiction on the Tax Tribunal over a matter that would not otherwise come within its jurisdiction.

g) In the case of an issue of fact, the taxpayer shall have the burden of persuasion by a preponderance of the evidence in the record, except that the [department of revenue] shall have the burden of persuasion in the case of an assertion of fraud and in other cases provided by law.

h) Proceedings before the Tax Tribunal, except those before the Small Claims Division as provided in Section 14 of this Act, shall be officially reported. The state shall pay the expense of reporting from the appropriation for the Tax Tribunal.

Section 12 Commentary

This section addresses the hearing before the tribunal.

Subsection 12(a) provides that hearings shall be without a jury and *de novo*.

Subsection 12(c) provides that the hearing is open to the public. While some jurisdictions currently provide that the hearing is open to the public, *e.g.*, Maryland and Massachusetts, others do not allow the public to attend, *e.g.*, New York State and New York City. Recognizing that occasionally there will be the need for a protective order or for an order closing part or all of the hearing to the public, the Model Act provides for such orders upon a showing of good cause.

Inasmuch as the hearing is public, the state's statutes concerning the confidentiality of taxpayer information may need to be amended to permit the department of revenue to present taxpayer documents and testimony in the tribunal.

Subsection 12(d) provides that the tribunal is not bound by the rules of evidence and that all relevant evidence, including hearsay, is admissible. At the same time, the Act provides that the rules of privilege shall apply to proceedings before the tribunal.

The Model Act thus reflects the conclusion that, on balance, the value of reaching a correct conclusion outweighs the risks associated with admitting evidence that violates the traditional rule against hearsay. While sometimes unreliable, hearsay evidence is often credible and in some cases is the only evidence available to prove a material fact.

A number of state tax courts and tribunals, *e.g.*, the New York State Division of Tax Appeals, routinely admit and rely upon such evidence. In the absence of a jury, the tribunal should be able to evaluate such evidence and to discount it where appropriate.

Subsection 12(f) is taken from Rule 41 of U.S. Tax Court's Rules of Practice and Procedure. That rule ensures that a party's failure to plead facts as to which evidence is subsequently presented at the hearing will not be grounds for excluding the evidence, unless the objecting party demonstrates that its ability to defend its position is unfairly compromised thereby or unless allowing the pleadings to conform to the proof would confer jurisdiction on the tribunal over a new matter.

Section 13. Decisions

a) The Tax Tribunal shall render its decision in writing, including therein a concise statement of the facts found and the conclusions of law reached. The Tax Tribunal's decision shall, subject to law, grant such relief, invoke such remedies and issue such orders as it deems appropriate to carry out its decision.

b) The Tax Tribunal shall render its decision no later than six months after submission of the last brief filed subsequent to completion of the hearing or, if briefs are not submitted, then no later than six months after completion of the hearing. The Tax Tribunal may extend the six-month period, for good cause, up to three additional months.

c) If the Tax Tribunal fails to render a decision within the prescribed period, either party may institute a proceeding in the [general trial] court to compel the issuance of such decision.

d) The Tax Tribunal's decision shall finally decide the matters in controversy, unless any party to the matter timely appeals the decision as provided in Section 15 of this Act.

e) The Tax Tribunal's decision shall have the same effect, and shall be enforced in the same manner, as a judgment of a [general trial] court of the state.

f) The Tax Tribunal's interpretation of a taxing statute subject to contest in one case shall be followed by the Tax Tribunal in subsequent cases involving the same statute, and its application of a statute to the facts of one case shall be followed by the Tax Tribunal in subsequent cases involving similar facts, unless the Tax Tribunal's interpretation or application conflicts with that of an appellate court or the Tax Tribunal provides satisfactory reasons for reversing prior precedent.

Section 13 Commentary

Following the example of the New York State Division of Tax Appeals, subsections (a) and (b) require that the tribunal issue a written decision within six months after the submission of briefs subsequent to completion of the hearing (which time can be extended for an additional three months) or, if briefs are not submitted, within six months after completion of the hearing.

Subsection (c) provides that, if the tribunal fails to render a timely decision, either party may institute a proceeding in the judicial branch to compel the issuance of a decision. Consideration should be given to penalizing the judge for failing to issue a decision in a timely manner unless the failure is for good cause. For example, §271.20 of the Minnesota Statutes provides that a judge of the Minnesota Tax Court must ordinarily file a decision within three months after submission and that no part of the judge's salary shall be paid unless the judge has certified full compliance with this requirement.

Pursuant to subsection (e), the Tax Tribunal's decision shall have the same legal effect as a judgment of the state's general trial court. Since the Model Act allows the losing party to obtain judicial branch review of an adverse tribunal decision, this provision should not create a separation-of-powers issue in an enacting state.

Subsection (f) provides that the Tax Tribunal's decisions are to be considered as precedent in other proceedings before the tribunal. The tribunal is to follow its decisions in all future proceedings unless the decision conflicts with the decision of an appellate court or the Tax Tribunal provides satisfactory reasons for reversing its decision.

It is not the intention of the Model Act that a decision by one Tax Tribunal judge should bind another Tax Tribunal judge in a proceeding involving a different taxpayer. If the tribunal has more than one judge, the tribunal should adopt rules providing for *en banc* decisions that would settle the rule to be applied to pending cases and in future cases that come before one of the tribunal's judges.

It has been suggested that, in order to lessen the judges' workload, the Model Act should not require the tribunal to issue a written decision in certain cases, *e.g.*, proceedings in the small claims division or cases involving no substantial question of law or fact. The Model Act reflects the conclusion that relaxing this requirement would not significantly impact the tribunal's workload, but would hinder the Model Act's goal of increasing the public's confidence in the fairness of the state's tax dispute resolution process. The Model Act requires only that the tribunal's opinion include a concise statement of its legal conclusions and the principal facts (or failures of proof) underlying those conclusions.

If a written decision is not provided, it would be difficult for the losing party to determine whether to appeal a regular tribunal decision and for an appellate court to know whether the decision is correct under the applicable standard of review. Moreover, a taxpayer who has incurred the time and expense of litigation deserves a written statement of the reasons for the Tax Tribunal's determination.

STUDY QUESTIONS

---

17. The evidentiary rule of hearsay applies to hearings before the tax tribunal. *True or False?*

18. Based on the material in this chapter, in which of the following states must the Tax Court judge ordinarily file a decision within three months or risk not being paid?
- **a.** New York
- **b.** Maryland
- **c.** Minnesota
- **d.** None of the above

Section 14. Small Claims Division: Establishment, Jurisdiction

a) There is hereby established a Small Claims Division of the Tax Tribunal.

b) The judge[s] of the Tax Tribunal shall sit as the judge[s] of the Small Claims Division.

c) If the taxpayer timely elects, the Small Claims Division shall have jurisdiction over any proceeding with respect to any calendar year for which the net amount of the tax deficiencies and claimed refunds in controversy does not exceed $25,000, exclusive of interest and penalties.

d) A taxpayer may elect to proceed in the Small Claims Division of the Tax Tribunal by filing a petition in the form prescribed by the Tax Tribunal no later than 90 days after the taxpayer's receipt of written notice of the determination that is the subject of the petition. A taxpayer may not revoke an election to proceed in the Small Claims Division.

e) No later than 30 days after receipt of notice that the taxpayer has filed a petition in proper form, or at such other time as the Tax Tribunal may order, the [department of revenue] shall file with the Tax Tribunal an answer similar to that required by Section 9 of this Act.

f) At any time prior to entry of judgment, a taxpayer may dismiss a proceeding in the Small Claims Division by notifying the clerk of the Tax Tribunal in writing. Such dismissal shall be with prejudice, and shall not have the effect of revoking the election made in accordance with subsection (d) of this section.

g) Hearings in the Small Claims Division shall be informal, and the judge may receive such evidence as the judge deems appropriate for determination of the case. Testimony shall be given under oath or affirmation.

h) A judgment of the Small Claims Division shall be conclusive upon all parties and may not be appealed. A judgment of the Small Claims Division shall not be considered as precedent in any other case, hearing or proceeding.

i) Sections 1 to 13 and Sections 15 to 20 of this Act shall apply to proceedings in the Small Claims Division unless expressly inapplicable thereto or inconsistent with the provisions of this section.

Section 14 Commentary

This section concerns proceedings in the small claims division of the tribunal. Some states may wish to change the jurisdictional limits.

The purpose of this section is to give the local drafter the recommended framework which can be adapted to the local situation. As with subsection (a) of Section 9, if the state currently provides for different time frame within which to protest the department's actions, the times provided in the Model Act may have to be adjusted.

Section 15. Appeals

a) The taxpayer or the [department of revenue] shall be entitled to judicial review of a final decision of the Tax Tribunal, except a final decision of the Small Claims Division, in accordance with the procedure for appeal from a decision of the [general trial] court, but without regard to the sum involved. The taxpayer or the [department of revenue] may obtain judicial review of an interlocutory decision of the Tax Tribunal under the same conditions and in the same manner as an interlocutory decision of the [general trial] court.

b) The record on judicial review shall include the decision of the Tax Tribunal, the stenographic transcript of the hearing before the Tax Tribunal, the pleadings and all exhibits and documents admitted into evidence.

Section 15 Commentary

This section requires that Tax Tribunal decisions be subject to appeal in the same manner as decisions of the state's courts of general civil trial jurisdiction, except that decisions of the tribunal's small claims division are not appealable. In other words, decisions of the Tax Tribunal shall generally be entitled to the same right of nondiscretionary appellate court review as decisions of the state's [general trial] court. Given the Tax Tribunal's independence and tax expertise, it makes sense to eliminate any existing "review" or "appellate" role for the state's [general trial] courts in relation to tax matters within the tribunal's jurisdiction.

Section 16. Representation

a) Appearances in proceedings conducted by the Tax Tribunal may be by the taxpayer, by an attorney admitted to practice in this state (including an attorney who is a partner or member of, or is employed by, an accounting or other professional services firm), by an accountant licensed in this state, or by an enrolled agent authorized to practice before the IRS. The Tax Tribunal may allow any attorney or accountant authorized to practice or licensed in any other jurisdiction of the United States to appear and represent a taxpayer in proceedings before the Tax Tribunal for a particular matter. In addition, the Tax Tribunal may promulgate rules and regulations permitting a taxpayer to be represented by an officer, employee, partner or member.

b) The [department of revenue] shall be represented by an authorized representative in all proceedings before the Tax Tribunal.

Section 16 Commentary

This section specifies the persons who may represent the taxpayer in Tax Tribunal proceedings. As is the practice within the IRS, before the U.S. Tax Court, and in the formal hearing process in most state revenue departments, this section allows the taxpayer to represent himself or herself, or to select as a representative an attorney, accountant or enrolled agent.

The department of revenue may be represented by any authorized person. If the jurisdiction of the Tax Tribunal includes taxes administered by other state or local officials, such as assessors, subsection 16(b) would have to be modified to allow those officials to appoint persons to represent them before the tribunal.

Section 17. Publication of Decisions

Except for decisions issued by the Small Claims Division, the Tax Tribunal shall index and publish its final decisions in such print or electronic form as it deems best adapted for public convenience. Such publications shall be made permanently available and constitute the official reports of the Tax Tribunal.

Section 17 Commentary

This section requires decisions of the tribunal be to be indexed and published in a manner that makes them "permanently available" to the public. This provision would authorize publication on a state-maintained Web site, as an alternative to publication in print.

Decisions rendered by the tribunal's small claims division are exempt from the publication requirement, since such decisions involve smaller tax amounts, are generally less developed cases, and cannot be appealed.

The drafters decided against an alternative rule under which some regular tribunal decisions would not be published, *e.g.*, cases involving no substantial question of law or fact. Other taxpayers have a legitimate interest in knowing how the tribunal handles issues, even issues that are relatively unimportant or uncontroversial in the eyes of tax experts. Since every tribunal decision will necessarily be available to the revenue department, failure to publish certain regular tribunal decisions only ensures that taxpayers and their representatives might remain unaware of prior tribunal decisions on issues of importance to them. Moreover, deciding which cases are not to be published involves the application of a necessarily vague standard, a process that itself would unnecessarily consume judicial effort.

Section 18. Service of Process, etc.

a) Mailing by first class or certified or registered mail, postage prepaid, to the address of the taxpayer given on the taxpayer's petition, or to the address of the taxpayer's representative of record, if any, or to the usual place of business of the [department of revenue], shall constitute personal service on the other party. The Tax Tribunal may by rule prescribe that notice by other means shall constitute personal service and may in a particular case order that notice be given to additional persons or by other means.

b) Mailing by registered or certified mail and delivery by a private delivery service approved by the IRS in accordance with Sec. 7502(f) of the Internal Revenue Code of 1986, as amended, shall be deemed to have occurred, respectively, on the date of mailing and the date of submission to the private delivery service.

Section 18 Commentary

This section allows service by mail or private delivery service, as alternatives to personal service. The tribunal may, by rule, allow filings by facsimile or e-mail.

Section 19. Rules and Forms

The Tax Tribunal is authorized to promulgate and adopt all reasonable rules and forms as may be necessary or appropriate to carry out the intent and purposes of this Act.

Section 19 Commentary

This section authorizes the tribunal to adopt rules, regulations and forms to carry out the intent of the Model Act.

The tribunal should consider adopting motion practice and other rules similar to those in effect in the state's [general trial] courts. As to discovery, the tribunal should consider the Rules of Practice and Procedure of the U.S. Tax Court as an informed source.

Section 20. Effective Dates

This Act shall take effect January 1, 200_, except that the provision in Section 2 of this Act for the appointment of [a] judge[s] to the Tax Tribunal shall take effect on _____, 200_. This Act shall apply to (a) all proceedings commenced in the Tax Tribunal on or after such date, and (b) all administrative proceedings commenced prior to such date that have not been the subject of a final and irrevocable administrative action as of such effective date, to the extent this Act can be made applicable thereto. Any administrative proceeding in which a hearing has commenced prior to the effective date of this Act shall be transferred to the Tax Tribunal, which shall render the decision in such proceeding unless there is a prior settlement. This Act shall not affect any proceeding, prosecution, action, suit or appeal commenced in the judicial branch before its effective date.

Section 20 Commentary

This section sets forth the effective date of the Model Act. Suits pending in the judicial branch at the time the Model Act becomes effective will not be affected. Proceedings pending in an administrative tax tribunal will generally be transferred to the new tribunal.

Coordination with Administrative Statutes

Legislation adopting the Model Act should also include amendments to tax and other statutes, including any statutory provisions governing the review of administrative tax determinations, to ensure that all intended tax contests will be handled by the new Tax Tribunal.

STUDY QUESTIONS

19. The taxpayer must file a petition with the small claims division within how many days of receiving a written notice of determination from the department of revenue?

a. 90
b. 30
c. 25
d. 20

20. All of the following are true statements about publishing the tax tribunal's decisions *except:*

a. All decisions made by the tribunal must be available to the public.
b. The tribunal is required to publish all of its decisions.
c. The tribunal's Small Claims Division is exempt from publishing its decisions.
d. None of the above is untrue.

CONCLUSION

As the Joint Committee on Taxation noted: "Perhaps above all, the government objective should be to strive to maintain a tax system that is broadly viewed as fair to all." A survey of the state tax appeal process currently available in each of the states, the District of Columbia, and New York City is included (Exhibit A). Some states still have a long way to go to reach the goal, but it is critical that states' efforts continue.

If history has taught those who study tax structures anything, it is that unfairness in tax administration can be fatal to a society's longevity. Even if people are not long-sighted, fairness in tax administration is simply the right thing to do.

EXHIBIT B SURVEY OF STATES' TAX APPEALS PROCESSES

The following chart discusses the tax appeals processes available in the states and pertains solely to corporation income and franchise tax disputes, unless otherwise noted. It is important to remember that many states have different processes to which a taxpayer can avail itself, and that this chart does not encompass all such avenues of redress. For example, under certain circumstances, a taxpayer may bring a declaratory judgment action in the New York courts as opposed to pursuing an administrative remedy. Similarly, a taxpayer may pay a purported North Carolina tax liability and, if its refund claim is denied, pursue redress in the courts as opposed to making its record before the secretary of revenue. Therefore, the reader should independently confirm the process of a given state, and determine the process most appropriate to its circumstances, as opposed to relying solely on this chart.

State	Level at Which Record is Made	Is level at which record made independent of the department?	Bond-to-Play or Pay-to-play?
Alabama	Circuit Court*	Yes	Yes—must post bond
Alaska	Office of Tax Appeals	Yes	No
Arizona	Tax Court	Yes	No
Arkansas	Circuit Court	Yes	Yes—must post bond
California	Superior Court	Yes	Yes—must pay tax.
Colorado	District Court	Yes	Yes—must post bond
Connecticut	Superior Court, Tax Session	Yes	No
Delaware	Tax Review Board	Yes	No

State	Level at Which Record is Made	Is level at which record made independent of the department?	Bond-to-Play or Pay-to-play?
District of Columbia	Office of Administrative Hearings	Yes	No
Florida	Circuit Court	Yes	Yes— must post bond
Georgia	Superior Court	Yes	Yes—must post bond
Hawaii	Tax Appeals Court	Yes	No
Idaho	District Court	Yes	Yes—must pay 20 percent of the amount assessed
Illinois	(1) Dept. of Revenue or (2) Circuit Court (if tax is paid into an escrow fund)	(1) No (2) Yes	(1) No (2) Yes—must pay tax to escrow fund
Indiana	Tax Court	Yes	No
Iowa	Department Director	No	No
Kansas	Board of Tax Appeals	Yes	No
Kentucky	Board of Tax Appeals	Yes	No
Louisiana	(1) Board of Tax Appeals or (2) District Court (if Department sues)	(1) Yes (2) Yes	(1) No (2) No
Maine	Superior Court	Yes	No
Maryland	Tax Court	Yes	No
Massachusetts	Appellate Tax Board	Yes	No
Michigan	Tax Appeals Tribunal	Yes	No
Minnesota	Tax Court	Yes	No
Mississippi	Chancery Court	Yes	Yes—bond-to-play
Missouri	Administrative Hearing Commission	Yes	No
Montana	State Tax Appeal Board	Yes	No
Nebraska	State Tax Commissioner	No	No
Nevada (sales and use tax)	Dept. of Taxation	No	No
New Hampshire	Superior Court	Yes	No
New Jersey	Tax Court	Yes	No
New Mexico	Secretary of Taxation and Revenue	No	No
New York City	Tax Appeals Tribunal, Administrative Law Division	Yes	No
New York State	Division of Tax Appeals, Administrative Law Division	Yes	No
North Carolina	Secretary of Revenue (§105-241.2)	No	No
North Dakota	Office of the State Tax Commissioner	No	No
Ohio	Board of Tax Appeals	Yes	No

State	Level at Which Record is Made	Is level at which record made independent of the department?	Bond-to-Play or Pay-to-play?
Oklahoma	Tax Commission, Administration Proceedings Section	No	No
Oregon	Tax Court, Magistrate Division	Yes	No
Pennsylvania	Commonwealth Court	Yes	Yes—bond-to-play
Rhode Island	District Court	Yes	Yes—must pay tax, penalty and interest
South Carolina	Administrative Law Judge Division	Yes	No
South Dakota (sales and use tax)	Office of Hearing Examiners, Administrative Law Judge	Yes	No
Tennessee	Chancery Court	Yes	Yes-must post bond of 150 percent of challenged amount
Texas	District Court	Yes	Yes—pay-to-play
Utah	District Court	Yes	Yes—must post bond
Vermont	Dept. of Taxes, Commissioner or representative	No	No
Virginia	Circuit Court	Yes	No
Washington (business and occupation tax)	Board of Tax Appeals	Yes	No
West Virginia	Office of Tax Appeals	Yes	No
Wisconsin	Tax Appeals Commission	Yes	No
Wyoming (sales and use tax)	State Board of Equalization	Yes	No

* If the parties consent, judicial review may be on the administrative record and transcript.

See Ala. Code §40-2A-9(g)(2).

SOURCE: A Lawmaker's Guide to State Tax Appeals Process: Suggestions for Improvement, by Paul Frankel, Craig Fields and Amy Nogid of Morrison & Foerster LLP, published by The Deloitte Multistate Tax Center

MODULE 2 — CHAPTER 6

Valuation of Real Estate

This chapter describes different approaches used in the valuation of real estate and state court decisions that explain when each approach may be appropriate.

LEARNING OBJECTIVES

Upon completion of this chapter, you should be able to:
- Apply the economic principles affecting property valuation;
- Describe the three valuation approaches;
- Understand the common issues that arise in applying the three valuation approaches; and
- State which valuation approach typically applies to each type of property.

INTRODUCTION

The basis for the assessment of real property is market value. Various underlying economic principles affect the value of real estate and are given commensurate weight by appraisers. Appraisers traditionally use three approaches to arrive at an accurate estimate of value: the cost approach, the income approach, and the sales-comparison approach. The chapter examines uses of these three approaches in the valuation of real estate (whether exclusively or in combination) from case law in Connecticut, Illinois, and Minnesota.

Seemingly simple to define, the subjective nature of an opinion of market value often is modified by administrative bodies and/or by judicial review due to the failure of a valuation approach to address the unique characteristics of a property. It is the function of a real estate appraiser to determine the market value of a property, sometimes referred to as *fair market value (FMV)*.

Fair market value embodies certain requisite elements:
- The transaction is an arm's-length transaction;
- Determination of the most probable price that a property will bring (not the average or highest price but a normal consideration for the property sold, unaffected by special financing amounts or terms, services, fees, costs, or credits incurred in the market transaction);
- The buyer and seller must be unrelated and must act without undue pressure;
- The buyer and the seller must be well informed about market conditions and the property's use and potential, including its defects and its advantages;

- The property must be exposed to the open market for a reasonable period of time; and
- Payment must be made in cash or its equivalent (Gerald R. Cortesi, *Mastering Real Estate Principles (4th Ed. 2004)*; Fillmore W. Galaty, Wellington J. Allway & Robert C. Kyle, *Modern Real Estate Practice in Illinois (Update) (2005))*.

ECONOMIC PRINCIPLES THAT AFFECT VALUE

Anticipation, Change, and Competition

Numerous economic principles affect the value of real estate. The principle of anticipation may affect value, i.e., the increase or decrease of value in anticipation of some future benefit or detriment, such as the knowledge that a major highway interchange will soon be built close to a commercial property. Moreover, because physical and economic real estate conditions do not remain constant, change affects value. For instance, normal wear and tear, sudden changes such as fire or storms, zoning, and tax laws all have an effect on market value. Also, when substantial profits are being made, competition is drawn to the area, such as when a successful retail store entices other investors who open similar stores in the same area. Increased competition between investors may result in less profit in the long term (Cortesi, *Mastering Real Estate Principles*).

Conformity and Contribution

Another economic principle that affects value is *conformity*, i.e., the maximum value for a property is reached when it conforms to the surrounding land use. For instance, a single-family residence may not reach its full value if it is located in an industrial area. Pursuant to the principle of *contribution,* the value of any part of a property is measured by its effect on the value of the whole. For instance, the addition of a swimming pool, deck, greenhouse, or garage may not add value to the property that is equal to the cost of the improvement, whereas remodeling an outdated bathroom or kitchen might add value that is greater than the cost of the improvement (Galaty, Willington, and Kyle, *Modern Real Estate Practice in Illinois*).

Highest and Best Use

One of the most important economic principles that affects value is the *highest and best use* of the property, i.e., the most profitable single use to which a property may be put or the use that is most likely to be in demand in the near future. This principle bears heavily on appraisers, because estimating the value of a property according to its current use may not indicate its true value. Property may be used for several purposes, and the existing use of a property may not be its highest and best use (Galaty, Wellington, and Kyle, *Modern Real Estate Practice in Illinois*).

Increasing and Diminishing Returns

Increasing and diminishing returns are likewise an economic principle in the valuation of real estate. The addition of more improvements to land and structures increases total value only to the asset's maximum value; beyond that point, additional improvements have no further effect on the value of a property. For instance, the addition of a second bedroom to a one-bedroom house should substantially increase its value, but as more bedrooms are added, the increase in value diminishes to a point at which eventually no additional value is added. As long as improvements produce an increase in income or value, the law of increasing returns is applicable—it is of economic benefit to make those improvements. However, when additional improvements no longer increase the income a property earns or its value, the law of diminishing returns is applicable, and the property's value will no longer keep pace with the expense of the improvements (Cortesi, *Mastering Real Estate Principles;* Galaty, Wellington, and Kyle, *Modern Real Estate Practice in Illinois*).

Plottage

The merger or consolidation of adjacent lots into a single large one produces a greater total land value than the sum of the two sites valued separately. This economic principle is known as *plottage. Assemblage* is the process of the merger of two adjoining lots. For instance, zoning laws may allow the construction of a two-story office building on a 50,000 square-foot lot, but if two adjoining lots are combined, zoning would allow a 10-story office building. In this manner, the combination of two lots increases the total value (Cortesi, *Mastering Real Estate Principles*).

Regression and Progression

Simply stated, the value of a better-quality property is adversely affected by the presence of a lesser-quality property, such as the presence of a larger, better-maintained, or more luxurious property in a neighborhood of more modest homes. Although the better-quality property may have been more expensive to build than the properties surrounding it, the better-quality property will tend to be valued in the same range as the lesser properties. On the other hand, the value of a modest home increases if it is near better properties (Galaty, Willington, and Kyle, *Modern Real Estate Practice in Illinois*).

Substitution and Supply and Demand

Under the tenet of *substitution,* the maximum value of a property is equal to the cost of the purchase or construction of an equally desirable and valuable property. The final important economic principle that affects the valuation of real estate is *supply and demand.* Basically, property value is affected by both the supply of property and buyers' demand for that type of property.

Value rises as supply decreases or demand increases, and value declines as supply increases or demand decreases. Other factors also play a role in the supply and demand of real estate and its effect on valuation, including the price of other properties, the number of prospective purchasers, and the price buyers are willing to pay (Cortesi, *Mastering Real Estate Principles*; Galaty, Wellington, and Kyle, *Modern Real Estate Practice in Illinois*).

These economic principles that affect value are discussed in the cases cited throughout this course, as appropriate and relevant.

STUDY QUESTIONS

1. Knowledge that a major highway interchange will be built near commercial property is an example of the _____ economic principle affecting real estate valuation.

   a. Anticipation
   b. Change
   c. Contribution
   d. Increasing returns

2. The merger or consolidation of adjacent lots into a single large lot is an example of the economic principle of:

   a. Progression
   b. Conformity
   c. Plottage
   d. Competition

THE THREE VALUATION APPROACHES AS APPLIED IN THREE STATES

Appraisers traditionally use three approaches to arrive at an accurate estimate of value: the cost approach, the income approach, and the sales-comparison approach. It is generally acknowledged that there are different types of property that are best suited for each type of valuation approach. The use of the cost, income, and sales-comparison approaches as applied to properties in Connecticut, Illinois, and Minnesota is discussed here, with emphasis on the different types of property appraised under each approach. In addition, common issues that arise in the application of each of the approaches are explored, such as:

- The use of two or more approaches in combination to arrive at a value (as opposed to the use of only one inappropriate or ill-fitting approach);
- Conflicts that arise over the amount of depreciation and/or obsolescence of property to be applied; and
- When appraisers disagree on the type of approach to use and the approach used is later found to be unreliable.

Cost Approach

In the cost approach, the following steps are taken to arrive at a value:

1. The current cost of constructing buildings and other improvements on the property are estimated;
2. The amount of accrued depreciation is estimated (three types of depreciation are included within this step—physical deterioration, functional obsolescence, and economic obsolescence);
3. The amount of accrued depreciation is then deducted from the construction costs; and
4. The value of the land is added (land value is determined under the assumption that the land is vacant and has been put to its highest and best use).

The cost approach to determine value can be used for any improved property, but it is best when used in the appraisal of special-purpose buildings such as schools, churches, and government property. Moreover, this approach may also be used on newly constructed houses and manufacturing property (Cortesi, *Mastering Real Estate Principles*).

STUDY QUESTION

---

3. Common issues that arise in the application of each of the three valuation approaches include all of the following *except:*

   a. Conflicts over the amount of depreciation to be applied
   b. Use of two or more approaches in combination
   c. Disagreements among appraisers about the type of approach used
   d. Current costs of construction

The Cost Approach as Applied in Connecticut. Conclusion: Cost approach credible. In Connecticut, the cost approach is often found to be a credible and reliable method of valuation. In *General Electric Co. v Fairfield* (Conn. Sup. Ct, No. CV02 0392891S, July 22, 2005 (CONN. TAX REP. (CCH) ¶401-073)), the court held that the cost approach was the most effective way to determine the value of a corporation's national headquarters that consisted of land and three buildings). The sales-comparison and income valuation methods were dismissed because evidence of sales of other corporate property lacked credibility, and the land did not produce income. Moreover, a guest house on the property was inaccurately considered a hotel when zoning laws prohibited the land from being used as a hotel, and the corporation used the guest house exclusively for business purposes. Considering the property as a single unit, the court held that the best use of the property was a single, owner-occupied corporate headquarters and not income-producing property.

In *National Amusements, Inc. v East Windsor* (Conn. Sup. Ct, No. CV000503380 S, Feb. 10, 2003, *aff'd*, 854 A. 2d 58, Conn. Ct. App., Aug. 17, 2004 (CONN. TAX REP. (CCH) ¶400-774)), a 12-screen movie theater, land, and site improvements were valued using the cost approach that incorporated the actual costs of new construction, as opposed to an amount provided by a national cost-estimating service, because the theater construction and site improvements were completed approximately one year before the valuation date. The value of the land was the sales price of the subject property shortly before construction began.

The cost method was the most credible valuation approach for special use property in *Southern New England Telephone Co. v East Hartford* (Conn. Sup. Ct, No. CV020515610S, July 19, 2004 (CONN. TAX REP. (CCH) ¶400-976)). The property's highest and best use was as a telephone-switching station and was, consequently, classified as commercial property. The taxpayer attempted to reclassify the property as industrial and used comparable sales of industrial property as a basis for the reduction of the property's value. The comparable properties, however, were not credible because they were industrial as opposed to commercial properties. The court held that because of the lack of similar special-use commercial properties on the market, the cost method was more credible than the sales-comparison method.

In *Services Development Corp. v. Willington* (Conn. Sup. Ct, No. CV980066947S, Oct. 14, 2003 (CONN. TAX REP. (CCH) ¶400-888)), the cost approach was the most reliable approach to value a transit warehouse. In coming to a conclusion regarding value, the court first segregated the value of the warehouse and the land, then valued the property as a whole. In regard to the warehouse, the highest and best use of the warehouse was as a transit-package or transit-warehouse facility, and as such, there was a very limited market of potential buyers for the property and few comparable properties that could be used for valuation purposes under the sales-comparison approach. Consequently, the cost approach was most reliable, and in applying that approach, reproduction costs were a more accurate indicator of value than replacement costs, because the improvements to the facility to convert the property into a transit warehouse were new and made the property unique.

An unusually large commercial office building and surrounding land was best valued by use of the reproduction-cost approach, because it more clearly fit the building objective of the taxpayer as a corporate employer, rather than the replacement-cost approach applicable to a typical investor. The property's unusually large size made the comparable-sales approach unfeasible because there were no similar comparable sales. In addition, the income approach would also have proven unreliable because of the size of the property, the 25-year lease contract involved, and the use of the entire facility by one tenant (*Aetna Life Insurance Co. v. Middletown*, Conn. Super. Ct., Feb. 14, 2002, *aff'd*, 822 A.2d 330, Conn. Ct. App., May 27, 2003 (CONN. TAX REP. (CCH) ¶400-656)).

The cost approach may be used in combination with other approaches. Many times, more than one approach is used to determine value when multiple approaches will prove the final valuation results more reliable. For example, in another Connecticut case, the town's assessor used comparable sales in neighboring towns in conjunction with the cost approach to determine the fair market value of a residential property that was uniquely overbuilt for the area. The owner's assessor used only the sales-comparison approach, and despite his attempt to provide reliable evidence of value in this way, the only fact that he wound up proving to the court was that the property was overbuilt for the area. The assessor's valuation applied instead (*DeSarbo v. Madison*, Conn. Super. Ct., No. CV990426189S, Dec. 21, 2001 (CONN. TAX REP. (CCH) ¶400-634)).

Conflicts may arise regarding the amount of obsolescence or depreciation of the property in question. Proof of a specific amount of obsolescence or depreciation is a difficult task to accomplish sometimes, even for very experienced appraisers and assessors. A town assessor overvalued property when he failed to depreciate the value of a barn on the property. Although both the taxpayer's and the town's appraisers used the cost approach, the town's appraiser used a 70-percent depreciation factor when he valued the residences on the land, but he failed to depreciate the barn's value. The court applied that same depreciation factor to the 13-year-old barn (*Fedus v. Colchester*, Conn. Super. Ct., No. CV020125210S, Dec. 26, 2003 (CONN. TAX REP (CCH) ¶ 400-912)).

In other circumstances, the cost approach is held to be an unreliable indicator of value. A Connecticut property that contained a building originally constructed for use as a telephone-switching facility with upgrades to accommodate a cable television application was not unique enough to be a special-purpose property that required a cost/market valuation. The property could be converted to other uses, such as office or retail space, even though the building did not include an elevator or loading dock because of applicable zoning restrictions. As a result, the court found the sales-comparison approach more appropriate (*Southern New England Telephone Co. v. Milford*, Conn. Super. Ct., No. CV02-0078344S, Nov. 4, 2003 (CONN. TAX REP. (CCH) ¶400-896)).

The Cost Approach as Applied in Illinois. In *Cook County Collector v. Illinois Bell Telephone Co.* (Ill. App Ct, First District, Second Division, No. 85-0555, 1987 161 Ill. App. 3d 860, 515 N.E. 2d 731 (ILL. TAX REP. (CCH) ¶400-266)), the Illinois appellate court ruled that the approach to be used in the valuation of property is not a question of law to be determined by a judge. Consequently, the county appraiser's assessment of a telephone company's office and computer building using the reproduction-cost approach was upheld absent a finding of fraud. A state constitutional provision as well as case precedent forbids interference with an assessment unless fraud is involved. The appraiser chose the reproduction-cost approach because the building was designed to ensure the continuance of communications in the event of a natural catastrophe, sabotage, or enemy action. The building, composed of exceptionally unique features, such as the absence of windows, a deep foundation, high ceilings, and a well that acted as a backup to the city water supply, indicated the building was special-purpose property without independent marketability and was not convertible or adaptable to other uses without a large capital investment.

The Cost Approach as Applied in Minnesota. In Minnesota, the use of the cost approach has received a mixed response from the courts. Often, the use of one approach is discouraged and use of multiple approaches is preferred and considered more reliable. In some cases, however, the cost approach is considered reliable. For instance, in *Federal Reserve Bank of Minneapolis v. Hennepin* (Minn. 372 N.W.2d 699, 1985), the unique characteristics of a building that housed a Federal Reserve Bank were deemed to create special-purpose property that was properly assessed using the reproduction-cost approach to valuation. An updated historical cost-of-reproduction approach took into account functional obsolescence as well as the building's super-adequacies, and this approach was preferred over the replacement-cost approach.

However, in *Shepard Park Office Center Limited Partnership v. Ramsey* (Minn. Tax Ct., No. 464980, July 26, 1984 (MINN. TAX REP. (CCH) ¶201-461)), the Minnesota Tax Court found that, although the cost approach generally provides the best indication of the value of newer properties, the income and market-data approaches should also still be considered. Consequently, the assessor's sole reliance on the cost method in the valuation of a new office building was in error in light of the glut of office space at that location that could increase the vacancy rate or cause lower rental rates.

Again, there are occasions in which using multiple approaches is best. Use of both the sales and cost approaches in the valuation of a taxpayer's combined corporate headquarters and turkey-processing facility resulted in a reduced market value for property tax purposes. An analysis under either method did not accurately reflect the value of the relatively unique property (*Jennie-O Foods, Inc. and Heartland Foods v. Kandiyohi*, Minn. Tax Ct., Nos. C8-99-0404 and CX-00-0492, September 11, 2001 (MINN. TAX REP. (CCH) ¶ 201-011)).

At other times, the income method is found to be unreliable. The income method, rather than the cost approach, was the preferable way to value a boarding house for the elderly because the property was not adaptable to any other use, and it was unlikely that anyone would reconstruct a similar structure due to zoning restrictions and economic considerations (*Nouis v. Morrison*, Minn. Tax Ct., No. 24654, Dec. 3, 1982 (MINN. TAX REP. (CCH) ¶201-322).

The market approach, as opposed to the cost approach, was the preferred method for the valuation of a building that had been specifically designed as a car and farm machinery sales-and-service business, There was practically no market for the building due to economic conditions, and according to the Minnesota Tax Court, economic obsolescence is better quantified using the market approach (*Schmitz Garage, Inc. v. Otter Tail*, Minn. Tax Ct., No. 32445, Aug. 19, 1981 (MINN. TAX REP. (CCH) ¶ 201-115)).

In another case that rejected the use of the cost approach, the Minnesota Tax Court held that the cost method was an unreliable indicator of value for an industrial facility built in 1966 that produced manufacturing display and storage racks for retailers. The value was determined using the sales and income approaches, with the heavier weight placed on the sales approach, which the experts agreed was the most reliable. The cost approach was rejected because the building's layout was inefficient, the building required extensive repairs, and the extent of the building's depreciation and functional obsolescence was difficult to determine (*Cannon Falls Partnership v. Goodhue*, Minn. Tax Ct., Nos. C5-94-639 and C0-95-462, Dec. 14, 1995 (MINN. TAX REP. (CCH) ¶202-639)).

STUDY QUESTIONS

4. In which Connecticut case did the court determine that an unusually large commercial office building was best valued using the reproduction-cost approach rather than the replacement-cost approach?

   a. *Aetna Life Insurance*
   b. *Services Development Corp.*
   c. *General Electric Co.*
   d. *Fedus*

5. In which case did the Minnesota court determine the cost approach was reliable?

   a. *Shepard Park Office Center Limited Partnership*
   b. *Federal Reserve Bank of Minneapolis*
   c. *Cannon Falls Partnership*
   d. *Schmitz Garage, Inc.*

Income Approach

The income approach to valuation involves the determination of:

- An estimate of the property's annual *potential gross income* (which includes income from rent in addition to income from other sources, such as vending machines and laundry facilities);
- An estimate of the annual *effective gross income* from the property (with allowances for anticipated vacancies and uncollectible rent);
- An estimate of the annual *net operating income* (NOI) (mortgage or debt expense is not included in NOI);
- An estimate of the *capitalization rate, rate of return, or yield* an investor may expect from investment in the property (the capitalization rate is determined by dividing NOI by the sales price of similar buildings recently sold: net income divided by value equals rate); and
- An estimate of the property value by application of the capitalization rate to the subject property's annual NOI (net income divided by rate equals value).

The types of properties that are best suited for an income approach to valuation are income-producing property (such as apartment buildings) and commercial properties (such as shopping centers, office buildings, and smaller manufacturing facilities).

The Income Approach as Applied in Connecticut. Conclusion: Income approach credible. In Connecticut, the income approach is often found to be credible and reliable. For instance, an apartment building was valued according to its highest and best use as an apartment building using the income approach. Comparable sales of similar motel-style or efficiency-type apartment buildings were unavailable for comparison. A 20-percent vacancy and collection loss rate was applied to the formula because neighborhood conditions and the motel-style layout of the building gave rise to a higher-than-normal rate of unrented apartments and loss rate. The inclusion of income from a laundry room, as recommended by the town's appraiser, was rejected because no evidence was presented that the laundry facilities provided a source of income (***Primus v. East Hartford***, Conn. Super. Ct., No. CV 980492276S, June 29, 2000 (CONN. TAX REP. (CCH) ¶400-439)).

The income approach was the best method to use to value an aged manufacturing facility. The building had substantial physical and functional depreciation that rendered the cost approach inadequate, and comparable sales used by the appraisers were insufficiently comparable to the subject property (***Brame v. Plymouth***, Conn. Super. Ct., No. CV980487854S, Oct. 11, 2000 (CONN. TAX REP. (CCH) ¶400-484). Similarly, the income approach was deemed the most credible in the valuation of a hotel, both before and subsequent to significant renovations (***Winthrop Plaza Assoc. v. New London***, Conn. Super. Ct., Aug. 21, 2002 (CONN. TAX REP. (CCH) ¶400-710)).

In another Connecticut case that found the income approach to be a reliable indicator of value, the court held that the income or market approach is more appropriate to determine the assessed value of older, small, multiunit residential buildings in average condition that are subject to a high rate of deterioration and obsolescence. That approach is more likely to take those factors into account. New or nearly new improvements are best suited to valuation using the cost approach (*Yale Church of Truth v. Windsor Locks*, Conn. Super. Ct., No. CV 980492301S, Jan. 12, 2001 (CONN. TAX REP. (CCH) ¶400-509).

Industrial property was valued at its highest and best use as multitenant property by use of the income-capitalization valuation method. The valuation was based on comparable properties close in size to the subject property. In addition, the approach was adjusted for vacancy, collection, and expense factors (*Corbin Russwin, Inc. v. Berlin*, Conn. Super. Ct., No. CV 980492452S, July 7, 2000 (CONN. TAX REP. (CCH) ¶400-444)).

The income approach was also used to value a tennis club. The market-sales approach was inadequate because comparable properties were lacking, and the cost approach was equally inadequate because of the difficulty in determining an appropriate depreciation rate. In the application of the income approach, the court accepted the lease rate on the property, despite it being for a lease between related parties, because a comparable tennis club charged a similar rent per square foot in a lease that was between unrelated parties. Also, both appraisers were in agreement regarding the vacancy and collection loss factors (*Parotta v. Newington*, Conn. Super. Ct., No. CV010508277S, July 8, 2004 (CONN. TAX REP. (CCH) ¶400-971)).

As indicated earlier for the cost approach, many courts consider the use of multiple approaches to be the most reliable way to determine the fair market value of a property. Sometimes, however, even the use of two or more approaches results in a modified assessment. For instance, in *The Old Pin Shop, LLC v. Waterbury* (Conn. Super. Ct., No. CV03-0172751S and CV03-0179824S, July 19, 2004 (CONN. TAX REP. (CCH) ¶400-978)), although both appraisers used the income approach to value an industrial/commercial property in overall poor condition with high functional obsolescence, and they reconciled their valuations against comparable sales, the city's appraiser produced a valuation of the property that was almost twice as high as the value determined by the taxpayer's appraiser. Both appraisers were criticized for the rationale behind their calculations. The city appraiser included the square footage of elevators, stairways, corridors, and bathroom facilities as leasehold space, disregarded the building's actual rental history, and instead applied a theoretical market rent to the first through the fourth floors. The taxpayer's appraiser in turn placed no value on the vacant space in his analysis of potential gross income, then deducted a vacancy rate from the actual income. So, although both appraisers used two approaches to determine value, the court found neither one of them compelling and came to its own conclusion regarding value.

For *Prudential Insurance Co. of America v. Norwalk* (Conn. Super. Ct., No. CV010184994S, Dec. 11, 2003 (CONN. TAX REP. (CCH) ¶400-903)) using the income approach was not reliable. Property purchased for use as a management training center that was valued using the income-capitalization approach was not credible. The appraiser had to rely on many projections because the property was never used as an income-producing property, and special permit and zoning regulations contemplated a corporate owner/operator's use as opposed to that for an income-producing investment property.

The capitalization-of-net-income approach was likewise found inappropriate in the valuation of a parking lot. The taxpayer's appraiser had applied a reduced rental rate to the taxpayer's lot because it was further from the downtown area than other such lots, but the court found this application invalid. Several buildings owned by the taxpayer as well as numerous other businesses in the area created a demand for off-street parking that would allow the taxpayer to ask and get the same downtown rental rate (*Consiglio v. New Haven*, Conn. Super. Ct., No. CV02-0465292, May 28, 2004 (CONN. TAX REP. (CCH) ¶400-957)).

The Income Approach as Applied in Illinois. The income approach was the best way to value a hydroelectric-generating plant in Illinois, but the basis of the approach was the plant's capacity income as opposed to its actual income. The Property Tax Appeal Board was not bound to apply a vacancy factor in the calculation of the income-producing potential of the property based on the difference between the average amount of water that flowed through the turbines and the amount of water the power plant was judicially restricted to using (*Board of Education of Township High School District 205 v. Illinois Property Tax Appeal Board*, 142 Ill App. 3d 853, 491 NE2d 454 (1986)).

The Income Approach as Applied in Minnesota. The property of one of Minnesota's celebrity residents was involved in a case regarding the use of the income approach. Prince's recording studios, production sound stage, and related offices were valued using the cost-replacement and income approaches. The income approach was appropriate because:

- The property was special-purpose property; and
- Market-rate rents were being received from unrelated tenants, and Prince himself paid the rental rate charged to all other artists when he used the recording studio space (*PRN Music Corp. v. Carver*, Minn. Tax Ct., Nos. C8-92-523, C6-93-742, and CX-94-642, Oct. 2, 1995 (MINN. TAX REP. (CCH) ¶ 202-633)).

In *KMart Corp. v. Crow Wing*, Minn. Tax Ct., No. CX-00-768, July 19, 2001 (MINN. TAX REP. (CCH) ¶202-998)) the use of the income approach reduced the taxable value of a discount retail store in a shopping mall. The store was located in an area having potentially reduced traffic due to a highway bypass that limited the appeal of the property for retail stores. Moreover, the store's attachment to the mall had a negative impact on its value because the majority of big box discount retail stores were freestanding buildings that made for optimal positioning in the market, and the relatively short period of time remaining on the store's lease contributed to a higher capitalization rate.

Undeveloped property was properly assessed using a discounted-cash-flow analysis because although the land had been improved with water and sewer lines, it probably would not be developed for several years (*Cooley and Lakeville Land Ltd. v. Dakota*, Minn. Tax Ct., Nov. 16, 1994 (MINN. TAX REP. (CCH) ¶202-580)).

STUDY QUESTIONS

---

6. The income approach is best suited to value new or nearly new improvements. *True or False?*

7. In which Connecticut case was the income approach not credible because the property was never used as income-producing property?

    a. *Prudential Insurance Co. of America*
    b. *Yale Church of Truth*
    c. *Primus*
    d. *Parotta*

Sales-Comparison Approach

The sales-comparison approach involves two steps: data is collected on sales of similar properties that have recently been sold (the comparables), and adjustments are made to those comparables to reflect the differences between the subject property and the comparables. Amounts are added to the sales price of the comparable if features are present (are superior) in the subject property that are not present in the comparable, and amounts are deducted from the sales price of the comparable if features are not present (are inferior) in the subject property but are present in the comparable (Cortesi, *Mastering Real Estate Principles*).

Adjustments to comparables for the following must be made:

■ Property rights when less than the fee simple or the full legal bundle of rights (the rights of possession, control, enjoyment, exclusion, and disposition) is being conveyed;

- Financing concessions or terms, including differences such as mortgage-loan terms and owner financing;
- Conditions of sale or motivations that affect the sale, such as foreclosure, interfamily sales, and nonmonetary incentives;
- The date of the sale to accommodate economic changes that occur between the date of the sale of the comparable and the date of the appraisal;
- Location; and
- Physical features and amenities (Galaty, Willington, and Kyle, Modern Real Estate Practice in Illinois).

The sales-comparison approach (or *market approach, market-data approach,* or *direct-market-comparison approach*) is best suited to, and is the most reliable in, the appraisal of single-family homes. However, it is also useful in the appraisal of smaller rental properties, smaller commercial properties, and light industrial properties, and the approach may be used for any type of property for which there are other similar properties available for comparison.

The Sales-Comparison Approach as Applied in Connecticut. Conclusion: Sales-comparison approach credible. The sales-comparison approach was the best way to determine the fair market value of an obsolete manufacturing plant and various utility and storage buildings, based on the highest and best use of improved property for multitenant industrial occupancy. The court considered the property as an integral unit rather than assigning a value to each of its eight parcels and applied the sales-comparison method to only one of the properties. Other properties were not comparable to the subject property, which was a functionally obsolescent, oversized manufacturing plant (*United Technologies Corp. v. Southington*, Conn. Super. Ct., No. CV 95-0550309, July 14, 1997 (CONN. TAX REP. (CCH) ¶400-240)).

The sales-comparison approach was also credible in the valuation of a commercial/industrial facility. The income approach was rejected because the appraisers submitted vacancy rates that differed by 12.5 percent, and the rental market data submitted was not comparable to the subject property's layout or location (*Equity 96, LLC v. Newington*, Conn. Super. Ct., Nos. CV 980492466S and CV990495197S March 20, 2002 (CONN. TAX REP. (CCH) ¶400-661)). The Connecticut Superior Court found the sales-comparison approach preferable for the valuation of an office building. The income approach was inappropriate because the lease agreements were between related entities, which would make it difficult to determine what the maximum income would be for the subject property (*Professional Arts Group v. New Haven*, Conn. Super. Ct., No. CV020462632S, March 11, 2003 (CONN. TAX REP. (CCH) ¶ 400-807)).

In another case involving the suitability of the sales-comparison approach as well as the economic principle of competition (which affects valuation), the court found that when numerous industrial properties are being offered for sale in a competitive market, the lowest appraisal of substantially similar properties in that market is the most credible indicator of the property's market value (*Cadle Properties of Connecticut II, Inc. v. Windsor*, Conn. Super. Ct., No. CV040527794S, Dec. 17, 2004 (CONN. TAX REP. (CCH) ¶401-031)).

Conflicts may arise regarding the property's amount of obsolescence or depreciation. Claims by a taxpayer's appraiser that the subject residential property was functionally obsolete and posed environmental threats and should, therefore, receive a reduced valuation were rejected by the court. The appraiser claimed the property was functionally obsolete because the property had only two bedrooms, which reduced the property's marketability, and contained a 1,000-gallon underground oil tank that posed a potential environmental hazard and detracted from the property's market value. The claims of functional obsolescence were not credible, according to the court, because the property contained a guest house that supplied an additional bedroom and full bath. The court did reduce the property's valuation slightly for the underground oil tank, however, after it reviewed comparable sales of residential property (*Wolman v. Deep River*, Conn. Super. Ct., No. CV020099002S, Aug. 5, 2004 (CONN. TAX REP. (CCH) ¶400-981)).

Another court ruled the sales-comparison approach not credible. Although a town appraiser used comparable properties located near the subject properties, the comparables were much larger both in size of the building structure and lot size, and were also in much better condition than the taxpayer's properties; as such, subject properties and other properties were not truly comparable. The taxpayer's appraiser used comparables of similar size and condition in nearby towns and those comparables were, consequently, accepted by the court over those of the city appraiser (*Sullivan v. Westbrook*, Conn. Super. Ct., No. CV020098896S, Jan. 23, 2004 (CONN. TAX REP. (CCH) ¶400-915)).

The comparable properties were likewise not credible in the valuation of a residential property. The taxpayer's appraiser argued that the property's best use was as a tear-down property because the property was in poor condition and lacked a foundation, but the comparable properties he chose were sold with residences that were not torn down but were rehabilitated (*Beechwood v. New Haven*, Conn. Super. Ct., No. CV02-0465505S, Aug. 11, 2004 (CONN. TAX REP.).

The comparable-sales method was inappropriate in the determination of the value of an island composed of unimproved land with limited accessibility and no docks. Comparables offered were islands that were accessible and provided docks and utilities. As such, there were no truly comparable properties. The island's fair market value was ultimately determined to be the island's last sales price, adjusted upward for inflation and with the recognition that the last sales price was possibly not the result of an arm's-length transaction, plus probable appreciation (*Madison Beach Club, Inc. v. Board of Assessment Appeals*, Conn. Super. Ct., No. 400680, May 11, 2001 (CONN. TAX REP. (CCH) ¶400-554)).

The Sales-Comparison Approach as Applied in Illinois. Upholding the use of the sales-comparison approach in Illinois has been somewhat uneven. For instance, the sales price of property acquired by a railroad could not be used as the market value for tax purposes when there was no true contemporaneous sale. The sales price of property may be used as an indication of market value when the transaction is between a willing buyer and a willing seller, neither of whom is under a compulsion or obligation to buy or sell. In this instance, it was practically mandatory that the railroad acquire the property for its business operations regardless of price. In addition, there was an interlocking of stock ownership between the parties and a mutual use of the property under the lease. The sale, therefore, was inadmissible as evidence of the fair market value of the property (*Belt Railway Co. of Chicago v. Korzen*, 226 N.E. 2d 265 , 37 Ill. 2d 158 (1967)).

In another case, the applicability of the sales-comparison approach in addition to the replacement value approach to determine the value of an automobile-assembly plant resulted in a rejection of the appraiser's exclusive use of the reproduction-cost-minus-depreciation method to value the subject property. The Illinois Appellate Court held:

> Nonetheless, the constitutional provision highlights the strong public interest in treating taxpayers in a uniform manner. Relying solely on reproduction cost when another method is used to value all other property in a county is a practice that should be tightly limited. Likewise, characterization of one piece of property among 12,000 as special-purpose property is something that should be done only as a last resort. When something like a bridge or railroad is involved, reproduction, minus depreciation minus obsolescence, may be the only way to obtain a valuation for taxing purposes; it must be used despite its similarity to the prohibited value in use method. If, however, some other method, based on a more objective value to the prospective buyer or renter, is available, that more objective value must be given at least some weight in the valuation process. Here, Mr. Romito has testified that the property could be sold for use as something besides an automobile manufacturing plant for a price in excess of $22 million. Messrs. Byer, Ferguson, Townsley, and Rodge all produced appraisals within $6 million of that figure and Mr. Ferguson at least, tied his estimate to the market value of the plant at sale. We hold, therefore,

that there was sufficient credible evidence of comparable sales for these sales to be given significant weight as evidence of market value. It follows that the Property Tax Appeal Board's assignment of a valuation herein based solely on a reproduction-cost method was incorrect as a matter of law (*Chrysler Corp. v. State Property Tax Appeal Board*, 387 N.E. 2d 351 , 69 Ill. App. 3d 207 (1979)).

Had the valuation included multiple approaches, presumably the court would have decided upon a value.

The Sales-Comparison Approach as Applied in Minnesota. Often, properties selected as comparables are found to be insufficiently similar and are rejected. The closer the comparables are to the subject property, the greater their credibility; the more adjustments that have to be made to comparables, the less reliance can be placed on the comparative results. For instance, comparable sales offered by the county's appraiser were insufficient to uphold the presumption of correctness of the estimate of market value. The county appraiser failed to quantify the differences between the comparables and the subject property, and the comparables were not nearly identical to the subject property (*Grove v. Pope*, Minn. Tax Ct., No. CX-00-112, Jan. 23, 2001 (MINN. TAX REP. (CCH) ¶202-974)).

In a case that involved a large industrial manufacturing plant, the Minnesota Tax Court held that the application of an evidentiary rule that barred out-of-state comparables in the use of the sales-comparison approach violated the trial court's duty to use its independent judgment in the evaluation of all evidence to assess property at market value. The Minnesota Supreme Court found that the reliability of comparable sales could not be limited by physical proximity, and the exclusion of out-of-state sales ultimately distorted the valuation process (*McNeilus Truck & Manufacturing, Inc. v. Dodge* (Minn, No. A05-121, Nov. 10, 2005 MINN. TAX REP. (CCH) ¶203-185) *Rev'g* Minn. Tax Ct., Nos. C4-03-287 and C5-02-241, Aug. 6, 2004 (MINN. TAX REP. (CCH) ¶203-134)).

In another case, for a number of reasons a residence was valued at an amount higher than the selling price. The assessment value of a single-family residence was set at an amount significantly higher than the price at which the residence was sold. The extraordinarily long period of time the house was listed for sale, the several price reductions, the out-of-state relocation of the sellers prior to the sale of their property, and a high original list price that frightened potential buyers were all evidence that indicated that a below-market sale may have occurred. The value of the residence was ultimately determined by consideration of comparable sales of residences similar in age, neighborhood location, date of sale, quality, and amenities (*Merz v. Hennepin County*, Minn. Tax Ct., Nos. TC-26517 and TC-27158, Nov. 16, 1998 (MINN. TAX REP. (CCH) ¶202-845)).

Both the sales and income approaches were used by both the taxpayer's and the county's expert witnesses to determine the market value of a manufacturing facility, but the taxpayer's expert did not rely heavily on the income approach because the property was an owner-occupied, single-tenant building. The court held that the income approach was unreliable in this instance because of the lack of true market data for the property and true comparables. In addition, the property was unequally assessed relative to comparable properties in the same area, and in order to equalize the property with other similar commercial/industrial property in the county, adjustments were made to the estimated market value to arrive at a taxable value (*Johnson Matthey Advanced Circuits, Inc. v. Wright*, Minn. Tax Ct., Nos. C7-00-869, C9-01-981, and C5-01-2954, May 22, 2003 (MINN. TAX REP. (CCH) ¶201-081)).

STUDY QUESTIONS

8. In which Connecticut case did the court determine that the sales-comparison approach was the best way to determine fair market value of an obsolete manufacturing plant and various other buildings?

   a. *Sullivan*
   b. *United Technologies Corp.*
   c. *Madison Beach Club, Inc.*
   d. *Equity 96, LLC*

9. In which state did the court indicate valuing property relying solely on reproduction costs when another method is used to value all other property in the county should be a very limited practice?

   a. Illinois
   b. Connecticut
   c. Minnesota
   d. None of the above is the state

10. In which case did the Minnesota Supreme Court determine comparable sales could not be limited by physical proximity?

    a. *Merz*
    b. *Grove*
    c. *McNeilus Truck & Manufacturing, Inc.*
    d. None of the above

CONCLUSION

What becomes evident after an examination of property valuations for property-tax purposes in different states is that there are advantages and disadvantages to all three approaches to valuation. Experts often disagree on many issues, including the type of approach to use and the factors to consider and/or apply in forming their opinion of the fair market value of a property. Considering the severe distaste most people have for property taxes, however, it is likely that property assessments and the three approaches to the valuation of real estate will continue to be questioned, challenged, accepted, and rejected.

MODULE 2 — CHAPTER 7
Short Term Investments

LEARNING OBJECTIVES

Upon completion of this chapter, you should be able to:

■ Understand the implications of a nondomiciliary corporation's use of gross receipts from the sale of short-term security investments in the sales factor denominator;

■ Anticipate arguments made by state taxing authorities to minimize distortion in the taxpayer's apportionment formula resulting from the sale of short-term security investments;

■ Discuss recent cases in California and Illinois that discuss whether taxpayers may use gross receipts from the sale of short-term security investments in the sales factor denominator; and

■ Articulate issues that taxpayers may face when deciding whether to amend the sales factors in their corporate income tax returns for open years in California, Illinois, and any other states that follow this line of cases.

INTRODUCTION

One of the more contentious issues in many state income tax audits is the question of whether a nondomiciliary corporation should be able to include the gross receipts—or just the net gains—from its short-term investments in securities in the denominator of the sales factor that the corporation utilizes to apportion business income within and without the taxing state. The treasury departments of large corporations often invest excess cash in marketable debt or equity securities that the corporation may hold for less than a month so that this capital will be available for use in the corporation's business operations, as needed. Because these short-term investments turn over so often in the tax year, they can generate an enormous amount of gross receipts compared with the sales revenue that the corporation earns from its core business operations.

Based on a plain reading of the apportionment statutes, many corporations include the *gross receipts* from their short-term securities investments in the denominator of the sales factor. This reporting position can be quite beneficial to the corporation because it will significantly reduce the sales factor—and the amount of taxable income—that the corporation reports on the tax returns that it files with the states where it does not conduct its investment activities. State tax auditors who review those tax returns often will attempt to mitigate the dilution of the corporation's sales factor by limiting the corporation to including only the *net gains* from its short-term securities investments in the sales factor.

Over the past 20 years, two lines of cases have developed on this issue. The first line of cases has held that taxpayers are entitled under the literal wording of the sales factor statute to include gross receipts from their short-term securities investments in the sales factor even if it results in a significant reduction of the sales factor (*See, e.g., American Tel. & Tel. Co. v. Tax Appeal Board*, Mt. SCt, 241 Mont. 440, 787 P2d 754, 757-59 (1990); *Sherwin-Williams Co. v. Department of Revenue*, Ore. SCt, 329 Ore. 599, 996 P2d 500, 501 (2000); *Sherwin-Williams Co. v. Johnson*, Tenn. Ct. App., 989 S.W.2d 710, 712-15 (1998); *United States Steel Corp. v. Wisconsin Department of Revenue*, Wis. Tax App., 1985 Wis. Tax LEXIS 89).The other line of cases has allowed the state tax administrator to limit the corporation to including net gains from short-term securities investments in the sales factor in order to avoid distortion of the sales factor (*See, e.g., American Telephone & Telegraph Co. v. Taxation Division Director*, NJ Super., 194 N.J. Super. 168, 476 A.2d 800, 802-803 (1984); *Walgreen Arizona Drug Co. v. Arizona Department of Revenue*, Ariz. Ct. App., 209 Ariz. 71, 97 P3d 896, 899-902 (Ariz. 2004); *Sherwin-Williams Co. v. Department of Revenue*, Ind. Tax Ct., 673 NE2d 849, 851-53 (1996)).

Because the courts have been evenly divided on this issue, the state tax community has been keenly watching two California Supreme Court cases to see how that influential court would decide the issue. The California Supreme Court has now weighed in on the issue in the *Microsoft* (*Microsoft Corp. v. Franchise Tax Board*, Cal. SCt, 39 Cal. 4th 750, 139 P3d 1169 (Aug. 17, 2006)) and *General Motors* (*General Motors Corp. v. Franchise Tax Board*, Cal. SCt, 39 Cal. 4th 773, 139 P3d 1183 (Aug. 17, 2006)) decisions discussed below. In these two cases, the California Supreme Court held that while the wording of the California sales factor statute would allow Microsoft and General Motors to include the gross receipts from short-term securities investments held to redemption in their sales factors, the California Franchise Tax Board (FTB) could limit the companies to including net gains in the sales factor under the "alternative relief" provision of the California franchise tax statutes if the FTB could show that the companies were distorting their sales factors. Alternative relief provisions require the taxpayer to show the state tax administrator that the taxpayer's modification of the standard sales factor would not distort the apportionment of the taxpayer's net income. The California Supreme Court found the requisite distortion in the *Microsoft* case and remanded the *General Motors* case to give the FTB the opportunity to present its distortion argument.

The Illinois Appellate Court reached a similar conclusion in the *Mead* (*Mead Corp. v. Illinois Department of Revenue*, No. 1-03-1160 (Ill. App. Ct., 1st Dist., Jan. 12, 2007)) case discussed below. Although not as thoroughly reasoned as the *Microsoft* decision, the *Mead* decision will lend additional support to state auditors who object to nondomiciliary corporations including gross receipts from short-term securities investments in their sales factors.

STUDY QUESTIONS

> **1.** Which of the following methods of reporting short-term investments in securities is most likely, from a state tax administrator's perspective, to distort a nondomiciliary corporation's sales factor?
>
> **a.** Alternative relief
> **b.** Net gains
> **c.** Gross receipts

THE MICROSOFT CASE

Microsoft Corporation is an international computer software company headquartered in the State of Washington (*Microsoft Corp. v. Franchise Tax Board*, 39 Cal. 4th 750, 757, 139 P3d 1169 (Aug. 17, 2006)). In order to earn additional income, Microsoft's treasury department in Washington State invested the company's excess cash in various short-term marketable securities, including commercial paper, corporate bonds, United States Treasury bills and notes, discount notes, United States money market preferred securities, United Kingdom money market preferred securities, fixed rate auction preferred securities, floating rate notes, loan participations, municipal bonds and loan repurchase agreements (*Microsoft* at 757 fn. 6). Microsoft generally held these securities to maturity, which, in the case of approximately 80 percent of these securities investments, meant a period of 30 days or less (*Microsoft* at 757).

In the 1991 tax year at issue in the case, Microsoft earned $10.7 million of income and generated $5.7 billion of revenue—or a 0.2 percent margin—from its short-term securities transactions (*Microsoft* at 767). In comparison, Microsoft's sales of software products generated $659 million of income and gross receipts of $2.1 billion, for a margin of roughly 31 percent (*Microsoft* at 767). In overall percentage terms, the short-term securities investments produced less than 2 percent of Microsoft's income, but as much as 73 percent of its gross receipts (*Microsoft* at 765 fn. 17).

Microsoft filed an amended 1991 California franchise tax return that included the entire $5.7 billion of gross receipts from its sales and redemptions of marketable securities in the denominator of its California sales factor (*Microsoft* at 757). Microsoft did not include any portion of the $5.7 billion of short-term investment receipts in the numerator of the California sales factor because these investment receipts had been generated in Washington State, where Microsoft's treasury function was located. Including the gross receipts in the denominator of the sales factor reduced Microsoft's 1991 California sales factor from approximately 11 percent to 3 percent and cut Microsoft's California franchise tax liability nearly in half (*Microsoft* at 757).

When the California FTB audited Microsoft's 1991 amended tax return, the auditor agreed with Microsoft's inclusion of the gross receipts from its *sales* of securities in the denominator of the California sales factor. The auditor took the position, however, that in situations in which Microsoft had held a security *to maturity*, Microsoft could only include the *net gain* from the short-term securities redemption (*i.e.,* the difference between the redemption price and the purchase price) in the denominator of the California sales factor. The auditor viewed the excluded portion of the gross receipts as the return of capital on Microsoft's securities redemptions (*Microsoft* at 757). The FTB assessed more than $1 million of California franchise tax and interest against Microsoft, largely as a result of increasing the company's sales factor back to 11 percent.

Microsoft exhausted its administrative remedies and then filed a refund suit to recover its payment of the California franchise tax assessment. After a bench trial, the California Superior Court for the City and County of San Francisco entered judgment in Microsoft's favor, holding that the entire amount of receipts that Microsoft had received from redeeming securities at maturity was includible in the California sales factor and that the FTB had not demonstrated that distortion of the sales factor would result if Microsoft were permitted to include more than the net gain from its securities redemptions in the sales factor (*Microsoft* at 757-58).

The California Court of Appeals reversed the trial court's decision, however, concluding that Microsoft's inclusion of the gross receipts from its securities redemptions in the denominator of its California sales factor had seriously diluted the sales factor. Based on this factual finding, the Court of Appeals allowed the FTB to invoke the "alternative relief" provision of Section 25137 of the California franchise tax statutes (Cal. Rev. & Tax Code §25137) to exclude the return of capital portion of Microsoft's investment receipts from its sales factor (*Microsoft,* 39 Cal. 4th at 758). The California Supreme Court agreed to review the Court of Appeals decision.

The California Supreme Court turned first to the question of what the California sales factor statute itself provides as the measure of the securities redemption proceeds to be included in the sales factor. Under the California franchise tax statutes, the sales factor is a ratio of the taxpayer's "sales" in a given state to its total sales everywhere (Cal. Rev. & Tax Code §25134). The term "sales" is then defined in the California franchise tax statutes to mean "*all gross receipts* of the taxpayer not allocated [as nonbusiness income] under Sections 25123 through 25127 of this code." (Cal. Rev. & Tax Code §25120(e)) Unfortunately the critical term "gross receipts" is not defined either in the California franchise tax statutes or in the Uniform Division of Income for Tax Purposes Act ("UDITPA") (UNIFORM DIVISION OF INCOME FOR TAX PURPOSES ACT, 7A part 1 (U.L.A. 2002) p. 141) on which the California franchise tax statutes are based.

The California Supreme Court agreed, however, with Microsoft's argument that "the meaning of 'gross receipts' in the UDITPA more naturally includes the entire redemption prices of marketable securities. 'Gross' implies the whole amount received, not just the amount received in excess of the purchase price. To only consider the net price difference as 'gross receipts' is an awkward fit with the statutory language, at best." (*Microsoft*, 39 Cal. 4th at 759. As support for its interpretation of the plain meaning of the California and UDITPA statutes, the California Supreme Court cited the following dictionary definitions of "gross receipts": BLACK'S LAW DICTIONARY 722-23 (8th ed. 2004) ("gross receipts" are "[t]he total amount of money or other consideration received by a business taxpayer for goods or services performed in a year, before deductions," *citing* 26 USC §448); AMERICAN HERITAGE DICTIONARY 578 (2d college ed. 1982) ("gross" means "exclusive of deductions; total"))

The California Supreme Court rejected the FTB's argument that notwithstanding the generally accepted meaning of "gross receipts," the California franchise tax meaning of the term should only include amounts that the taxpayer received *as consideration* for an income-producing transaction. The FTB contended that amounts that Microsoft had received as a return of principal or capital on its securities investments were not consideration received for making the investment. However, the California Supreme Court considered the example of a 28-day Treasury bill transaction in which the investor exchanges $9,900 now for the right to receive a $10,000 payment from the federal government in 28 days and concluded that:

> The Federal Reserve's consideration is the entire amount it receives now; the investor's consideration is the entire larger, but deferred, amount it receives upon redemption. The transaction occurs because the Federal Reserve views the money it receives now as more valuable than the money it must pay later, while the investor views the money it will receive later as more valuable than the money it has now. The difference between the purchase and redemption price

is a measure of either gross income or net receipts, not a measure of consideration. (*Cf. Gray v. Franchise Tax Board* (1991), 235 Cal. App. 3d 36, 42 [286 Cal. Rptr. 453] (gross income is 'the excess of the sales price over the cost of goods sold'); *MCA, Inc. v. Franchise Tax Board* (1981), 115 Cal. App. 3d 185, 197-198 [171 Cal. Rptr. 242] (gross receipts differs from gross income in that the latter subtracts the cost of goods sold).) (*Microsoft*, 39 Cal. 4th at 759)

The California Supreme Court determined that the legislative history of UDITPA supported a broad measure of the term "gross receipts." An early draft of UDITPA had defined the term "sales" as "all *income* of the taxpayer" not otherwise allocated, but this "sales" definition was later revised to read "all *gross receipts* of the taxpayer" not otherwise allocated (*Microsoft* at 760 (emphasis added) (*comparing* Proceedings of Com. of Whole for UDITPA, transcript of Aug. 22, 1956, p. 5 ("income" definition) with Proceedings of Com. of Whole for UDITPA, transcript of July 9, 1957, p. 28 ("gross receipts" definition)). The California Supreme Court concluded that the drafters of UDITPA had intentionally defined the term "sales" in terms of "gross receipts" instead of "income," with the result that "the drafters had in mind a definition of 'sales' that encompassed more than just gross income." (*Microsoft* at 760 (emphasis added) (*comparing* Proceedings of Com. of Whole for UDITPA, transcript of Aug. 22, 1956, p. 5 ("income" definition) with Proceedings of Com. of Whole for UDITPA, transcript of July 9, 1957, p. 28 ("gross receipts" definition))

The California Supreme Court drew additional support for its statutory construction of the term "gross receipts" from decisions of the California State Board of Equalization (SBE), the administrative tribunal that decides California franchise tax cases. In *Appeal of Pacific Telephone & Telegraph* (*Appeal of Pacific Telephone & Telegraph Co.*, Cal. SBE, [Cal.] St. Tax Rep. (CCH) ¶ 205-858, (May 4, 1978)), the taxpayer's treasury department had invested idle cash in short-term securities such as Treasury bills, certificates of deposit, and commercial paper. Pacific Telephone and Telegraph held most of these investments to maturity, just as Microsoft had done. The California Supreme Court noted that the SBE had held that "the gross receipts from these activities come within the literal definition of 'sales' that are includible in the sales factor, and allowed Pacific Telephone and Telegraph to include all of the gross receipts in the determination of its California sales factor." (*Microsoft*, 39 Cal. 4th at 760 (*quoting from Pacific Telephone & Telegraph*, [Cal.] St. Tax Rep. (CCH) ¶ 205-858 at p. 14,907-42))

The California Supreme Court also rejected the FTB's reliance on certain court decisions in other states that had limited the term "gross receipts" to net gains from short-term securities investments. In fact, one line of these out-of-state cases had interpreted "gross receipts" the same way that the California Supreme Court was doing in its *Microsoft* decision (*See, e.g., American Tel. & Tel. Co. v. Tax Appeal Board*, Mt. SCt, 241 Mont. 440, 787 P2d 754, 757-59 (1990); *Sherwin-Williams Co. v. Department of Revenue*, Ore. SCt, 329 Ore. 599, 996 P2d 500, 501 (2000); *Sherwin-Williams Co. v. Johnson*, Tenn. Ct. App., 989 S.W.2d 710, 712-15 (1998); *United States Steel Corp. v. Wisconsin Department of Revenue*, Wis. Tax App., 1985 Wis. Tax LEXIS 89). The other line of out-of-state cases had found that interpreting the term "gross receipts" to include the gross receipts from short-term securities investments would produce "absurd results." (*Supra* note 2) However, the California Supreme Court observed that:

> There are two problems with these 'absurd results' cases. First, they do violence to the language of the statutes they interpret. In each case, the same language governs both sales of off-the-shelf products and sales of securities. *AT & T* and its progeny offer no explanation why in one instance that language should require inclusion of gross proceeds and in the other require inclusion of only net proceeds. Second, they overlook the fact no absurd result is required. As the Tennessee Court of Appeals has explained: 'With deference to sister jurisdictions, this court is reluctant to apply the same 'absurd result standard.' An absurd result is not necessary for, in spite of the plain language of [the sales factor statute], the commissioner may opt for a different scheme of assessment whenever the resulting apportion-ment does not fairly represent the taxpayer's business in this state.' *Sherwin-Williams Co. v. Johnson, supra*, 989 S.W.2d at p. 715. The UDITPA contains an equitable relief provision so that, in cases where application of the statutory sales definition results in exces-sive distortion, an 'absurd result' may be avoided. (See §25137.) (*Microsoft*, 39 Cal. 4th at 763)

For all of these reasons, the California Supreme Court concluded, as an initial matter, that the meaning of the term "gross receipts" in the Cali-fornia and UDITPA sales factor statutes included the entire amount of proceeds that Microsoft had received from redemptions of short-term securities at maturity.

However, the Supreme Court then went on to explain that "[o]ur con-clusion that the full redemption price constitutes gross receipts does not end matters. The UDITPA includes a relief provision for dealing with any unreasonable calculations rote application of the three-factor formula may yield." (*Microsoft*, 39 Cal. 4th at 764) The Supreme Court was referring to Section 25137, the "alternative relief" provision of the California franchise tax statutes, which provides:

> If the allocation and apportionment provisions of this act do not fairly represent the extent of the taxpayer's business activity in this state, the taxpayer may petition for or the Franchise Tax Board may require, in respect of all or any part of the taxpayer's business activity, if reasonable:
> (a) Separate accounting;
> (b) The exclusion of any one or more of the factors;
> (c) The inclusion of one or more additional factors which will fairly represent the taxpayer's business activity in this state; or
> (d) The employment of any other method to effectuate an equitable allocation or apportionment of the taxpayer's income (Cal. Rev. & Tax Code §25137).

As the party seeking alternative relief under Section 25137, the FTB bore the burden to demonstrate, *by clear and convincing evidence,* that apportioning Microsoft's business income with a sales factor that included the gross receipts (instead of the net gain) from Microsoft's redemptions of short-term securities investments would "not fairly represent the extent of the taxpayer's business activity [in California]." (*Microsoft,* 39 Cal. 4th at 765) The California Supreme Court rejected Microsoft's contention, based on certain language in the United States Supreme Court's *Container Corporation* decision (*Container Corporation v. Franchise Tax Board,* SCt, 463 US 159, 170, 103 SCt 2933 (1983)), that the FTB needed to show that "the income attributed to [California] is in fact 'out of all appropriate proportions to the business transacted ... in that State,' or has 'led to a grossly distorted result." (*Microsoft,* 39 Cal. 4th at 765 n. 16) The California Supreme Court explained that Microsoft was attempting to hold the state to the constitutional standard that a taxpayer must meet to persuade a court to strike down a tax under the Due Process Clause or Commerce Clause of the United States Constitution. The California Supreme Court determined that the FTB only needed to meet the statutory standard described in Section 25137 in order to utilize an alternative method for computing Microsoft's sales factor.

Having decided the burden of proof that the FTB was required to meet, the California Supreme Court determined that apportioning Microsoft's business income with a sales factor diluted by the gross receipts from the company's short-term securities investments would indeed distort the computation of Microsoft's California taxable income by reducing income attributable to California by more than 50 percent. In determining whether Section 25137 could be applied in the treasury operations context, the California Supreme Court discussed the California SBE's decision in *Appeal of Pacific Telephone & Telegraph* (*Appeal of Pacific Telephone & Telegraph Co.,* Cal. SBE, [Cal.] St. Tax Rep. (CCH) ¶ 205-858, (May 4, 1978)), in which:

[A]s here, the taxpayer corporate group maintained an out-of-state treasury department that invested in short-term securities. These investments produced less than 2 percent of the company's business income, but 36 percent of its gross receipts. The SBE described the sales factor as intended to 'reflect the markets for the taxpayer's goods and services' and asked whether inclusion of all investment receipts would serve that function. *Id.* at p. 14,907-43. It answered in the negative: 'The inclusion of this enormous volume of investment receipts substantially overloads the sales factor in favor of New York, and thereby inadequately reflects the contributions made in all other states, including California, which supply the markets for the ... services provided by [taxpayer]. *Moreover, we are unable to accept, even for a moment, the notion that more than 11 percent of [taxpayer's] entire unitary business activities should be attributed to any single state solely because it is the center of working capital investment activities that are clearly only an incidental part of one of America's largest, and most widespread, businesses. We conclude, therefore, that UDITPA's normal provisions "do not fairly represent the extent of the taxpayer's business activity in this state," and that [the Board] is authorized, under Section 25137, to require a deviation from the normal rules* (**Microsoft**, 39 Cal. 4th at 765-66 (*quoting from* **Pacific Telephone & Telegraph**, [Cal.] St. Tax Rep. (CCH) ¶ 205-858 at p. 14,907-43)).

The California Supreme Court found that the facts of the Microsoft case presented even greater distortion than the Pacific Telephone case did because Microsoft's short-term securities investments were producing less than two percent of the company's overall income, but 73 percent of its gross receipts (**Microsoft**, 39 Cal. 4th at 765 n. 17). Moreover, the inclusion of the gross receipts from Microsoft's short-term securities investment activity in the numerator and denominator of the Washington State sales factor would result in 24 percent of Microsoft's business income being apportioned to Washington State solely as a result of Microsoft's corporate treasury department being located in that state. This distortion was produced, in the California Supreme Court's view, by the significant difference in the profit margins of Microsoft's investment function and its core business of selling computer software products:

When a short-term marketable security is sold or redeemed, the margin will often be, in absolute terms, quite small (though of course the annualized returns may well be perfectly respectable). Microsoft's treasury activities provide a perfect illustration. Its 1991 redemptions totaled $5.7 billion, while its income from those investments totaled only $10.7 million—a less than 0.2 percent margin. In contrast, its nontreasury activities produced income of $659 million and gross receipts of $2.1 billion, for a margin of more than 31 percent, roughly 170 times greater (*Microsoft* at 767).

Of course, disparities between the profit margins of a taxpayer's different lines of business arise in countless numbers of unitary business cases, yet the courts have allowed states (and taxpayers) to apportion the combined business income of the unitary group with the group's apportionment fraction. However, the California Supreme Court clearly was more troubled by a corporate treasury department contributing to the disparity in the profit margins and gross receipts of the business segments involved in the apportionment computation and determined that Section 25137 could be applied.

Relying on the more-than-50-percent reduction in income attributable to California resulting from inclusion of Microsoft's gross receipts from treasury operations, the California Supreme Court held that the "stipulated evidence establishes that mixing the gross receipts from Microsoft's short-term investments with the gross receipts from its other business activity seriously distorts the standard formula's attribution of income to each state ... . The distortion that the Board has shown here is of both a type and size properly addressed through invocation of Section 25137." (*Microsoft* at 770-71) The California Supreme Court cautioned, however, that it was not giving the FTB a free hand to limit taxpayers' sales factors to net gains from short-term securities investments. This is a facts and circumstances issue and:

In other cases the Board's approach may go too far in the opposite direction and fail the test of reasonableness. By mixing net receipts for a particular set of out-of-state transactions with gross receipts for all other transactions, it minimizes the contribution of those out-of-state transactions to the taxpayer's income and exaggerates the resulting California tax. If, unlike here, treasury operations provide a substantial portion of a taxpayer's income, this exaggeration may result in an apportionment that does not fairly represent California business activity (*Microsoft*. at 771. The California Supreme Court also noted that unacceptable levels of distortion are less likely to arise in situations where investment activity is the taxpayer's principal business activity.).

The Supreme Court cited with approval the California SBE's rejection, in *Appeal of Merrill Lynch, Pierce, Fenner & Smith, Inc.*, Cal. SBE, [Cal.] St. Tax Rep. (CCH) ¶ 401-740, (June 2, 1989), of the FTB's argument that

Merrill Lynch should include only net gains from its securities investments in its California sales factor.

STUDY QUESTIONS

2. Microsoft's sales of software products generated a gross profit margin of roughly what percent?
   a. 31
   b. 2
   c. 0.2
   d. 73

3. According to the California FTB, what was Microsoft's proper sales factor percentage in California?
   a. 11
   b. 31
   c. 3
   d. 2

4. In which California case was it found proper to include the taxpayer's gross receipts from its investment activities in the sales factor denominator?
   a. *Microsoft*
   b. *Appeal of Pacific Telephone & Telegraph*
   c. *Sherwin-Williams*
   d. *Merrill Lynch*

THE GENERAL MOTORS CASE

On the same day that the California Supreme Court decided the *Microsoft* case, the court dealt with similar apportionment factor issues in the companion case of *General Motors Corp. v. Franchise Tax Board* (*General Motors Corp. v. Franchise Tax Board*, Cal. SCt, 39 Cal. 4th 773, 139 P3d 1183 (Aug. 17, 2006)). General Motors' treasury department in New York invested the company's idle cash in short-term marketable securities (*General Motors* at 777-78 and 779). The General Motors investments included U.S. Treasury bonds, notes and bills, and bank certificates of deposit, which typically turned over every 3.25 days (*General Motors* at 779). During the 1986-1988 audit period, the gross proceeds from the treasury department's short-term securities investments amounted to almost $1 trillion, producing $550 million of General Motors' total $7 billion of net income for those three tax years (*General Motors* at 779 and 780). General Motors derived about 90 percent of its short-term investment proceeds from repurchase agreements, commonly referred to as "repos." (*General Motors* at 779 and 780)

Repo transactions are financing arrangements in which one party provides funds to another party for a short period of time, using marketable securities as collateral. The repurchase agreement describes two interrelated transactions. First, the seller-borrower agrees to transfer securities shares to the buyer-lender in exchange for an amount of cash. Shortly thereafter, or upon demand, the seller-borrower agrees to repurchase the securities from the buyer-lender at the original price plus an agreed amount of "interest." (*General Motors* 781; the California Supreme Court addressed repos in greater detail in *Bewley v. Franchise Tax Board,* Cal. SCt, 9 Cal. 4th 526, 529, 886 P2d 1292 (1995).) General Motors principally engaged in "reverse repos," which means that it was the party that provided the cash in the transaction and agreed to sell the securities back to the seller-borrower on the date specified in the repurchase agreement (*General Motors,* 39 Cal. 4th at 782).

As in *Microsoft,* the California Supreme Court had to determine what portion of the proceeds that General Motors received from its repo transactions was includible in the denominator of General Motors' California sales factor. General Motors and the FTB agreed that in a transaction involving an actual sale of a marketable security, the entire sales price would constitute the "gross receipts" that belonged in the sales factor. The parties also agreed that in a loan transaction, only the interest proceeds would be treated as "gross receipts" that were includible in the sales factor (*i.e.,* the lender's recovery of the capital it had loaned to the borrower was not a gross receipt) (*General Motors* at 784). The question was where repo transactions fit within these parameters.

The FTB contended that General Motors' repo transactions were really secured loans, citing the United States Supreme Court's statement in *Nebraska Department of Revenue v. Loewenstein* (*Nebraska Department of Revenue v. Loewenstein,* 513 US 123, 115 SCt 557 (1994)) that "in economic reality, the [buyer-lenders] receive interest on cash they have lent to the Seller-Borrower." (*General Motors,* 39 Cal. 4th at 784 (*quoting from Loewenstein,* 513 US at 134)) The U.S. Supreme Court concluded in *Loewenstein* that because this interest was paid by the seller-borrower rather than the federal government, the interest was not exempt from the Nebraska income tax. Several months after the *Loewenstein* case was decided, the California Supreme Court reached the same conclusion in *Bewley v. Franchise Tax Board* (*Bewley v. Franchise Tax Board,* 9 Cal. 4th 526, 531-32 (1995)), characterizing repos as secured loans for California personal income tax purposes.

General Motors argued, on the other hand, that its repo transactions involved sales of securities, with title passing, first, from the lender-borrower to General Motors, and then back to the lender-borrower on the date specified in the repurchase agreement. General Motors cited a number of federal cases that had characterized a repo as a purchase and sale of a security, although it does not appear any of these were tax cases (*General Motors,* 39 Cal.4th at 785 n.6 (*citing In re County of Orange*, DC Cal., 31 FSupp2d 768, 778 (1998) (repos are not secured loans for purposes of debt-limit provisions of California Constitution); *Granite Partners L.P. v. Bear, Stearns & Co.*, DC N.Y., 17 F. Supp. 2d 275, 302, 1998-2 TRADE CAS. (CCH) ¶72,301 (repos are purchase and sale agreements and thus not subject to Uniform Commercial Code (UCC) article 9 secured loan obligations); *In re Comark*, CA-BR-9, 145 B.R. 47, 53-54, BANKR. L. REP. (CCH) ¶74,956 (1992) (repos are securities transactions, not secured loans, under particular bankruptcy law provisions); *In re Residential Resources Mortgage Investments*, DC BR Ariz., 98 B.R. 2, 23, BANKR. L. REP. (CCH) ¶72,723 (1989) (repos involve sale and repurchase of security); 44 Ops. Cal. Atty. Gen. 140, 143 (1964) (State Treasurer is authorized to enter repos because they involve sale, not loan)).

The California Supreme Court observed that there was some merit to both parties' arguments:

> In some circumstances, [a repo transaction] is properly characterized as a secured loan; in others circumstances, it is properly characterized as a purchase and sale of a security. Which characterization fits depends mainly on context; those features of a repo salient in its characterization for bankruptcy purposes, or securities law purposes, or UCC purposes, or even federal tax purposes, are not necessarily the features that will be most salient in characterizing it under UDITPA (*General Motors* at 785).

The California Supreme Court concluded that in a true sale of securities, the amount of money that the taxpayer pays for the securities and receives from the redemption of the securities would depend on the changing value of the securities. From this perspective, the Supreme Court concluded that:

> [F]or gross receipts purposes, a repo has the characteristics of a loan, not a sale of a commodity. In a repo, the amount paid depends not on the value of the surrendered security, but on the amount of money the repo buyer paid the repo seller in the front end of the transaction .... This means, in a repo, the seller is 'buying' cash (*i.e.,* receiving a loan), while in a sale or redemption, the buyer/issuer is paying for a commodity. Thus, a repo is properly characterized as a secured loan for gross receipts purposes (*General Motors* at 787).

Having found that General Motors' repo transactions had the characteristics, for California tax purposes anyway, of a secured loan, the California Supreme

Court held that only the interest that General Motors received from the repo sellers-borrowers was a gross receipt includible in General Motors' California sales factor (*General Motors* at 788). Therefore, the FTB auditor had correctly handled the repos in the franchise tax audit of General Motors.

However, citing the *Microsoft* case, the California Supreme Court reversed the Court of Appeals' determination that only the net proceeds that General Motors received from securities held to redemption were includible in General Motors' sales factor. The California Supreme Court remanded this issue to the trial court to allow the FTB to present its argument that including the gross receipts from securities redemption transactions in General Motors' sales factor would distort the apportionment of its income within and without California (*General Motors* at 789). On January 29, 2007, the California Court of Appeals remanded the case to the trial court with instructions to consider the FTB's argument. (*General Motors Corp. v. Franchise Tax Board*, California Court of appeal, Second Appellate District, No. B 165665 (unpublished Decision), (January 29, 2007)).

STUDY QUESTIONS

5. General Motors engaged in reverse repo transactions. *True or False?*

6. In *General Motors*, the California Supreme Court determined that:
   a. In the sale of a marketable security, net gain belongs in the sales factor.
   b. In a loan, the gross receipts include the entire amount paid by the borrower to the taxpayer.
   c. Repo transactions have the characteristics of a secured loan.
   d. Under the California sales factor statutes, only the net proceeds from securities held to redemption should be included in General Motors' sales factor denominator.

THE MEAD CORP. CASE

In *Mead Corp. v. Illinois Department of Revenue* (*Mead Corp. v. Illinois Department of Revenue*, No. 1-03-1160 (Ill. Ct. App., 1st Dist., Jan. 12, 2007)), the Illinois Appellate Court limited the taxpayer to including the net gains from its sales of investments in the denominator of its Illinois sales factor. Mead Corporation sold the stock of its Mead Data Central, Inc., Lexis, Inc. and Nexis, Inc. subsidiaries (collectively, "Lexis/Nexis") in 1994 for a gain of more than $1 billion (*Mead*, slip op. at 1). Mead excluded this $1 billion gain on its 1994 Illinois corporate income tax return, taking the position that the gain was nonbusiness income that was allocable to Ohio where Mead's commercial domicile was located. Mead further reduced its 1994 Illinois taxable income by including $4,846,382,229 of gross receipts from its sales of interest-bearing financial instruments in the denominator of its Illinois sales factor. Again, Mead took the position that none of this $4.8 billion of gross receipts from the sales of financial instruments belonged in the numerator of the Illinois sales factor because Mead's investment activities occurred outside Illinois.

The Illinois Department of Revenue reclassified the $1 billion gain from the sale of the stock of the Lexis/Nexis subsidiaries as apportionable business income (*Mead*, slip op. at 4). The Department also concluded that Mead should only be including the net gain rather than the gross receipts from the sales of the financial instruments in its sales factor denominator citing an Illinois income tax regulation providing that "[i]n the case of sales of business intangibles ... gross receipts shall be disregarded and only the net gain (loss) therefrom shall be included in the sales factor." (86 Ill. Admin. Code §100.3380(b)(6)) As a result of these audit adjustments, the Department assessed more than $4 million of Illinois income tax and interest against Mead for its 1994 tax year (*Mead*, slip op. at 5).

The Illinois Appellate Court held that the gain from Mead's sale of the stock of the Lexis/Nexis subsidiaries was subject to formulary apportionment under the "operational function test" of the United States Supreme Court's *Allied-Signal* decision (*Allied-Signal, Inc. v. Director, Division of Taxation*, SCt, 504 US 768, 112 SCt 2251 (1992)). The Illinois circuit court had found that Mead had spent considerable resources developing the Lexis/Nexis businesses since 1968 (*Mead*, slip op. at 4). Indeed, Mead had repeatedly converted the Lexis/Nexis' business from a corporate division to a corporate subsidiary and back, depending on which structure was more beneficial to Mead (*Mead*, slip op. at 2). Mead had also retained tax benefits and control over the excess cash of the Lexis/Nexis businesses. Based on these findings, the Appellate Court upheld the circuit court's conclusion that Lexis/Nexis served an operational purpose within Mead's business operations, thereby allowing Illinois to apportion the gain from Mead's sale of Lexis/Nexis under Illinois' statutory definition of "business income," which incorporates the "operational function test" of *Allied-Signal* (*Mead*, slip op. at 18. The Appellate Court also rejected Mead's argument that the gain from the sale of Lexis/Nexis was nonbusiness income under the *Blessing/White* "cessation of business" principle, because Mead had reinvested the $1 billion gain in its ongoing business operations. *Blessing/White, Inc. v. Zehnder*, Ill. App., 329 Ill. App. 3d 714, 768 2d 332 (2002)).

As for the sales factor issue, the Appellate Court held that although the Illinois Income Tax Act (the "IITA") defines "sales" to mean "gross receipts," (35 ILCS 5/1501(a)(21)) this statutory definition had been modified by the Department's regulation providing that "[i]n the case of sales of business intangibles ... gross receipts shall be disregarded and only the net gain (loss) therefrom shall be included in the sales factor." (86 Ill. Admin. Code

§100.3380(b)(6)) The Appellate Court explained that this regulation had the "force and effect of law." Perhaps more significant to the outcome of the issue, however, was the Appellate Court's finding that:

> The inclusion of the gross receipts from the sale of financial instruments in Mead's sales factor denominator would not have resulted in a fair representation of its business activity; the gross receipts add approximately $4.8 billion to Mead's sales factor denominator when it actually earned only about $1.9 million on those investments. Accordingly, we believe summary judgment was properly granted in favor of the Department on this issue (*Mead*, slip op. at 21).

Consequently, the Appellate Court held that, even if the Department's regulation did not limit Mead to including the net gains from its sales of business intangibles in the sales factor, the Department was still authorized to take this position under the "alternative relief" provision of Section 304(f) of the IITA (35 ILCS 5/304(f)).

STUDY QUESTIONS

---

7. Which case did Mead rely on when it claimed that the proceeds it received from the sale of Lexis/Nexis was nonbusiness income allocable to Ohio?

   a. *Merrill Lynch*
   b. *Blessing/White*
   c. *Allied Signal*
   d. *Microsoft*

8. In determining that Mead could only include the net gains from its short-term securities investments in the sales factor denominator, the Illinois Appellate Court relied on the Department's regulation. ***True or False?***

CONCLUSION

There are a number of important points in the California Supreme Court's *Microsoft* and *General Motors* opinions that should not be lost on taxpayers and state income tax auditors. First, the parties and the California Supreme Court agreed that if taxpayers sell marketable securities—as opposed to holding those securities to maturity—UDITPA allows the taxpayer to include the gross receipts from these sale transactions in the taxpayer's sales factor. When corporate treasury departments engage in long-term investments in securities, it is likely that the treasury department will sell securities from time to time. Under the holding of the *Microsoft* case, the gross receipts from such securities sale transactions would be includible in the corporation's California sales factor as long as the state cannot show that distortion of the apportionment computation will result.

Second, it is significant that even in situations where short-term securities investments are held to maturity, the California Supreme Court correctly determined that the UDITPA statutes provide for the inclusion of the gross receipts from those investment transactions in the denominator of the sales factor. Companies may be able to continue to include the gross receipts from their short-term securities transactions in the sales factor in California and other states if their short-term securities investment activity is not comparable to that of Microsoft. After all, Microsoft derived 73 percent of its gross receipts, but only two percent of it net income from its treasury department function.

The state tax agency bears the burden to prove that distortion of the apportionment formula will result if a taxpayer is allowed to include gross receipts instead of net gains from short-term securities investments in the denominator of the sales factor. The California Supreme Court cautioned in *Microsoft* that the California FTB cannot reflexively limit taxpayers to including net gains from short-term securities transactions in the sales factor because that administrative position might distort the apportioned computation in favor of the state in certain cases. California FTB auditors undoubtedly will pressure taxpayers to agree to modify their California sales factors so that they only include net gains from short-term securities held to maturity, but taxpayers should carefully analyze their facts before conceding this issue.

The Illinois Appellate Court did not see any problems in the *Mead* case with how the Illinois Department of Revenue had issued a broad regulation providing that only net gains from sales of business intangibles are includible in the Illinois sales factor. This regulation is arguably contrary to the IITA's "sales" definition, which is identical to the UDITPA provision that the California Supreme Court interpreted in *Microsoft* and *General Motors*. Depending on the facts, companies may be able to argue that the application of this "one size fits all" approach to this apportionment issue in Illinois results in over-taxation of multistate taxpayers.

Taxpayers that do have short-term securities investment activity comparable to Microsoft and Mead are going to have to decide whether to amend the sales factor in their corporate income tax returns for open tax years in California, Illinois and any other states that follow the *Microsoft* and *Mead* decisions. This will not be an easy decision in California and Illinois because both of these states may impose significant amounts of penalties and interest if the open tax years were eligible for the California and Illinois tax amnesty programs.

STUDY QUESTIONS

9. All of the following are true statements, *except*:
   a. Gross receipts from the sale of short-term security investments are always includible in the corporation's California sales factor.
   b. Gross receipts from the sale of long-term security investments are includible in the corporation's California sales factor.
   c. Under the UDITPA statutes, gross receipts from short-term securities held to maturity are includible in the sales factor denominator.
   d. When a state tax auditor adjusts the taxpayer's sales factor, the state agency has the burden of proving that the taxpayer is distorting the apportionment formula.

10. When deciding whether to amend corporate income tax returns, multistate taxpayers with short-term securities investment activity comparable to *Microsoft* will only have a difficult decision to face in California, due to its earlier tax amnesty program. *True or False?*

CPE NOTE: When you have completed your study and review of chapters 5-7, which comprise this Module, you may wish to take the Quizzer for the Module.

For your convenience, you can also take this Quizzer online at **www. cchtestingcenter.com.**

TOP MULTISTATE TAX ISSUES FOR 2008 CPE COURSE
Answers to Study Questions

MODULE 1: PASSIVE INVESTMENT COMPANIES AND PASS-THROUGH ENTITIES—CHAPTER 1

1. a. Correct. The South Carolina Supreme Court upheld an income tax assessment against Geoffrey, an out-of-state corporation, mainly because Geoffrey was a passive investment company created by a corporation with physical nexus in South Carolina.

b. Incorrect. The *Quill* court required an out-of-state corporation to have physical presence in the taxing state before that state could impose sales and use tax.

c. Incorrect. In *Complete Auto*, the Supreme Court established the substantial nexus standard.

d. Incorrect. Toys 'R Us established the Geoffrey PIC and had physical presence in South Carolina.

2. True. Correct. Nevada is attractive as a PIC site because that state does not have a corporate income tax.

False. Incorrect. PICs are created to avoid physical nexus with states imposing corporate income taxes, and Nevada is a state that does not impose such taxes.

3. d. Correct. The *Geoffrey* court determined Geoffrey had substantial nexus with South Carolina based on three factors that became known as economic nexus.

a. Incorrect. *Quill* requires physical presence before a state may impose sales and use taxes on out-of-state corporations.

b. Incorrect. The *Kmart* court determined *Quill's* physical presence standard did not apply to income taxes and declined to rule on whether the Kmart PIC had economic nexus.

c. Incorrect. *Complete Auto* requires substantial, not economic, nexus before a taxing state may impose tax on an out-of-state corporation.

4. c. Correct. Kmart's PIC was a Michigan corporation.

a. Incorrect. New Mexico determined Kmart's PIC had substantial nexus with New Mexico even though it did not have a physical presence in New Mexico.

b. Incorrect. The Gap's PIC was located in California.

d. Incorrect. Louisiana determined that the intangibles in Gap's California PIC had a business situs in Louisiana.

5. b. Correct. An income tax obligation is imposed on an out-of-state corporation's use of in-state property to derive income from the state.

a. Incorrect. One factor in determining an out-of-state corporation's sales tax obligations is whether the corporation's activities involve in-state purchasers.

c. Incorrect. If an out-of-state corporation performs activities within the state, it may have a sales tax obligation in that state.

d. Incorrect. An out-of-state corporation's sales tax activities within a state may justify the corporation's duty to collect the tax.

6. c. Correct. Lanco did not have physical presence in New Jersey.

a. Incorrect. New Jersey argued that the long-term licensing agreement increased Lane Bryant's in-state retail sales.

b. Incorrect. New Jersey asserted that it protected the intangible property rights by protecting the tangible assets to which the trademarks were affixed.

d. Incorrect. Based on increased in-state sales by Lane Bryant, New Jersey argued that this burdened the state by increasing traffic, requiring the state to provide police and fire protection, and imposing demands on the local workforce.

7. a. Correct. Lanco followed other cases using economic nexus as a proxy for physical presence.

b. Incorrect. The Lanco court described what substantial nexus is not but provided no real understanding of this nexus standard.

c. Incorrect. Lanco did not have physical presence in New Jersey.

d. Incorrect. This author defines attributional nexus as more precisely describing nexus based on attributing the in-state affiliate's physical nexus to the out-of-state PIC.

8. c. Correct. The court described the physical presence standard as only applying to sales and use taxes.

a. Incorrect. The court indicated the nexus analysis starts with substantial nexus, not physical presence.

b. Incorrect. The court determined the *Quill* physical presence standard applies only to sales and use taxes.

d. Incorrect. One of the statements was not made by the court in *Geoffrey II.*

9. d. Correct. California's unitary-combined reporting offsets the royalty expense deduction and royalty income creating a "wash" for income tax purposes.

a. Incorrect. Indiana is a noncombined reporting state.

b. Incorrect. Ohio has adopted legislation denying gross income deductions for interest, royalties, and licensing fees paid to PICs.

c. Incorrect. New York is a noncombined reporting state.

10. a. Correct. A successful taxpayer's proof must include economic and policy analysis, rather than merely claiming no physical presence in the taxing state.

b. Incorrect. Courts must currently consider how, and how extensively, out-of-state corporations exploit a taxing jurisdiction's market.

c. Incorrect. Many courts have determined that *Quill's* physical presence standard does not apply to income taxes.

d. Incorrect. Courts must address whether the nature of the out-of-state corporation requires it to have no more than *de minimis* physical presence in the state and whether a corporation's lack of physical presence poses a significant barrier to market penetration in the taxing jurisdiction.

MODULE 1—CHAPTER 2

1. b. Correct. Maryland advised Delaware holding companies owing taxes in Maryland to pay the tax soon or face heavy penalties.

a. Incorrect. In 2002, New Jersey enacted the Business Tax Reform Act, which raised taxes and fees on most businesses by disallowing business deductions and expenses of inter-affiliated companies.

c. Incorrect. New Jersey created an alternative minimum assessment tax in an effort to alleviate its annual revenue shortfall crisis.

d. Incorrect. New Jersey has been challenging the physical presence standard and using economic nexus to show out-of-state PICs are subject to New Jersey's corporate income tax.

2. c. Correct. PICs are only an appropriate tax savings strategy in states that require separate company returns.

a. Incorrect. Many companies use PICs as a state tax planning strategy to shift taxable income from an affiliated company in a high tax rate state to an affiliated company in a lower tax rate or no tax state.

b. Incorrect. PICs are defined as companies organized to manage and protect intangible assets, including patents, trademarks, trade names, stocks, bonds, and other nonoperating assets.

d. Incorrect. PICs may make loans and pay dividends to other companies as another state tax planning strategy.

3. d. Correct. Voluntary compliance is a way states target companies for state income tax compliance.

a. Incorrect. Before a state may tax income earned in interstate commerce, it must show nexus or a connection between the state and the activities from which the income is derived.

b. *Incorrect.* A minimal connection is another way of describing the required connection between the state and the activities it wants to tax.

c. *Incorrect.* The Commerce Clause and the Due Process Clause prohibit state taxation of interstate activities unless there is a rational relationship between the income attributed to the state and the intrastate value of the multinational corporation.

4. d. *Correct.* The Interstate Income Tax Act, P.L. 86-272, limits income tax nexus on out-of-state businesses when business activity in that state is restricted to solicitation of sales.

a. *Incorrect.* The Due Process Clause is a constitutional provision limiting state taxation of interstate activities.

b. Incorrect UDITPA is a uniform act, codified, at least in part, by some states and that divides receipts into business and nonbusiness income.

c. *Incorrect.* The Commerce Clause is a constitutional provision limiting state taxation of interstate activities.

5. False. *Correct.* Separate company return filing does not allow one affiliate to offset its losses against another affiliate's profits.

True. *Incorrect.* One disadvantage of consolidated tax return filing is the inability to develop defensible arm's-length prices for intercompany transactions.

6. c. *Correct.* States do not deny legitimate business expenditures but do recharacterize transactions that are not legitimate.

a. *Incorrect.* States may challenge PICs by arguing they lack legitimate economic substance or a business purpose.

b. *Incorrect.* Some states adopt new rules and regulations that disallow specific intercompany transactions that distort taxable income or add back certain tax deductions.

d. *Incorrect.* Some states assert nexus over the PIC by showing that the intangible assets are really being used in the state.

7. b. *Correct.* West Virginia's Supreme Court determined that MBNA's business activities of direct mail, telemarketing, and advertising in the state were sufficient to create economic nexus.

a. *Incorrect.* New Mexico's court determined that Kmart's PIC had agency nexus in New Mexico because an independent representative present in the state satisfied the physical presence test and Commerce Clause concerns.

c. *Incorrect.* New Jersey's *Lanco* decision reiterated that *Quill's* physical presence requirement is applicable only to sales and use taxes, not income taxation.

d. Incorrect. North Carolina determined that *A&F Trademark* met the requirements of doing business in the state pursuant to its tax rules in conducting a business activity for economic gain using tradenames and trademarks.

8. a. Correct. The overall purpose of the PIC is to limit the states in which the PIC has nexus, but doing so is not a due diligence requirement.
b. Incorrect. For due diligence, the PIC should have separate employees, board of directors, and meetings.
c. Incorrect. To show a legitimate business purpose, the PIC should have its own separate offices and separate stationery.
d. Incorrect. For due diligence, the PIC should have separate tangible assets, accounting records, and financial statements.

9. b. Correct. Some state regulations have changed to disallow specific intercompany transactions that distort taxable income, but this has not decreased state income tax revenues.
a. Incorrect. As reported in State Tax Notes, the federal tax base has declined by increasing depreciation expense deductions, among other factors.
c. Incorrect. States decrease their revenues by offering tax incentives and credits to expanding businesses.
d. Incorrect. According to the MTC, tax shelters have lowered state tax revenues by one-third.

10. a. Correct. The Business Activity Tax Simplification Act was reintroduced in the 109th Congress to codify the physical presence standard for income, franchise, and other taxes.
b. Incorrect. The Streamlined Sales and Use Tax Act sought to expand the collection of sales and use taxes for some remote sellers.
c. Incorrect. H.R. 3184 was one of the bills introduced in the 108th Congress that attempted to clarify the nexus standards for sales tax and state income taxes.
d. Incorrect. The 109th Congress attempted to expand the scope of P.L. 86-272.

MODULE 1—CHAPTER 3

1. d. Correct. Section 409 of RULLCA does not limit fiduciary duties to those of care and loyalty and the operating agreement may not eliminate any other fiduciary duty.
a. Incorrect. Section 404(a) of RUPA states the only fiduciary duties owed by a partner are those of loyalty and care.
b. Incorrect. ULLCA states the only fiduciary duties a member owes other members are the duty of loyalty and the duty of care.

c. Incorrect. ULPA (2001) indicates a limited partner does not have any fiduciary duty to the limited partnership because limited partners have no power justifying the imposition of fiduciary duties.

2. a. Correct. RULLCA applies the ordinary negligence standard of care, which will likely create controversy with the application of the business judgment rule.

b. Incorrect. Under §404(c) of RUPA, a partner's duty of care is limited to refraining from engaging in grossly negligent or reckless conduct, intentional misconduct, or a knowing violation of the law.

c. Incorrect. ULPA imposes a gross negligence standard of care upon general partners based on RUPA §404(c).

3. b. Correct. Delaware's LLC Act affords each member and each manager the statutory apparent agency authority to bind the LLC.

a. Incorrect. RULLCA §301 specifically states that a person is not an agent of the LLC solely by reason of being a member.

c. Incorrect. Kentucky's LLC Act links the internal management structure of the LLC with statutory apparent authority.

d. Incorrect. ULLCA §301 links the internal management structure of the LLC with statutory apparent authority.

4. d. Correct. Illinois' series LLC statute was influenced by Delaware, but also contains additional provisions designed to further the separateness of each series.

a. Incorrect. Delaware was the first state to have series LLCs and most states enacting a series LLC statute have followed Delaware.

b. Incorrect. Iowa's series LLC provisions closely follow Delaware.

c. Incorrect. Tennessee's series LLC provisions mostly follow Delaware.

5. c. Correct. Although a series LLC structure is comparable to a parent with multiple subsidiaries, the master LLC does not necessarily have to own an interest in each series.

a. Incorrect. To maintain the liability limitation, the series must maintain separate and distinct records from the records of the master LLC and other LLCs in the series.

b. Incorrect. Not only must the master LLC's Articles of Organization provide notice of the limitation of liability of the series but its operating agreement must also provide for such limitation of liability.

d. Incorrect. The series must hold its assets separate from both the master LLC and others in the series.

6. c. *Correct.* Although naming each series separately helps maintain firewall liability protection in other states, only seven states have legislation providing for firewall liability protection of foreign series LLCs.

a. *Incorrect.* Only the master LLC is required to file an annual report and each series will be in good standing as long as the master LLC is in good standing.

b. *Incorrect.* The only concrete advantage of the series LLC is the lower filing fee compared to that for multiple separate entities.

d. *Incorrect.* Illinois explicitly states that the master LLC has one registered agent, which serves the master LLC and each series. This is implicit in the other states' statutes.

7. True. *Correct.* Each series in a series LLC may dissolve without affecting the viability of the other series or the master LLC.

False. *Incorrect.* Dissolution of the master LLC causes the dissolution of all of the series of the LLC.

8. False. *Correct.* One commentator has concluded that a Delaware series LLC may not hold title because it is not a separate entity under the statute; the statute merely provides a mechanism for segregating assets, but does not actually provide for separate ownership of assets.

True. *Incorrect.* While the Illinois statute clearly states that each series is a separate entity and that each series may hold legal title, the Delaware statute does not clearly state this.

9. c. *Correct.* The only definitive advantage of using a series LLC instead of separate LLCs is the cost savings associated with filing fees.

a. *Incorrect.* Although series LLC statutes do not require separate operating agreements, they may be required as a practical matter if each series has different members or managers or to preserve the firewall liability protection.

b. *Incorrect.* If the series LLCs are treated as a single entity for real estate transfer tax purposes, they may transfer property within the jurisdiction without paying transfer tax, but they may lose firewall liability protection.

d. *Incorrect.* If each series LLC has separate operating agreement, books, management, etc. as would be needed to preserve the firewall liability protection, there will be no administrative cost savings.

10. c. *Correct.* The Full Faith and Credit Clause requires states to respect transactions governed by the law of another state unless the law is against that state's public policy. The series LLC may be against a state's public policy because it is merely a device to reduce the filing fees owed in that state.

a. Incorrect. Whether a series in a series LLC needs to qualify to transact business in another state is governed by the laws of the other state.

b. Incorrect. Creditors contracting with the master LLC to do work for all the series in a series LLC are encouraged to have each series sign the contract because the series LLC statutes state that each series is not liable for the liabilities of the master LLC.

d. Incorrect. The series LLC statutes provide that each series maintain separate records and hold assets separately as conditions to liability protection, commingling of funds would arguably dissipate the firewall liability protection because the statutory conditions would no longer be met.

11. d. Correct. One element in determining a series trust is a separate entity is that each series had its own investment objective.

a. Incorrect. One element in determining that each series trust is a separate entity is that upon redemption, liquidation, or termination, the holders of each series were limited to the assets of that series only.

b. Incorrect. A series trust would likely be considered a separate entity when each holder's interest in a series was determined by reference to its capital account in that series without regard to any capital account in another series.

c. Incorrect. One element in determining that a series trust is a separate entity is that the liabilities of each series were limited to the assets of that series.

12. b. Correct. If the series of a series LLC are not treated as separate entities, then some complex tax accounting would likely be needed to keep track of the flow of income to all of the different members of each series.

a. Incorrect. If each series is treated separately for federal tax purposes, then a transfer between two series would be treated as a transaction between separate entities and not as an internal transfer.

c. Incorrect. The entity classification rules would apply separately to each series, such that some series could be classified as partnerships, some as corporations, and others as disregarded entities.

d. Incorrect. If the IRS rules that each series is a separate entity, then each series would separately be able to engage in reorganization transactions.

13. False. Correct. The provisions of state LLC statutes are not binding on a bankruptcy court.

True. Incorrect. There is currently no authority indicating whether the separateness of a series will be respected in bankruptcy.

14. b. Correct. The issuer integration problem of series LLCs is important in determining the $1,000,000 limitation of the Rule 504 limited offering exemption.

a. Incorrect. Rule 501 provides that an "entity" is considered one purchaser for purposes of the Regulation D limited offering exemptions.

c. Incorrect. Among other things, Rules 505 and 506 discuss determining the 35 nonaccredited investors for purposes of the limited offering exemptions.

15. True. Correct. Until the various open issues are addressed and the series LLC becomes more accepted, organizations are best advised to use separate LLCs as opposed to series LLCs because the only current real advantage with the series LLCs is lower filing fees.

False. Incorrect. Unless, for example, a group of investors owned so many parcels of real estate that creating separate LLCs would be very expensive and the group would not otherwise create separate LLCs.

MODULE 1—CHAPTER 4

1. a. Correct. The goal of FIN 48 is more consistent reporting of tax positions by setting forth separate recognition and measurement standards.

b. Incorrect. Recognizing current tax consequences, whether payable or refundable, is one objective of accounting for income taxes.

c. Incorrect. One objective of accounting for income taxes is accounting for future tax consequences of events that have been recognized, whether payable or refundable.

d. Incorrect. Defining recognition standards is only one part of FIN 48, not the overall goal.

2. d. Correct. Before beginning the two-step process, the enterprise must determine the appropriate unit of account based on the individual facts and circumstances of the tax position in light of all available evidence.

a. Incorrect. The first step of the two-step process is recognition, in which the enterprise determines whether it is more likely than not that a tax position, based on technical merits, will be sustained upon ultimate resolution in the court of last resort.

b. Incorrect. The second step of the two-step process is measurement, where the tax position is measured to determine the amount of the benefit to recognize in financial statements.

c. Incorrect. Deciding not to file a tax return is a "tax position" and the two-step process evaluates an enterprise's uncertain tax position.

3. b. Correct. With the more-likely-than-not recognition threshold, a legal tax opinion is not required although such opinion may be external evidence supporting management's assertion.

a. Incorrect. The more-likely-than-not recognition threshold assumes the tax position will be examined by the relevant tax authority and that the tax authority has full knowledge of all relevant information.

c. Incorrect. One assumption about the more-likely-than-not recognition threshold is that the tax position is evaluated without considering the effect of offset or aggregation with other tax positions.

d. Incorrect. The more-likely-than-not threshold assumes the technical merits of the tax position derive from sources of tax authority and facts and circumstances are applicable to the tax position, including administrative practices and precedents.

4. c. Correct. The look-back issue occurs when the enterprise determines its non-filing position is not "more likely than not" to be sustained under examination in a particular state.

a. Incorrect. A state taxing authority may use the income reallocation approach by using a general statute or regulatory authority to reallocate income between the two related entities.

b. Incorrect. A state taxing authority may use the forced combination approach to tax the combined income of Company A and Company B.

d. Incorrect. A state taxing authority may use the economic nexus approach to assert that Company B has economic nexus with its state based on a statute, regulation, case law, or other applicable authority.

5. a. Correct. A state taxing authority may attack the transactions between the two companies in an attempt to reduce Company A expenses. A current transfer pricing study may support these expenses.

b. Incorrect. If Company B cannot reach a more-likely-than-not threshold that it can preclude a state taxing authority's attempted forced combination, then the companies must accrue a FIN 48 liability.

c. Incorrect. A state taxing authority may assert that Company B has economic nexus based on a state statute, regulation, case, or other applicable authority.

d. Incorrect. A state taxing authority may rely on general statutory or regulatory authority to reallocate income between the two related entities.

MODULE 2: OTHER CURRENT
STATE TAX ISSUES—CHAPTER 5

1. b. Correct. Per the counterpoints, pay-to-play and/or bond-to-play will ensure that the taxpayer will mount its best defense to an assessment.

a. Incorrect. Per the counterpoints, a large corporation can afford to pay a few million dollars based solely on an auditor's assertion. If the auditor is wrong, the corporation will receive a refund. Therefore, no harm, no foul.

c. Incorrect. Per the counterpoints, if a taxpayer pays-to-play, the financial risk to a tax authority due to business setbacks is eliminated.

d. Incorrect. One of the choices reflects the justification for a pay-to-play system.

2. d. Correct. Impartiality is critical to the review process; taxpayers should have decisions rendered by an independent hearing officer who will render determinations based on their objective evaluation of the law to the facts presented.

a. Incorrect. Paying the members of the reviewing forum a fair and reasonable salary is helpful in attracting the best and the brightest, but a forum may be effective even if members are paid less than the prevailing salaries of private practitioners.

b. Incorrect. Judicial experience is not required; however, many states specify the qualifications necessary for appointment, requiring federal or state tax expertise. Often a minimum number of years of such experience is needed.

c. Incorrect. Pay-to-play should not be required.

3. c. Correct. In order to attract qualified individuals, the compensation should be reasonable.

a. Incorrect. There is no need for compensation to be consistent with that offered by other jurisdictions.

b. Incorrect. Compensation need not be tied to the salaries of judges sitting in the jurisdiction's highest court; in some jurisdictions, however, compensation is tied to that offered to a particular level of the judiciary.

d. Incorrect. Members of a forum can be paid different salaries based upon their level of experience and responsibilities.

4. d. Correct. To remain impartial, appointed hearings officers should be instructed that they are not appointed to protect the state's revenue.

a. Incorrect. Partisan political appointments demean the system and tax appeals positions should not be awarded for political patronage.

b. Incorrect. In order to employ well-qualified individuals, they must be fairly and reasonably compensated.

c. Incorrect. Unless appointees are fully tax compliant, the review process may cause taxpayers to likewise flout the law.

5. a. Correct. Neither New York State nor New York City is permitted to appeal adverse determinations.

b. Incorrect. In Massachusetts, the Appellate Tax Board is required to issue a decision within three months after the record closes.

c. Incorrect. The California State Board of Equalization considered amending its briefing rules to prohibit revenue estimates.

d. Incorrect. In West Virginia, the Governor appoints the chief administrative law judge from a list of three qualified nominees submitted by the state bar's board of governors.

6. d. Correct. Although some states have requirements that a decision must be rendered within a given timeframe, courts have been loathe to enforce mandatory time limits.

a. Incorrect. Barring any substantial reason for a distinction, rules should be consistent regardless of the nature or type of tax involved.

b. Incorrect. Although a record may need to be made about a taxpayer's personal life, decisions can be rendered in a redacted format without compromising the review process.

c. Incorrect. Only the independent fact-finder can be aware of the variations of demeanor and tone of voice that bear on credibility; therefore, deference should be given to such fact-finder's credibility determinations.

7. b. Correct. In 2002, West Virginia created the Office of Tax Appeals and modeled its rules after those of the U.S. Tax Court.

a. Incorrect. In 1986, New York State revamped its tax appeals process and created a tribunal independent from the tax department.

c. Incorrect. Although several attempts have been made since 1979, California has still not established an administrative body whose sole function is to hear tax appeals.

d. Incorrect. In 1989, New York City revamped its tax appeals process and created a tribunal independent from its tax department.

8. a. Correct. When its foreign franchise tax was declared unconstitutional in *South Central Bell*, Alabama gave future tax credits to South Central Bell worth 19 percent of the refund sought.

b. Incorrect. To date, California has not successfully established an administrative body solely to hear tax appeals.

c. Incorrect. In 2000, Kentucky enacted retroactive legislation prohibiting corporate tax refunds based on the filing of unitary business tax returns.

d. Incorrect. In Texas, refunds of more than $250,000 would not be paid without a specific legislation appropriation.

9. a. Correct. The Council on State Taxation has identified five elements that, at a minimum, should be present in a state's tax administration process: even-handed statutes of limitation; equalized interest rates; adequate time to file a protest; automatic extension of state return filing dates beyond the federal due date; and whether federal audit changes open the entire state return to audit.

b. Incorrect. California's State Board of Equalization hears the appeal if a corporate income taxpayer claims a refund.

c. Incorrect. The American Bar Association's State and Local Tax Committee has drafted and approved a Model State Administrative Tax Tribunal Act, which incorporates its own desirable elements for a fair tax tribunal.

d. Incorrect. The Joint Committee on Taxation has noted that the government objective should be to strive to maintain a tax system that is broadly viewed as fair to all.

10. d. Correct. Lindholm and Kranz critique existing dispute resolution systems in the various states from the point of view of larger, multistate business taxpayers in the *Tax Management Multistate Tax Report.*
a. Incorrect. An article by Coffin in the *State and Local Tax Lawyer* analyzes the characteristics and advantages of the various types of independent judicial and administrative tax courts and tribunals now in existence.
b. Incorrect. The Committee on State and Local Taxation of the ABA's Section of Taxation has proposed the Model State Administrative Tax Tribunal Act.
c. Incorrect. Comprehensive surveys of the tax appeal regimes in the various states and their salient characteristics may be found in Ocasal and Federation of Tax Administrators, *State Tax Appeal Systems,* 1700 Tax Management Portfolio (BNA).

11. b. Correct. In 1957, the American Bar Association's study of state tax courts prompted the National Conference of Commissioners on Uniform State Laws to promulgate a Model State Tax Court Act.
a. Incorrect. The American Bar Association's Committee on State and Local Taxation has proposed the current Model State Administrative Tax Tribunal Act.
c. Incorrect. The Federation of Tax Administrators has a comprehensive survey of the tax appeal regimes in the various states and their salient characteristics.
d. Incorrect. The Joint Committee on Taxation has noted that the government objective should be to strive to maintain a tax system that is broadly viewed as fair to all.

12. False. Correct. The state shall provide an independent agency with tax expertise to resolve disputes between the department of revenue and the taxpayer prior to requiring taxpayer's payment or posting of a bond, but after the taxpayer has had a full opportunity to attempt settlement with the department.
True. Incorrect. Even though states make several arguments in favor of pay-to-play, the Model Act does not require such payment or bond.

13. b. Correct. The Model Act recommends placing the Tax Tribunal in the executive branch, while simultaneously ensuring the tribunal is separate and independent from the department of revenue.

a. Incorrect. Many state constitutions require judicial branch judges to be elected, making it impossible to ensure the court has tax expertise.

c. Incorrect. Many state constitutions do not permit the legislature to establish a specialized court within the judicial branch without a constitutional amendment.

d. Incorrect. Authority is not to be shared among multiple branches.

14. True. Correct. The Model Act does not grant jurisdiction over tax collection actions initiated by the state, which must be brought in the regular courts. Because the tax liability in such cases has been finalized and cannot be contested by the taxpayer, there are generally no "questions of law and fact arising under the tax laws of this state" to be determined.

False. Incorrect. Collection actions by states are generally governed under existing statutory provisions, and the proposed jurisdiction the tax tribunal only extends to "questions of law and fact arising under the tax laws of this state."

15. c. Correct. The tax tribunal would decide all questions of law and fact arising under the tax laws of the state.

a. Incorrect. The taxpayer may file a petition with the tax tribunal covering all issues and then appeal the decision to the appropriate appellate court, at which time the taxpayer would present the constitutional issue.

b. Incorrect. The taxpayer may proceed directly through the judicial system addressing the constitutional issue and have the tax tribunal address the remaining tax issues.

d. Incorrect. The taxpayer may commence a declaratory action in the state court with respect to the constitutional challenge and have the remaining issues in the tax tribunal stayed pending final resolution of the constitutional issue.

16. a. Correct. The petition shall be filed in the Tax Tribunal no later than 90 days after receipt of the department of revenue's determination imposing a liability for tax, penalty, or interest.

b. Incorrect. The taxpayer has 30 days in which to reply to the department of revenue's answer in the proceeding. The taxpayer's period to file a petition has a different duration.

c. Incorrect. The department of revenue must answer or reply to an amended pleading no later than 75 days after filing of the amended petition. The taxpayer's period to file a petition has a different duration.

d. Incorrect. The department of revenue may have a 15-day extension to file its answer. The taxpayer's period to file a petition has a different duration.

17. False. *Correct.* The Model Act reflects the conclusion that, on balance, the value of reaching a correct conclusion outweighs the risks associated with admitting evidence that violates the traditional hearsay rule.
True. *Incorrect.* The Model Act provides that the tribunal is not bound by the rules of evidence and that all relevant evidence, including hearsay, is admissible.

18. c. *Correct.* A judge in the Minnesota Tax Court must ordinarily file a decision within three months of the hearing and not part of the judge's salary shall be paid unless the judge has certified full compliance with this requirement.
a. *Incorrect.* The Model Act follows the New York State Division of Tax Appeals with the requirement that the Tax Tribunal must issue a decision within six months after submission of briefs subsequent to completion of the hearing.
b. *Incorrect.* Maryland is one of the states currently providing that tax hearings are open to the public.
d. *Incorrect.* One of the choices is the state requiring the judge to file his or her decision or risk not being paid.

19. a. *Correct.* A taxpayer who elects to proceed in the small claims division must file a petition no later than 90 days after the taxpayer's receipt of the written notice of determination.
b. *Incorrect.* The department must respond no later than 30 days after receipt of notice that the taxpayer filed a petition in proper form. The taxpayer's filing period for the petition is different than 30 days.
c. *Incorrect.* The suggested jurisdiction for the small claims division is any net amount of tax deficiencies and claimed refunds that do not exceed $25,000 exclusive of interest and penalties.
d. *Incorrect.* Experience over the last 20 years demonstrates that executive-branch state tax tribunals can efficiently achieve the Model Act's principal goals of providing every taxpayer faced with a tax dispute a pre-payment opportunity to make his factual record before an independent forum of tax experts.

20. d. *Correct.* All three choices are true statements about the dissemination of the tribunal's decisions.
a. *Incorrect.* The Model Act requires that decisions of the tribunal be indexed and published in a manner that makes them permanently available to the public.
b. *Incorrect.* The drafters of the Model Act decided against an alternative rule whereby certain decisions involving no substantial question of law or fact would not be published because other taxpayers have a legitimate interest in know how the tribunal handles issues.

c. Incorrect. Decisions rendered by the tribunal's Small Claims Division are exempt from the publication requirement because such decisions involve smaller tax amounts, are generally less developed cases, and cannot be appealed.

MODULE 2—CHAPTER 6

1. a. Correct. Knowledge that a major highway interchange will be built near commercial property is an example of an anticipated increase or decrease of value based on a future benefit or detriment.
b. Incorrect. Examples of change affecting valuation include normal wear and tear and fire or storm damage.
c. Incorrect. The principle of contribution refers to the value of any part of the property as measured by its effect on the value of the whole.
d. Incorrect. Increasing returns means that the addition of improvements to the land and structures increases the total value only to the asset's maximum value.

2. c. Correct. Plottage occurs when adjacent lots are merged or consolidated into one larger lot that produces a greater total value than the sum of the two sites valued separately.
a. Incorrect. Progression refers to situations in which the value of a modest home increases if it is near better properties.
b. Incorrect. Conformity is the economic principle in which the maximum value for a property is reached when it conforms to surrounding land use.
d. Incorrect. Competition affects valuation when substantial profits are being made, drawing similar investors to the area.

3. d. Correct. Determining the current cost of constructing buildings and other improvements on the property is one step taken to arrive at the value using the cost approach.
a. Incorrect. Although the cost approach estimates the amount of accrued depreciation, determining the depreciation and/or obsolescence to be applied is a common issue arising in the application of each approach.
b. Incorrect. One common issue is combining two or more approaches instead of using only one ill-fitting or inappropriate approach.
c. Incorrect. One common issue that arises is when appraisers disagree over the approach to be used and the approach used is later found to be unreliable.

4. a. Correct. In *Aetna Life Insurance*, the court determined that the reproduction-cost approach best valued the office building and surrounding land because that approach more clearly fit the building objective of the taxpayer as a corporate employer.

b. Incorrect. In *Services Development Corp.*, the court determined that reproduction costs more accurately indicated the value of a transit warehouse because the improvements to the facility to convert the property into a transit warehouse were new and made the property unique.

c. Incorrect. In *General Electric Co.*, the court held that the cost approach was the most effective way to determine the value of a corporation's national headquarters.

d. Incorrect. In *Fedus*, the court concluded the town assessor had overvalued property when he failed to depreciate the value of a barn located on the property.

5. b. Correct. In *Federal Reserve Bank of Minneapolis*, the court concluded that the Federal Reserve Building was special-purpose property that was properly assessed using the reproduction-cost approach method of valuation.

a. Incorrect. Although the *Shepard Park Office Center Limited Partnership* court indicated the cost approach generally provides the best indication of value for newer properties, it also determined that the income and market-data approaches should be considered.

c. Incorrect. In *Cannon Falls Partnership*, the court rejected using the cost approach because it was an unreliable indicator of value for an industrial facility built in 1966.

d. Incorrect. In *Schmitz Garage, Inc.*, the court preferred the market approach over the cost approach for valuing a building that had been specifically designed as a car and farm machinery sales-and-service business.

6. False. Correct. In *Winthrop Plaza Assoc.*, the Connecticut court indicated the income approach was the best method to use when the building had substantial physical and functional depreciation.

True. Incorrect. In *Yale Church of Truth*, the Connecticut court found that the income or market approach is appropriate to determine the assessed value of older buildings in average condition that are subject to a high rate of deterioration or obsolescence.

7. a. Correct. In *Prudential Insurance Co. of America*, the appraiser had to rely on many projections because the property was never used as income-producing property and special permit and zoning regulations contemplated use by a corporate owner as opposed to use as an investment property.

b. Incorrect. In *Yale Church of Truth*, the income or market approach was appropriate to value older, small, multiunit residential buildings in average condition that were subject to a high rate of deterioration and obsolescence.

c. Incorrect. In *Primus*, an apartment building was valued according to its highest and best use as an apartment building using the income approach.

d. Incorrect. In *Parotta*, a tennis club was valued using the income approach because the lease rate on the property was comparable to lease rates charged by another tennis club.

8. b. Correct. In *United Technologies*, the court determined the sales-comparison approach was the optimal valuation method based on the highest and best use of improved property for multitenant industrial occupancy.

a. Incorrect. In *Sullivan*, the court found the town's appraiser had overvalued the property because the appraiser used comparables much larger and in better condition than was the taxpayer's property.

c. Incorrect. In *Madison Beach Club*, the comparable-sales method was inappropriate because there were no truly comparable properties.

d. Incorrect. In *Equity 96*, the sales-comparison approach was credible in valuing a commercial/industrial facility, and the income approach was rejected because vacancy rates differed by 12.5 percent.

9. a. Correct. In *Chrysler Corp.*, the Illinois Appellate Court rejected the appraiser's sole reliance on reproduction costs when there was sufficient credible evidence of comparable sales.

b. Incorrect. In *Equity 96*, the Connecticut court favored using the credible sales-comparison valuation and rejected using an income approach when vacancy rates differed by 12.5 percent and rental market data was not comparable to the subject property.

c. Incorrect. Minnesota rejects the sales-comparison approach when the comparables are insufficiently similar.

d. Incorrect. One of the choices is the state in which the court ruled reliance solely on such costs should be limited.

10. c. Correct. In *McNeilus Truck & Manufacturing*, the Minnesota Supreme Court overruled the Tax Court and determined that excluding out-of-state sales distorted the valuation process.

a. Incorrect. In *Merz*, a residence was valued substantially higher than its selling price because the house had been on the market for a long time, the sellers had reduced the price several times, and other factors indicated the prudence of conducting a below-market sale.

b. Incorrect. The *Grove* court rejected the appraiser's comparable sales because the appraiser failed to quantify the differences with the subject property and the comparables were not nearly identical to the subject property.

d. Incorrect. One of the choices is the case involving limitation of comparable sales.

MODULE 2—CHAPTER 7

1. c. *Correct.* Including gross receipts from short-term investments in the sales factor denominator can significantly reduce the sales factor of a nondomiciliary corporation.
a. *Incorrect.* Alternative relief provisions require the taxpayer to show the state tax administrator that the taxpayer's modification of the standard sales factor would not distort the apportionment of the taxpayer's net income.
b. *Incorrect.* State tax auditors attempt to mitigate dilution of the corporation's sales factor by arguing that net gains should be used in the sales factor denominator.

2. a. *Correct.* Microsoft's sales of software products generated $659 million of income and gross receipts of $2.1 billion, for a margin of roughly 31 percent.
b. *Incorrect.* In overall percentage terms, the short-term securities investments produced less than 2 percent of Microsoft's income.
c. *Incorrect.* From its short-term securities transactions, Microsoft earned $10.7 million of income and generated $5.7 billion of revenue for a gross profit margin of 0.2 percent.
d. *Incorrect.* In overall percentage terms, the short-term securities investments produced as much as 73 percent of Microsoft's gross receipts.

3. a. *Correct.* Prior to switching from net gain to including the gross receipts from its short-term securities investments in the sales factor denominator, Microsoft's California sales factor was approximately 11 percent. The FTB believed this was an accurate measure of Microsoft's sales factor in California.
b. *Incorrect.* Microsoft's sales of software products generated a gross profit margin of approximately 31 percent.
c. *Incorrect.* Microsoft's sales factor was reduced to approximately 3 percent after including gross receipts from short-term investments in the sales factor denominator. The FTB believed this use of gross receipts instead of net gain diluted the sales factor.
d. *Incorrect.* In overall percentage terms, the short-term securities investments produced less than 2 percent of Microsoft's income, but as much as 73 percent of its gross receipts.

4. d. *Correct.* In the *Microsoft* decision, the California Supreme Court noted that such distortions are less likely to arise in situations where investment activity is the taxpayer's principal business activity as it was in *Merrill Lynch*, where the California SBE rejected the FTB's argument that Merrill Lynch should include only net gains from its securities investments in its California sales factor.

a. Incorrect. In *Microsoft*, the California Supreme Court determined that the use of gross receipts from Microsoft's short-term investments distorted the standard apportionment formula's attribution of income to each state and allowed the FTB to require Microsoft to include only net gain from short-term investments in its sales factor.

b. Incorrect. In the *Appeal of Pacific Telephone & Telegraph,* the California SBE determined that including gross receipts from short-term securities transactions in the sales factor did not fairly represent the taxpayer's business in California because more than 11 percent of the taxpayer's business activities would be attributed to the state where Pacific Telephone's treasury function was located.

c. Incorrect. Neither of the *Sherwin-Williams* cases was decided in California. The Oregon *Sherwin-Williams* case allowed the taxpayer to include gross receipts from short-term investments in the denominator of the Oregon sales factor. The Tennessee *Sherwin-Williams* case allowed the state to limit the taxpayer to including net gain for short-term investments in the denominator of the Tennessee sales factor.

5. True. Correct. General Motors was the party that provided the cash in the transaction and agreed to sell the securities back to the seller-borrower on the date specified in the repurchase agreement.

False. Incorrect. If General Motors had been engaging in repo transactions, it would have been the seller-borrower that agreed to repurchase the securities from the buyer-lender at the original price plus an agreed amount of interest. This is referred to as a revenue repo.

6. c. Correct. The California Supreme Court determined that, for California tax purposes, General Motors' repo transactions had the characteristics of a secured loan and only the interest received from the seller-borrowers was a gross receipt includible in the sales factor.

a. Incorrect. General Motors and the FTB agreed that in a transaction involving an actual sale of a marketable security, the entire sales price would constitute gross receipts for purposes of the sales factor. The California Supreme Court seemed to agree that this was the correct treatment of sales of marketable securities in the California sales factor.

b. Incorrect. General Motors and the FTB agreed that in a loan transaction, the lender's recovery of the capital it had loaned to the borrower was not a gross receipt for purposes of the sales factor. Again, the California Supreme Court seemed to agree that only interest payments on loans were gross proceeds for purposes of the sales factor.

d. Incorrect. The California Supreme Court reversed the Court of Appeals' determination that, under the sales factor statute, only the net proceeds that General Motors received from securities held to redemption were includible in General Motors' sales factor and remanded this issue to the trial court, allowing the FTB to present evidence as to whether including the gross receipts from such short-term securities redemption transactions would distort the California sales factor.

7. b. *Correct.* Mead argued that *Blessing/White's* "cessation of business" principle applied and that the gain from the sale of Lexis/Nexis was properly characterized as nonbusiness income allocable to Ohio.
a. *Incorrect. Merrill Lynch* is the California case where the court rejected the FTB's arguments that Merrill Lynch should include only net gains from its securities investments in the California sales factor where investment activity was the taxpayer's principal business activity.
c. *Incorrect.* The Illinois Appellate Court held that Mead's gain from the sale of the Lexis/Nexis subsidiaries was subject to formulary apportionment under the "operational function test" of the United States Supreme Court's *Allied-Signal* decision.
d. *Incorrect.* In *Microsoft*, the California Supreme Court determined that Microsoft's short-term securities investments created a significant distortion in its California sales factor when gross receipts from these investments were included in the sales factor denominator.

8. True. *Correct.* The Department's regulation provides that for sales of business intangibles, gross receipts shall be disregarded and only the net gain (loss) should be included in the sales factor.
False. *Incorrect.* Even though the Illinois Appellate Court also held that limiting Mead to using net gain from the sale of the Lexis/Nexis business was appropriate under Illinois' statutory "alternative relief" provision.

9. a. *Correct.* Under the holding in *Microsoft*, gross receipts from the sale of short-term security investments would not be includible in the California's sales factor if the state can show that distortion of the apportionment computation will result.
b. *Incorrect.* Under *Microsoft*, gross receipts would be includible in the sales factor if it is unlikely that long-term securities transactions would be distorting the apportionment formula.
c. *Incorrect.* The California Supreme Court determined that the UDITPA statutes provide for the inclusion of the gross receipts from short-term securities investments held to maturity in the sales factor denominator, subject to the state tax auditor showing gross receipts would distort the sales factor.
d. *Incorrect.* State tax agencies bear the burden of proving that distortion of the apportionment formula will result if a taxpayer is allowed to include gross receipts instead of net gains from short-term securities investments in the sales factor denominator.

10. False. *Correct.* Illinois also imposes significant amounts of penalties and interest if the open tax years were eligible for its tax amnesty program. **True. *Incorrect.*** California is not the only state that has had a tax amnesty program that imposes significant penalties and interest if the taxpayer's open tax years were eligible for the tax amnesty program.

TOP MULTISTATE TAX ISSUES FOR 2008 CPE COURSE

Index

W

TOP MULTISTATE TAX ISSUES FOR 2008 CPE COURSE

CPE Quizzer Instructions

The CPE Quizzer is divided into two Modules. There is a processing fee for each Quizzer Module submitted for grading. Successful completion of Module 1 is recommended for **7 CPE Credits.*** Successful completion of Module 2 is recommended for **7 CPE Credits.*** You can complete and submit one Module at a time or all Modules at once for a total of **14 CPE Credits.***

To obtain CPE credit, return your completed Answer Sheet for each Quizzer Module to **CCH Continuing Education Department, 4025 W. Peterson Ave., Chicago, IL 60646**, or fax it to (773) 866-3084. Each Quizzer Answer Sheet will be graded and a CPE Certificate of Completion awarded for achieving a grade of 70 percent or greater. The Quizzer Answer Sheets are located after the Quizzer questions for this Course.

Express Grading: Processing time for your Answer Sheet is generally 8-12 business days. If you are trying to meet a reporting deadline, our Express Grading Service is available for an additional $19 per Module. To use this service, please check the "Express Grading" box on your Answer Sheet and provide your CCH account or credit card number **and your fax number.** CCH will fax your results and a Certificate of Completion (upon achieving a passing grade) to you by 5:00 p.m. the business day following our receipt of your Answer Sheet. **If you mail your Answer Sheet for Express Grading, please write "ATTN: CPE OVERNIGHT" on the envelope.** NOTE: CCH will not Federal Express Quizzer results under any circumstances.

NEW ONLINE GRADING gives you immediate 24/7 grading with instant results and no Express Grading Fee.

The **CCH Testing Center** website gives you and others in your firm easy, free access to CCH print Courses and allows you to complete your CPE Quizzers online for immediate results. Plus, the **My Courses** feature provides convenient storage for your CPE Course Certificates and completed Quizzers.

Go to **www.cchtestingcenter.com** to complete your Quizzer online.

---

* Recommended CPE credit is based on a 50-minute hour. Participants earning credits for states that require self-study to be based on a 100-minute hour will receive ½ the CPE credits for successful completion of this course. Because CPE requirements vary from state to state and among different licensing agencies, please contact your CPE governing body for information on your CPE requirements and the applicability of a particular course for your requirements.

Date of Completion: The date of completion on your Certificate will be the date that you put on your Answer Sheet. However, you must submit your Answer Sheet to CCH for grading within two weeks of completing it.

Expiration Date: December 31, 2008

Evaluation: To help us provide you with the best possible products, please take a moment to fill out the Course Evaluation located at the back of this Course and return it with your Quizzer Answer Sheets.

CCH is registered with the National Association of State Boards of Accountancy (NASBA) as a sponsor of continuing professional education on the National Registry of CPE Sponsors. State boards of accountancy have final authority on the acceptance of individual courses for CPE credit. Complaints regarding registered sponsors may be addressed to the National Registry of CPE Sponsors, 150 Fourth Avenue North, Suite 700, Nashville, TN 37219-2417. Web site: www.nasba.org.

CCH is registered with the National Association of State Boards of Accountancy (NASBA) as a Quality Assurance Service (QAS) sponsor of continuing professional education. State boards of accountancy have final authority on the acceptance of individual courses for CPE credit. Complaints regarding registered sponsors may be addressed to NASBA, 150 Fourth Avenue North, Suite 700, Nashville, TN 37219-2417. Web site: www.nasba.org.

CCH has been approved by the California Tax Education Council to offer courses that provide federal and state credit towards the annual "continuing education" requirement imposed by the State of California. A listing of additional requirements to register as a tax preparer may be obtained by contacting CTEC at P.O. Box 2890, Sacramento, CA, 95812-2890, toll-free by phone at (877) 850-2832, or on the Internet at www.ctec.org.

Processing Fee:	**Recommended CPE:**	
$84.00 for Module 1	7 hours for Module 1	
$84.00 for Module 2	7 hours for Module 2	
$168.00 for all Modules	14 hours for all Modules	
CTEC Course Number:	**CTEC Federal Hours:**	**CTEC California Hours:**
1075-CE-7502 for Module 1	N/A hours for Module 1	3 hours for Module 1
1075-CE-7512 for Module 2	N/A hours for Module 2	3 hours for Module 2
	N/A hours for all Modules	6 hours for all Modules

One **complimentary copy** of this Course is provided with copies of selected CCH Tax titles. Additional copies of this Course may be ordered for $29.00 each by calling 1-800-248-3248 (ask for product 0-0986-200).

TOP MULTISTATE TAX ISSUES FOR 2008 CPE COURSE

Quizzer Questions: Module 1

Answer the True/False questions by marking a "T" or "F" on the Quizzer Answer Sheet. Answer Multiple Choice questions by indicating the appropriate letter on the Answer Sheet.

1. Which of the following decisions found that a state could tax an out-of-state corporation if that corporation has "economic nexus"?

a. *Complete Auto*
b. *Geoffrey*
c. *Quill*
d. *Toys 'R Us*

2. All of the following are additional names for PICs ***except:***

a. Brass-plate headquarters
b. Special-purpose entities
c. Delaware holding companies
d. Intangible holding companies

3. In *Geoffrey*, the South Carolina Supreme Court concluded that all of the following in-state activities were sufficient for economic nexus ***except:***

a. Market exploitation
b. Physical presence
c. Protected activities
d. State benefits

4. In which of the following cases did the court determine the PIC's intangibles acquired a Louisiana "business situs"?

a. *Kmart*
b. *Quill*
c. *The Gap*
d. *Geoffrey*

5. In which of the following cases did the North Carolina court distinguish factors allowing a state to impose an income tax on an out-of-state corporation from factors allowing the state to impose a sales tax collection duty on an out-of-state corporation?

    a. *A&F Trademark*
    b. *Geoffrey*
    c. *The Gap*
    d. *Kmart*

6. In which state did the tax court determine that the state taxing authority could not impose an income tax obligation on an out-of-state PIC?

    a. North Carolina
    b. South Carolina
    c. New Jersey
    d. Delaware

7. In which of the following cases did the state try to impose income taxes on corporations lacking an in-state affiliate?

    a. *Lanco*
    b. *Kmart*
    c. *A&F Trademark*
    d. *J.C. Penney*

8. In which case did the court solely justify imposing an income tax on the out-of-state PIC based on income derived from Oklahoma customers?

    a. *Geoffrey*
    b. *Geoffrey II*
    c. *A&F Trademark*
    d. *Lanco*

9. Which of the following states has enacted legislation denying gross income deductions for interest, royalties, and licensing fees paid to PICs?

    a. Ohio
    b. Indiana
    c. New York
    d. California

10. What is the starting point for a state's taxation of out-of-state corporations?

   a. Substantial nexus
   b. Economic nexus
   c. Physical presence
   d. Dormant Commerce Clause

11. In which state did the court of appeals rule that two holding companies were taxable in *Syl, Inc.* and *Crown Cork & Seal Co.*?

   a. Maryland
   b. Delaware
   c. Florida
   d. New Jersey

12. All of the following are true statements about multinational company reporting *except:*

   a. Multinational corporations with several subsidiary corporations and publicly traded equity securities must report their financial condition on a consolidated basis.
   b. For federal income tax purposes, multinational corporations must file a consolidated tax return for their affiliated group of companies.
   c. For federal income tax purposes, multinational corporations may file either a consolidated return or separate company returns.
   d. A multinational corporation's consolidated statements reflect the practical reality that a group of commonly controlled corporations function as a single economic entity.

13. States target companies for state income tax compliance using all of the following methods *except:*

   a. Minimal connection
   b. Audit teams
   c. Referrals
   d. Questionnaires

14. Which of the following state income tax return filing options is the most advantageous to a PIC's tax-planning strategies?

   a. Elective consolidated returns
   b. Mandatory combined unitary reporting
   c. Mandatory separate company returns
   d. Discretionary combined unitary reporting

15. All of the following are true statements about PICs as a successful tax-planning strategy **except:**

    a. A PIC must demonstrate that it has a legitimate business purpose.

    b. A PIC must be careful to avoid establishing nexus in other states.

    c. A PIC should demonstrate a legitimate economic purpose.

    d. A PIC may engage in sham business transactions.

16. Decisions in all of the following cases unintentionally originated PICs **except:**

    a. *National Bellas Hess*

    b. *Quill Corporation*

    c. *Complete Auto*

17. In which of the following decisions did the court determine that the PIC had agency nexus?

    a. *Geoffrey*

    b. *Kmart Properties*

    c. *Quill*

    d. *Lanco, Inc.*

18. Which state's tax court held that Lane Bryant's PIC was not subject to the state's corporate business tax because the PIC lacked physical presence in the taxing state?

    a. North Carolina

    b. New Jersey

    c. New Mexico

    d. West Virginia

19. PICs are the most significant factor responsible for the drop in state income tax revenues. **True or False?**

20. All of the following are true statements **except:**

    a. The business community supports SSUTA.

    b. Most state and local government groups support SSUTA.

    c. The business community supports BATSA.

    d. Most state and local government groups support BATSA.

21. Based on the material in this chapter, all of the following states adopted the ULLCA of 1996, *except:*

    a. Illinois
    b. Iowa
    c. South Carolina
    d. West Virginia

22. Provisions for series LLCs are *not* included in the Revised Uniform Limited Liability Company Act. *True or False?*

23. In a series LLC, the master LLC must own an interest in each of the series LLCs. *True or False?*

24. Which of the following states was the first to enact legislation for series LLCs?

    a. Illinois
    b. Iowa
    c. Delaware
    d. Nevada

25. In which state must a series LLC file a different form with the Secretary of State, rather than the specific form of Articles of Organization for regular LLCs?

    a. Illinois
    b. Iowa
    c. Delaware
    d. Nevada

26. What is the only concrete advantage in creating a series LLC?

    a. Limited liability
    b. Transacting business in other states
    c. Lower real estate transfer taxes
    d. Lower filing fees

27. In which state is each series treated as a separate business entity for purposes of registering, paying fees, or transacting business in that state?

    a. Illinois
    b. Tennessee
    c. Delaware
    d. California

28. Which state requires the master LLC to file a Certificate of Designation to create each series, providing better notice to third parties?

a. Illinois
b. Tennessee
c. Delaware
d. California

29. Which is *not* a significant ambiguity facing the series LLC?

a. The franchise tax treatment of a series in a state in which the series LLC is organized
b. Whether firewall liability protection will be respected in states without a series LLC statute
c. How the bankruptcy courts will treat the series LLCs
d. Whether the series LLC will be treated as one entity or multiple entities for federal tax purposes

30. Commingling of funds between two regular LLCs is less likely to result in "piercing the LLC veil" than commingling the funds of two series LLCs in the same series. *True or False?*

31. For federal tax purposes, the IRS is most likely to treat which state's series LLCs as separate entities?

a. Delaware
b. Tennessee
c. Illinois
d. Nevada

32. If the IRS rules that each series is a separate entity, then each series must do all of the following, *except:*

a. File its own tax return
b. File a combined tax return
c. Distribute Schedule K-1s to its members
d. Obtain a tax identification number

33. California has specifically determined that which state's series LLCs will be treated as a separate business entity for income and franchise tax purposes?

a. Illinois
b. Tennessee
c. Delaware
d. California

34. Substantive consolidation, which is an equitable doctrine treating separate entities as if they were a single entity, applies to which legal area?

a. Bankruptcy Law
b. Securities Law
c. State Law
d. Tax Law

35. Which of the securities law rules provides that an "entity" is considered one purchaser for purposes of the Regulation D limited offering exemptions?

a. Rule 504
b. Rule 501
c. Rule 506
d. Rule 505

36. What accounting interpretation is applicable beginning December 15, 2006?

a. FASB 109
b. FASB 48
c. FIN 109
d. FIN 48

37. All of the following are tax positions *except:*

a. Decision not to file a tax return
b. Shift of income between jurisdictions
c. Decision to file a tax return
d. Characterization of income

38. What happens when the tax position no longer meets the more likely than not standard?

a. Recognition
b. Derecognition
c. Measurement
d. Audit

39. The unit of account for analyzing a tax position under FIN 48 will vary from state to state based, in part, on the approach the enterprise anticipates the taxing authority will take during an examination. *True or False?*

40. What is the second step of the two-step process?

    a. Audit
    b. Recognition
    c. Derecognition
    d. Measurement

Quizzer Questions: Module 2

> Answer the True/False questions by marking a "T" or "F" on the Quizzer Answer Sheet. Answer Multiple Choice questions by indicating the appropriate letter on the Answer Sheet.

41. States may justify having an internal hearing system for each of the following reasons *except:*

   a. Internal hearing officers are privy to internal tax department materials.

   b. Supervisors know when an auditor is overreaching.

   c. It is not a problem if the hearing officer is a little biased in favor of the tax department because many taxpayers are represented by qualified attorneys and accountants, which levels the playing field.

   d. States should be allowed to collect based on an auditor's assertion.

42. All of the following are attributes of a fair and effective tax appeals system *except:*

   a. Prompt resolutions

   b. Transparent process and public decisions

   c. Politically affiliated hearing officers

   d. Deference given to the fact-finder

43. In which state did the tax tribunal consider amending its briefing rules to prohibit revenue estimates or statements regarding revenue impacts?

   a. California

   b. Idaho

   c. Massachusetts

   d. New York

44. According to the text, in which state are members of the Board of Tax Appeals currently paid $200 per day?

   a. California

   b. Idaho

   c. Massachusetts

   d. New York

45. Based on the material in this chapter, which tax appeals board is required to render a decision within three to six months after the record is closed?

    a. Massachusetts Appellate Tax Board
    b. Idaho Board of Tax Appeals
    c. New York State Tax Appeals Tribunal
    d. New York City Tax Appeals Tribunal

46. Which jurisdiction has been having difficulties forming an independent tax appeals tribunal?

    a. New York State
    b. West Virginia
    c. California
    d. New York City

47. In which jurisdiction did one report indicate that 97 percent of all reviewed tax assessments were affirmed prior to the formation of an independent tax appeals tribunal?

    a. New York State
    b. West Virginia
    c. California
    d. New York City

48. According to the Council on State Taxation, all of the following elements should be included in a state's tax administration process *except:*

    a. Equalized interest rates
    b. Pay-to-play
    c. Even-handed statutes of limitations
    d. Adequate time to file a protest

49. Standards for judicial review of the internal hearing officer's factual determinations are often extremely onerous and include all of the following, *except:*

    a. Clearly erroneous
    b. More likely than not
    c. Arbitrary and capricious
    d. Without rational basis

50. The summary of the Model State Administrative Tax Tribunal Act notes that taxpayers desiring to contest a state tax authority's determination face several obstacles that seriously undermine the public's perception of fairness, including all of the following *except:*

    a. Unclear procedural rules
    b. Hearing officer employed by tax agency
    c. Onerous standard for judicial review
    d. Payment of expensive bond

51. Which of the following states has *not* enacted independent tax court and tribunal statutes?

    a. Maryland
    b. New Jersey
    c. California
    d. New York

52. In Section 1 of the Model Act, the legislative purpose language was derived from state legislation establishing all of the following *except:*

    a. New York State Division of Tax Appeals
    b. South Carolina Revenue Procedures Act
    c. California Tax Court
    d. West Virginia Office of Tax Appeals

53. Which of the following states has *not* implemented a successful executive-branch tribunal?

    a. Michigan
    b. Maryland
    c. New York
    d. South Carolina

54. According to the Model Act, a full-time judge of the tribunal may engage in all of the following pursuits *except:*

    a. Holding another income position within the government
    b. Holding passive interests in a business entity
    c. Holding an incidental teaching position
    d. Engaging in scholarly activities

55. The commentary on the Model Act suggests which type of taxes will likely be excluded by the legislature from the tax tribunal's jurisdiction?

   a. Sales and use taxes
   b. Local taxes
   c. Income taxes
   d. Property taxes

56. Which state's internal conference/appeals/settlement function is called the Informal Conference Board?

   a. New York
   b. Illinois
   c. California
   d. Massachusetts

57. The parties to a proceeding may rely solely on formal discovery mechanisms. *True or False?*

58. Based on the material in this chapter, which state does not allow the public to attend tax hearings?

   a. Maryland
   b. New York
   c. Massachusetts
   d. Illinois

59. All of the following are true statements about the Small Claims Division of the tax tribunal *except:*

   a. A final decision of the Small Claims Division may be appealed.
   b. A taxpayer may not revoke an election to proceed in the Small Claims Division.
   c. Hearings before the Small Claims Division are informal.
   d. The Model Act suggests a Small Claims Division threshold not exceeding $25,000.

60. The tax tribunal may promulgate a rule allowing the parties to serve their filings on the other party by e-mail. *True or False?*

61. What is one of the most important economic principles that affect property valuation?

   a. Substitution
   b. Conformity
   c. Plottage
   d. Highest and best use

62. All of the following are economic principles affecting real estate valuation *except:*

   a. Fair market value
   b. Supply and demand
   c. Highest and best use
   d. Competition

63. All of the following are approaches used by appraisers to accurately estimate the value of real estate *except:*

   a. Income approach
   b. Sales-comparison approach
   c. Fair market value approach
   d. Cost approach

64. In which Connecticut case did the town assessor overvalue the property using the cost approach method because he failed to depreciate the value of the barn?

   a. *Services Development Corp.*
   b. *Fedus*
   c. *General Electric Co.*
   d. *National Amusements, Inc.*

65. In which state did the appellate court rule that the state constitution and case precedence forbid judicial interference from an assessment unless fraud is involved?

   a. Illinois
   b. Connecticut
   c. Minnesota
   d. None of the above is the correct state

66. In which state is one approach discouraged in favor of using multiple approaches because the latter practice is considered more reliable?

a. Illinois
b. Connecticut
c. Minnesota
d. None of the above is the correct state

67. All of the following are types of property best suited for an income approach valuation **except:**

a. Apartment buildings
b. Shopping centers
c. Office buildings
d. Government property

68. In which state was the income approach valuation of Prince's recording studio found to be appropriate because it was special-purpose property and market-rate rents were being received from unrelated tenants?

a. Connecticut
b. Minnesota
c. Illinois
d. None of the above is the correct state

69. Which real estate valuation approach uses comparables?

a. Fair market value
b. Cost
c. Market
d. Income

70. For which type of property is the market approach is best suited?

a. Manufacturing property
b. Office buildings
c. Apartment buildings
d. Single-family homes

71. One of the more contentious issues in many state income tax audits is whether a domiciliary corporation should include the gross receipts from its short-term investments in the sales factor denominator. **True or False?**

72. In which of the following cases did the Illinois Appellate Court recently conclude that nondomiciliary corporations should include only the net gains from the sale of short-term investments in the denominator of the sales factor?

    a. *Microsoft*
    b. *Sherwin-Williams*
    c. *General Motors*
    d. *Mead*

73. Microsoft Corporation's treasury function was located in what state?

    a. Washington
    b. California
    c. New York
    d. Ohio

74. According to the California Supreme Court in the *Microsoft* decision, the statutory term "gross receipts" does not mean "net gains" from short-term securities investments. *True or False?*

75. General Motors' treasury function was located in what state?

    a. California
    b. New York
    c. Illinois
    d. Washington

76. Which of the following companies derived about 90 percent of its short-term investment proceeds from repurchase agreements or repos?

    a. General Motors
    b. Merrill Lynch
    c. Microsoft
    d. Mead

77. In which case did the California Supreme Court remand to the trial court the issue of whether net proceeds received from securities held to redemption were what was includible in the sales factor?

    a. *Mead*
    b. *Microsoft*
    c. *Sherwin-Williams*
    d. *General Motors*

78. In which case did the court decide whether the proceeds from the sale of Lexis/Nexis were properly characterized as apportionable business income in Illinois?

   a. *Microsoft*
   b. *Mead*
   c. *General Motors*
   d. *Merrill Lynch*

79. Mead's corporate domicile was located in what state?

   a. Illinois
   b. California
   c. Ohio
   d. New York

80. Based on the information provided in this chapter, which state has a regulation indicating that taxpayers with income from business intangibles shall disregard gross receipts and include only the net gain (loss) in the sales factor?

   a. New York
   b. Illinois
   c. California
   d. Ohio

TOP MULTISTATE TAX ISSUES FOR 2008 CPE COURSE   (0750-2)

Module 1: Answer Sheet

NAME _____

COMPANY NAME _____

STREET _____

CITY, STATE, & ZIP CODE _____

BUSINESS PHONE NUMBER _____

E-MAIL ADDRESS _____

DATE OF COMPLETION _____

CFP REGISTRANT ID (for Certified Financial Planners) _____

CRTP ID (for CTEC Credit only) _____ (CTEC Course # 1075-CE-7502)

On the next page, please answer the Multiple Choice questions by indicating the appropriate letter next to the corresponding number. Please answer the True/False questions by marking "T" or "F" next to the corresponding number.

A $84.00 processing fee wil be charged for each user submitting Module 1 for grading.

Please remove both pages of the Answer Sheet from this book and return them with your completed Evaluation Form to CCH at the address below. You may also fax your Answer Sheet to CCH at 773-866-3084.

You may also go to **www.cchtestingcenter.com** to complete your Quizzer online.

METHOD OF PAYMENT:

☐ Check Enclosed   ☐ Visa   ☐ Master Card   ☐ AmEx

☐ Discover   ☐ CCH Account* _____

Card No. _____ Exp. Date _____

Signature _____

* Must provide CCH account number for this payment option

EXPRESS GRADING: Please fax my Course results to me by 5:00 p.m. the business day following your receipt of this Answer Sheet. By checking this box I authorize CCH to charge $19.00 for this service.

☐ Express Grading $19.00   Fax No. _____

.CCH
a Wolters Kluwer business

Mail or fax to:
CCH Continuing Education Department
4025 W. Peterson Ave.
Chicago, IL 60646-6085
1-800-248-3248
Fax: 773-866-3084

TOP MULTISTATE TAX ISSUES FOR 2008 CPE COURSE   (0750-2)

Module 1: Answer Sheet

Please answer the Multiple Choice questions by indicating the appropriate letter next to the corresponding number. Please answer the True/False questions by marking "T" or "F" next to the corresponding number.

1. ___	11. ___	21. ___	31. ___
2. ___	12. ___	22. ___	32. ___
3. ___	13. ___	23. ___	33. ___
4. ___	14. ___	24. ___	34. ___
5. ___	15. ___	25. ___	35. ___
6. ___	16. ___	26. ___	36. ___
7. ___	17. ___	27. ___	37. ___
8. ___	18. ___	28. ___	38. ___
9. ___	19. ___	29. ___	39. ___
10. ___	20. ___	30. ___	40. ___

Please complete the Evaluation Form (located after the Module 2 Answer Sheet) and return it with this Quizzer Answer Sheet to CCH at the address on the previous page. Thank you.

TOP MULTISTATE TAX ISSUES FOR 2008 CPE COURSE   (0751-2)

Module 2: Answer Sheet

NAME _____

COMPANY NAME _____

STREET _____

CITY, STATE, & ZIP CODE _____

BUSINESS PHONE NUMBER _____

E-MAIL ADDRESS _____

DATE OF COMPLETION _____

CFP REGISTRANT ID (for Certified Financial Planners) _____

CRTP ID (for CTEC Credit only) _____ (CTEC Course # 1075-CE-7512)

On the next page, please answer the Multiple Choice questions by indicating the appropriate letter next to the corresponding number. Please answer the True/False questions by marking "T" or "F" next to the corresponding number.

A $84.00 processing fee wil be charged for each user submitting Module 2 for grading.

Please remove both pages of the Answer Sheet from this book and return them with your completed Evaluation Form to CCH at the address below. You may also fax your Answer Sheet to CCH at 773-866-3084.

You may also go to **www.cchtestingcenter.com** to complete your exam online.

METHOD OF PAYMENT:

☐ Check Enclosed   ☐ Visa   ☐ Master Card   ☐ AmEx

☐ Discover   ☐ CCH Account* _____

Card No. _____ Exp. Date _____

Signature _____

* Must provide CCH account number for this payment option

EXPRESS GRADING: Please fax my Course results to me by 5:00 p.m. the business day following your receipt of this Answer Sheet. By checking this box I authorize CCH to charge $19.00 for this service.

☐ Express Grading $19.00   Fax No. _____

®.CCH

a Wolters Kluwer business

Mail or fax to:
CCH Continuing Education Department
4025 W. Peterson Ave.
Chicago, IL 60646-6085
1-800-248-3248
Fax: 773-866-3084

TOP MULTISTATE TAX ISSUES FOR 2008 CPE COURSE   (0751-2)

Module 2: Answer Sheet

Please answer the Multiple Choice questions by indicating the appropriate letter next to the corresponding number. Please answer the True/False questions by marking "T" or "F" next to the corresponding number.

41. ___	51. ___	61. ___	71. ___
42. ___	52. ___	62. ___	72. ___
43. ___	53. ___	63. ___	73. ___
44. ___	54. ___	64. ___	74. ___
45. ___	55. ___	65. ___	75. ___
46. ___	56. ___	66. ___	76. ___
47. ___	57. ___	67. ___	77. ___
48. ___	58. ___	68. ___	78. ___
49. ___	59. ___	69. ___	79. ___
50. ___	60. ___	70. ___	80. ___

Please complete the Evaluation Form (located after the Module 2 Answer Sheet) and return it with this Quizzer Answer Sheet to CCH at the address on the previous page. Thank you.

TOP MULTISTATE TAX ISSUES FOR 2008 CPE COURSE   (0986-2)

Evaluation Form

Please take a few moments to fill out and mail or fax this evaluation to CCH so that we can better provide you with the type of self-study programs you want and need. Thank you.

About This Program

1. Please circle the number that best reflects the extent of your agreement with the following statements:

	Strongly Agree				Strongly Disagree
a. The Course objectives were met.	5	4	3	2	1
b. This Course was comprehensive and organized.	5	4	3	2	1
c. The content was current and technically accurate.	5	4	3	2	1
d. This Course was timely and relevant.	5	4	3	2	1
e. The prerequisite requirements were appropriate.	5	4	3	2	1
f. This Course was a valuable learning experience.	5	4	3	2	1
g. The Course completion time was appropriate.	5	4	3	2	1

2. This Course was most valuable to me because of:

    ____ Continuing Education credit   ____ Convenience of format
    ____ Relevance to my practice/   ____ Timeliness of subject matter
    employment   ____ Reputation of author
    ____ Price
    ____ Other (please specify) _____

3. How long did it take to complete this Course? (Please include the total time spent reading or studying reference materials and completing CPE Quizzer).

    Module 1 ____   Module 2 ____

4. What do you consider to be the strong points of this Course?

5. What improvements can we make to this Course?

TOP MULTISTATE TAX ISSUES FOR 2008 CPE COURSE   (0986-2)
Evaluation Form *cont'd*

General Interests

1. Preferred method of self-study instruction:
   ____ Text   ____ Audio   ____ Computer-based/Multimedia   ____Video

2. What specific topics would you like CCH to develop as self-study CPE programs? ___
   _____
   _____
   _____

3. Please list other topics of interest to you _____
   _____
   _____

About You

1. Your profession:
   ____ CPA   ____ Enrolled Agent
   ____ Attorney   ____ Tax Preparer
   ____ Financial Planner   ____ Other (please specify)
                                 _____

2. Your employment:
   ____ Self-employed   ____ Public Accounting Firm
   ____ Service Industry   ____ Non-Service Industry
   ____ Banking/Finance   ____ Government
   ____ Education   ____ Other _____

3. Size of firm/corporation:
   ____ 1   ____ 2-5   ____ 6-10   ____ 11-20   ____ 21-50   ____ 51+

4. Your Name _____
   _Firm/Company Name_____
   Address_____
   City, State, Zip Code_____
   E-mail Address_____

THANK YOU FOR TAKING THE TIME TO COMPLETE THIS SURVEY!

NOTES

NOTES

NOTES

NOTES